REGENERATING
THE INNER CITY

GEOGRAPHY, ENVIRONMENT AND PLANNING

Other titles include

Introduction to Urban Geography
J. R. Short

The Geographer at Work
P. Gould

Cities and Services
S. P. Pinch

Soil Landscape Analysis
F. D. Hole and J. B. Campbell

Nuclear Power: Siting and Safety
S. Openshaw

REGENERATING THE INNER CITY

GLASGOW'S EXPERIENCE

Edited by David Donnison and

Alan Middleton

Routledge & Kegan Paul
London

First published in 1987 by
Routledge & Kegan Paul Ltd
11 New Fetter Lane, London EC4P 4EE

Set in 10 on 12 pt Melior
by Columns of Reading
and printed in Great Britain
by T J Press (Padstow) Ltd
Padstow, Cornwall

British Library Cataloguing in Publication Data
Regenerating the inner city: Glasgow's
   experience. – (Geography, environment and
   planning)
   1. Urban policy – Scotland – Glasgow
   (Strathclyde) – Social conditions
   I. Donnison, David   II. Middleton, Alan
   III. Series
   307'.14'0941443   HT133

ISBN 0-7102-1116-3 (c)
ISBN 0-7102-1117-1 (p)

CONTENTS

Contents

PLATES

FIGURES

TABLES

NOTES ON CONTRIBUTORS

D. Miller Allan is a Lecturer in the Department of Town and Regional Planning, Glasgow University

David Clapham is Assistant Director at the Centre for Housing Research, Glasgow University

David Donnison is Professor of Town and Regional Planning at Glasgow University

Jean Forbes is a Senior Lecturer in the Department of Town and Regional Planning, Glasgow University

Keith Kintrea is a Research Fellow at the Centre for Housing Research, Glasgow University

Douglas Lamont was a Research Assistant at the Centre for Housing Research, Glasgow University

Roger Leclerc is a principal planner with Strathclyde Regional Council

Andrew McArthur is a Research Assistant in the Department of Town and Regional Planning, Glasgow University

Shiela T. McDonald is a Senior Lecturer in the Department of Town and Regional Planning, Glasgow University

Professor Duncan Maclennan is Director of the Centre for Housing Research, Glasgow University

Alan Middleton is Director of the International Programme of the Faculty of the Built Environment, City of Birmingham Polytechnic

Moira Munro is a Research Fellow at the Centre for Housing Research, Glasgow University

Isobel M. L. Robertson was, until her death in 1986, a Research Fellow in the Department of Town and Regional Planning, Glasgow University

Ivan Turok is a Lecturer in the Department of Town and Country Planning, Glasgow University

Notes on contributors

Urlan Wannop is Professor of Urban and Regional Planning at Strathclyde University

PREFACE

One after another, the more advanced market economies are finding that whole industries have to reorganise or close, shedding large numbers of workers as they do so. Older cities in which these industries are concentrated have been stricken; and along with their industries, the housing, the public and commercial services, the churches and the recreational resources of large areas have decayed.

It is in such areas, dubbed 'the inner cities', and in the big, peripheral housing estates, that the credibility of modern government is being tested. It is too early to say how many of these cities will realise the hopes expressed in the phrase 'urban renewal', and how many will sink deeper into poverty and brutalising social divisions to become no more than a policing and poor relief problem. Both options are real possibilities for many of them.

The east end of Glasgow is an area of this kind, now containing about 40,000 people – less than one third of the numbers who lived there a generation ago. It has experienced some of the most disastrous industrial closures and some of the biggest slum clearance projects in the world, and most of its people have fled or been rehoused elsewhere. The jagged population 'pyramid' representing the ages and sexes of the people left there looks much like that of Poland or Germany after the last world war. What this community has passed through is in some ways rather like a major war.

GEAR – the Glasgow Eastern Area Renewal project – was Scotland's response to the needs of this area. Started in 1976, it was one of the first and is still one of the largest urban renewal schemes in Europe. At the end of 1981 the central and local authorities responsible for this project decided they should reappraise it and make decisions about its future. Through the Scottish Development Agency (SDA) – the central government agency responsible for co-ordinating the project – they commissioned four studies, two by Glasgow's universities, and two by London-based consultancies. These four teams started work at the beginning of 1982, keeping in close contact with each other and with the SDA, and submitted reports with recommendations about different aspects of the GEAR project nine months later. Their reports were discussed by the central and local authorities and, by 1983, most of their recommendations had been accepted. Many of those who had worked on these studies had by then dispersed, but those remaining in the Department of Town and Regional Planning and the Centre for Housing Research at the University of Glasgow and in the Department of Urban and Regional Planning at the University of Strathclyde joined forces to present in this book the lessons to be learnt from the GEAR project which may help other cities in the western world which face similar problems. The work required to turn these studies into a book was made possible by a grant from the Leverhulme Trust to whom we are grateful.

This is not an academic evaluation of an urban renewal programme or a summary of the recommendations we made to the SDA about its future. We have had to omit important parts of our reports – on the social and community work services, on the assembly and marketing of land and on commercial development, for example – for which authors were not available. To extract useful lessons from Glasgow's experiences we have deliberately devoted more space to success than to failure, dealing with mistakes only when practical conclusions can be drawn from them.

We have tried to look at the east end of Glasgow from the bottom up. Had we confined our inquiries to the officials responsible for planning and carrying through the project we would have got a rather one-sided view, for practically none of them lived in the area. We talked with community groups of various kinds; we held public meetings to consult people about our research; and we conducted, through Social and Community Planning Research, a survey of a representative sample of the households. We interviewed those buying new houses built for sale in the east end, and the people running enterprises in the small workshops built there by the SDA, along with a similar group in Clydebank on the other side of Glasgow.

We offer our warmest thanks to all these people. Many east end residents gave us shrewd assessments of the area's problems and the policies of public authorities. We are grateful to many people in central and local government and in voluntary organizations who helped with our research, and to those who provided further help as we set about writing this book. John Condliffe at the SDA was our main link with the public services sponsoring the original studies on which this book is based. His dealings with us were a model for any official wanting to get the best out of a university and we are glad to have had the opportunity of working with him. Donald Draffen, responsible at that time for day-to-day management of the GEAR project, was also unfailingly helpful.

Margery Russell has helped us from start to finish with typing, the keeping of accounts and the general management of our research. We are enormously grateful to her, and to Isabel Burnside and Sally Young who have also done a great deal of typing for us.

This book is presented in three parts. Part I consists of two chapters which set the scene by describing the east end and the origins of the communities living there, and by tracing the evolution of British policies for inner city areas of this kind. Part II presents ten chapters dealing with different aspects of the renewal project, starting wth an account of how and why it was launched, followed by discussions of local economic initiatives, housing policies (three chapters), policies for renewing and 'greening' the environment, the location and accessibility of health services, policies for recreation, and for transport and communications, and concluding with a review of the management of the whole programme. The third and last part of the book turns again to wider perspectives with a discussion of local economic policies, proposals for an educational strategy which would combine the insights of planners and teachers, and a final chapter drawing conclusions from the whole project.

David Donnison and Alan Middleton
June 1986

PART I
The Setting

1 GLASGOW AND ITS EAST END*

Alan Middleton

Introduction

Glasgow, still the largest city in Scotland, was once the second city of the British Empire: producer of coal, steel, textiles, ships, railways and armaments; headquarters of firms trading throughout the world; a workshop in which skilled workers by the thousands were trained – men and women who were capable of mobilising to demand social and political changes which left a lasting mark upon their country's history.

That was the Glasgow of between sixty and a hundred years ago, now receding from living memory. Since then the city has lost one-third of its population – and an even larger proportion of its younger and more skilled workers. More than one-fifth of its labour force is unemployed, and only one-third of those still at work are producing manufactured goods; its mortality rates are high and its educational attainments low; its social classes live in separate neighbourhoods, segregated from each other to an unusually high degree . . . in short, it is a city in trouble.

But in recent years this has also become a city which has shown itself to be capable of healing the wounds of economic and social change: it has rebuilt itself on a bolder and larger scale than any other city in the world has attempted (attempted, that is to say, as a deliberate act of policy – not in the aftermath of destruction); it has created, in the process, a larger stock of publicly owned and subsidised housing, allocated on grounds of need, than is to be found in any other city in the market economies; it has rescued and repaired a marvellous heritage of Victorian parks, public buildings, houses and tenements, and enabled working people and pensioners who live in these buildings to stay there and enjoy the transformation; it has gone a long way to shed and surmount its reputation – only too well deserved – for

---

* Some of the information in this chapter comes from issues of the *Glasgow Eastern Standard*, consulted in the Glasgow Room of the Mitchell Library. We would like to thank the staff of the library for their assistance.

drunken violence; it has become a thriving centre – second within Britain only to London – for music, drama and the arts; and it has launched more innovative social projects, more imaginative new experiments in public enterprise, than are to be found in most cities of its size and character.

The story we are going to tell deals only with one part of this city and one aspect of these developments – Glasgow's east end and the scheme for renewing it. But the east end and its people stood once at the heart of the city's economy and its political life. This then became the most derelict and devastated quarter of the city. The same kind of thing has happened in many other big, old cities. In Glasgow, as in other places, the attempt to rebuild the city and the morale of its people had to begin here: a broader renewal programme which neglected the east end would carry no conviction. So our story has a significance which extends far beyond Glasgow. It must start, however, with a brief description of this city and its east end. Unless we understand the origins of the problems to be discussed, we will not understand their solutions.

Glasgow and the decline of urban Britain

Glasgow is the principal city in the west of Scotland, standing at the centre of a group of smaller industrial towns around the mouth of the river Clyde (Figure 1.1). It has an elected District Council which is responsible for housing, environmental health, local planning, city parks and other services. Of these, housing is the most important politically and in the scale of the resources it deploys. More than half the city's population live in public housing.

The Strathclyde Regional Council (SRC), covering the much larger area shown on our map, is another elected authority providing an upper tier of local government. It is responsible for strategic planning, education, personal social services, regional parks, major roads and other services. Of these, education is the most important in terms of the resources it wields, and probably in terms of its political significance.

Both these authorities are completely dominated by the Labour Party which in 1986 held fifty-nine of the sixty-six seats on the Glasgow District Council (GDC) and eighty-seven of the 103 seats on the Regional Council. Their similar political complexion does not prevent these authorities from

4

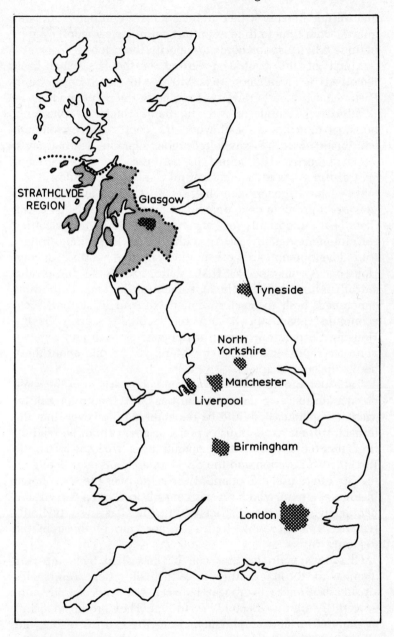

Figure 1.1 Britain's conurbations and Strathclyde Region

quarrelling fiercely when their interests conflict, and both quarrel from time to time with the central government, even in periods when Labour holds a majority there too.

Much of the central government's powers have been devolved to Ministers, accountable to the Cabinet and Parliament in London, who operate from the Scottish Office in Edinburgh. Central powers in fields such as planning, housing, education, social work, the courts and prisons are administered in this way, often under separate Scottish laws. Social security, tax collection and defence are the main central functions for which control remains in London.

The central government has set up various agencies with powers to promote development in particular fields. Of these, the most important for our purposes are the Scottish Development Agency (SDA), with powers to promote indus-trial development and urban renewal; the Scottish Special Housing Association (SSHA), with powers to build and subsidise housing with the agreement of the local authorities concerned, both to meet special needs and to support local economic development; and the Scottish branch of the Housing Corporation which has powers to fund and regulate voluntary housing associations. More will be said about these bodies in later chapters.

Table 1.1 provides an approximate comparison of the scale on which the two local authorities and the three central agencies operate. It should be remembered, however, that the impact of their expenditure upon Glasgow cannot be read off from this table because they operate over different areas: the Housing Corporation and the SSHA operate all over Scotland, the SDA over urban Scotland, the Region over the area shown in Figure 1.1 (in which 46 per cent of Scotland's 5.1 million people live) and the District within the Glasgow city limits (where 744,000 people live – 31 per cent of those in the Region).

Glasgow's main features can be described by comparing them with those of other large British cities. Tendencies already beginning to appear between the wars set in more powerfully after the Second World War. They produced a shift in population and employment from the centres of big, old cities to their suburbs, from larger conurbations to smaller free-standing towns, and from the north towards the south.

Table 1.1: Current and capital expenditure of some public
authorities, 1985-6 (£millions)

	Current	Capital
SRC	1,600,0	156.0
GDC	403.2	114.9
SDA	91.9	37.2
SSHA	89.4	45.3
Housing Corpn	1.9	104.2

The main result has been a decline of the older northern conurbations and growth of free-standing towns and suburbs of the southern half of England (Hall, 1981, p. 66). There has also been a smaller shift from the west to the east, due perhaps to the decline of ship-borne commerce with America, and the growing importance of trade with the continent and of development associated with North Sea oil and gas.

By the 1970s it was clear that local authorities forming the central cores of conurbations in Britain with populations over one million had declined dramatically since 1951. The rate of decline for the first decade was only 3.7 per cent; but between 1961 and 1971 these urban cores lost 9 per cent of their populations (Hall, 1981, p. 15). By 1971 inner Liverpool had lost 400,000 people in fifty years (a decline of 57 per cent); inner London had lost 1.5 million since 1951 (−30 per cent). The same patterns were to be seen in the USA, but although the American and British definitions of inner areas are not strictly comparable, we can safely say that the scale of the loss has been much greater in Great Britain (Kirwan, 1981, p. 72). Within Britain, during the next intercensal period, 1971-81, it was Glasgow which suffered the greatest percentage decline of population of all the major conurbations (Table 1.2).

The loss of population from central areas by itself need not present problems. Policies for slum clearance and the building of new towns and peripheral housing estates have actively promoted this since the end of the Second World War. The loss of population can mean a fiscal crisis for metropolitan government, but this too can be accommodated by adequate centrally planned redistribution of funds. More important are questions about those who are left behind and their prospects of obtaining a reasonable standard of living. Any migration is likely to draw off the younger, the more skilled and the more

Table 1.2: Population of Britain's major cities

	Total 1981 000ₛ	Change 1971-81 %
Glasgow City	766	−22.0
Greater London	6713	− 9.9
Birmingham MD	1007	− 8.3
Liverpool MD	510	−16.4
Manchester MD	448	−17.5
Newcastle MD	228	−19.9

Source: Census 1971, 1981; CURDS, *Functional Regions Factsheet*, No. 9, p. 1 (1984)

enterprising people, and policies for dispersal often reinforced these effects. Meanwhile, private sector investment policies, motivated by technological change, the need to redeploy workers, and hence a search for cheaper and more docile labour, led to the decline of manufacturing employment in the inner areas, growth at the periphery and in the new towns, and an increasing regional imbalance as profits were reinvested in southern parts of the country.

The outward flow of industrial investment and jobs from the centres of cities is now an accepted fact. Although Fothergill and Gudgin, for example, argue that the overall pattern of change in employment in Great Britain does not support the traditional north versus south view of regional imbalance, their own statistics show quite clearly that there is a north–south division – if one recognises that the north does not start at Watford and that Northern Ireland, where the growth of the state has produced peculiar employment circumstances, is not part of Great Britain (Fothergill and Gudgin, 1982).

This divide is now increasingly reflected in voting patterns and the concentration of support for the Labour Party in the northern parts of the country. The four British regions with the greatest employment growth between 1952 and 1979 were East Anglia, the South West, the East Midlands and the South East. Fothergill and Gudgin themselves acknowledge that East Anglia is one of the fastest growing regions in Europe, followed closely by the South West. They rightly remind us,

8

however, that Greater London has been losing people and jobs at an unprecedented rate, with the loss of over half a million manufacturing jobs in a period of twenty years – almost as many as Scotland ever had (*ibid.*, p. 6). They also show that while employment grew by 5.1 per cent in Great Britain as a whole between 1952 and 1975, it declined by 4.7 per cent in the six major conurbations and by 11.4 per cent in London.

The outward movement of new industrial development is not new. It was also a feature of urban growth in the nineteenth century. It is only since the Second World War, however, that departing industries have not been replaced by new and growing sources of employment. Meanwhile, the movement of people and jobs leapt beyond the green belts which have been placed around our cities, creating new spatial patterns for our labour markets and the urban systems based on them. While the decline of industry in cities and its growth in small towns and rural areas has been going on for many years, the steady deterioration in the conurbations has recently given way to collapse, with predictable repercussions for levels of unemployment, for the demands on public services and the resources available to support them, and for the morale of their populations.

The growth of unemployment in the British conurbations between the censuses of 1971 and 1981 can be seen in Table 1.3. Liverpool, Tyneside and Glasgow have been consistently worse than the other cities, but it is the increase in unemployment in Birmingham – hitherto the most prosperous – which is most striking.

Table 1.3: Unemployment in British conurbations, 1971-81

	1971 %	1981 %
Glasgow	7.51	14.81
Liverpool	8.24	16.09
Tyneside	8.05	14.88
Manchester	5.29	11.25
N. Yorkshire	4.84	10.85
London	4.71	9.25
Birmingham	4.17	11.79
Total Urban Britain	5.24	12.89

Source: Census, 1971, 1981. Data supplied by I.M.L. Robertson

The collapse of employment in manufacturing and construction in the conurbations is evident from Table 1.4. The structural changes which have occurred are remarkably similar across all the conurbations. Everywhere there has been a steady growth in the relative importance of the service sector. In 1971 the Birmingham, West Yorkshire, Manchester and Tyneside economies were still dominated by manufacturing, but by 1981 all except Birmingham had a larger percentage of their workforces in services than in secondary activities. Birmingham was the only city with more than 40 per cent of the labour force in secondary employment. Even this was a decline from 55 per cent in 1971 and it was only marginally higher than that for services.

Table 1.4: Percentage of economically active employed in secondary activities and services, 1971-81

	Secondary[1]		Services[2]	
	1971 %	1981 %	1971 %	1971 %
Glasgow	45.36	31.11	39.82	46.27
Birmingham	55.73	41.01	33.07	40.41
W. Yorkshire	51.71	39.06	37.00	42.62
Manchester	48.61	35.24	38.31	44.93
Tyneside	45.62	31.02	38.93	44.09
Liverpool	39.31	28.57	41.63	46.54
London	32.56	23.46	50.26	55.89
Total Urban Britain	42.95	31.98	42.66	47.79

1 SIC Divisions 2 to 5
2 SIC Divisions 6, 8 and 9

Source: Census 1971, 1981. Data supplied by I. M. L. Robertson

All cities except London and Liverpool also increased their percentage of the labour forces in transport and utilities, pointing to an even greater 'tertiarisation' of urban economies than figures for service employment alone would suggest. The decline in London and Liverpool, however, is probably related to the collapse of the docks in these cities and the consequent loss of much transport employment. Containerisation in shipping and the growth of air transport completely changed the transport map of Britain. The consequences of the 'rationalisation' of the docks have been very expensive for the taxpayers nationally and for these two major cities in particular.

The class structure of our cities has also been changing. Excluding retired persons and those for whom information is inadequate, all cities also show a decline in the proportion of skilled labour in their workforces (Table 1.5). There is a corresponding shift towards semi-skilled employment and the proportion in professional and managerial positions has shown a slight increase. However, the proportion of those who have either retired or for whom there is inadequate information has risen from 16 per cent to 21 per cent. This will be due partly to the increase in the proportion of people of pensionable age in the conurbations (by around 2 per cent) and partly to the larger proportion of 15-24 year olds in the labour force, many of whom will never have had a job.

Table 1.5: Skilled workers in the labour force, 1971-81
(percentages of labour force)

	1971 %	1981 %
Glasgow	35.79	34.20
Tyneside	42.43	38.47
Birmingham	41.13	36.98
W. Yorkshire	39.97	36.14
Manchester	37.43	34.15
Liverpool	33.68	32.31
London	30.16	27.10
Total Urban Britain	39.27	33.55

Source: Census 1971, 1981. Data supplied by I. M. L. Robertson

Of the cities we have compared, Glasgow has the second lowest percentage of the labour force in self-employment (Table 1.6). Just as the rate at which manufacturing declines depends on the characteristics of industry inherited from the past, so the structure of industry and the size of firms and plants influence the rate at which new firms are formed (Fothergill and Gudgin, 1982, p. 8). In areas where many large units are concentrated, such as Clydeside and Tyneside, few new small firms are founded. That may be because the workers in big enterprises rarely have opportunities for

11

learning the wide range of skills required by anyone setting up their own enterprise. New firms are usually formed by people from smaller enterprises. This has implications for any policy for the inner city which depends on the promotion of new enterprises, for it suggests that such policies will face the greatest difficulties just where they are most needed.

Table 1.6: Self-employment in British conurbations, 1981 (percentages of labour force)

	%
Glasgow	4.93
London	8.55
Manchester	7.17
W. Yorkshire	6.80
Birmingham	6.31
Liverpool	5.74
Tyneside	4.25
Total Urban Britain	6.85

Source: Census 1971, 1981. Data supplied by I. M. L. Robertson

As the large firms of the older cities have gone into permanent decline and as skilled workers, new investment and jobs have moved out beyond their green belts, the inner areas have been left with a surplus of traditional skills and of the unskilled; young people with no access to the new skills required by the growing service and manufacturing industries on the edge of town; and an elderly population whose younger relatives may have moved away. The inner city remains 'job rich' in that there is a surplus of employment over numbers in the labour force, but many of the young cannot break into this work. Meanwhile, for the increasingly numerous elderly population, of whom the majority are women, paid work is irrelevant. As policies for inner city regeneration have moved towards the promotion of private enterprise, the reality of the situation has in fact made people increasingly dependent on state support.

The role of the state will be considered in the following chapters. The economic collapse of cities like Glasgow and the devastating clearance schemes, which were the community's main response to the appalling housing in much of their inner cities, both arose from the unplanned and unregulated operation of free enterprise. Now the flight of private capital from the cities which used to be the main arenas of entrepreneurial activity is turning them into 'government towns', increasingly dependent upon the state. They are now heavily reliant on the state for unemployment and social security benefits and for services such as social work. In addition, a high proportion of their populations live in public housing, more so in Glasgow than elsewhere (Table 1.7). Living in council housing need not be a bad experience, any more than attending a state school or getting medical care from the National Health Service – which are other sectors of the economy in which these cities depend more heavily upon the state than the rest of urban Britain does. The towns in which most people own their own homes are of course also dependent on the state: the benefits conferred on house-buyers through tax relief are now greater in total than those provided by exchequer and rate-borne subsidies for council tenants. But the house-buyer gets his subsidies in a form which gives him far greater autonomy than the council tenant – greater freedom to choose where to live, to modify and subdivide his home, and to convert that asset and the loans raised upon it into other forms of capital. These house-buyers have increasingly moved beyond the boundaries of the older British cities, leaving tenants behind in areas such as Glasgow's east end.

Table 1.7: Proportion of households living in council housing 1981 (percentages)

	%
Glasgow	63.2
Tyneside	50.4
Manchester	32.8
Birmingham	32.4
London	32.4
Liverpool	31.4
W. Yorkshire	28.4
Total Urban Britain	34.1

Source: Census 1981. Data supplied by I. M. L. Robertson

The east end

Glasgow's east end is made up of a number of distinct though interrelated communities. Its recent official designation as the GEAR area treats it as a single entity and this has tended to disguise the complicated story underlying the crisis which led to large-scale state intervention in the 1970s. To regard the GEAR project as a technical solution to the physical problems of a decayed inner city area is to misunderstand a longer and more complex progress of growth and decline of different communities as they experienced the effects of the uneven development of capitalism. Nevertheless there is an underlying continuity about the successive problems and attempted solutions which is best understood as a result of capital accumulation and the response of the community to it. For ultimately, it is the investment and withdrawal of capital which determines the fate of cities. In this process, however, communities have not been passive. As the roles of these cities in the national and international economy changed, the people living in them fought to improve their living conditions and, in particular, fought for better housing. Their conflict with the owners of private capital led eventually to the provision of subsidised public housing and the creation of many welfare services. The fact that the people themselves played an important part in changing the face of our cities has been ignored and this has encouraged planners and other officials to evade questions about the role of ordinary people today.

Long before the GEAR scheme began, some of the communities of the east end had been defined out of existence by officialdom. Local people, however, continue to identify with the traditional communities. When, in our social survey, we asked them to identify the part of Glasgow they lived in, no-one said that they lived 'in the GEAR area' and only 14 per cent said 'the east end' before being prompted by interviewers for further information. More than half of them – 56 per cent – mentioned a part of the area which is not identified as a ward on the Registrar's valuation roll and when asked to confirm that they lived within the ward to which they had been assigned, two-thirds of these people categorically denied it.

Communities such as Calton have been artificially pushed

across the map by changes in ward boundaries, while others such as Bridgeton and Shettleston have disappeared from the official language of some local government departments. The people of the GEAR area still see themselves as belonging to the traditional communities which have their roots in the mining and weaving villages which lay outside eighteenth-century Glasgow and later became suburbs of the city before they were swallowed up in its expansion.

Figure 1.2 shows how the city grew, and Figure 1.3 shows Glasgow today and the GEAR area within it. If the reconstruction of the area depends on harnessing the energies of these communities, it should start by recognising the communities themselves. We try to do that by briefly tracing their history here.

Calton (see Figure 1.3) of which there is very little left now, was once a weaving village with a history of revolt against authority. From 1787 to 1820 there were various uprisings which resulted in the murder, execution and transportation of weavers. Bridgeton was also a weaving village. In the first half of the nineteenth century, most of its ground-floor properties were occupied by weavers' workshops and the village itself was surrounded by fields in which cloth was bleached, and into which coal pits were sunk. As the industrial revolution gathered pace, coal from the surrounding areas passed through the village, the fields gave way to railways and factories and the local water was used for whisky blending. Bridgeton's Public Washing Green became Glasgow Green and as a meeting place for large demonstrations it has a special place in Glasgow's social history.

As the city pushed eastwards in the nineteenth century it moved along the Edinburgh and London roads to meet the growing weaving and mining villages of Shettleston and Parkhead. In the mid-nineteenth century, four pits were situated right in the heart of Shettleston village. At this time, miners were tied to the pits through a form of debt peonage. The owners had stores situated beside the pit pay office, selling food and clothing. On certain days of the week the miners could get cash (a 'sub') which could be spent only in the owner's store. Through this 'truck' system the entire wages of the miner would be commandeered by the owners. Special permission had to be obtained to spend the money elsewhere,

15

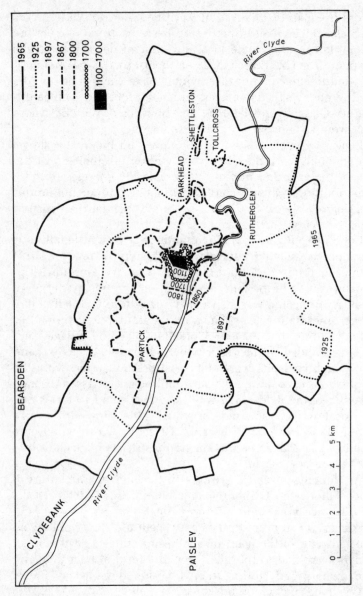

Figure 1.2 The growth of Glasgow from 1100 to 1965.

Glasgow and its east end

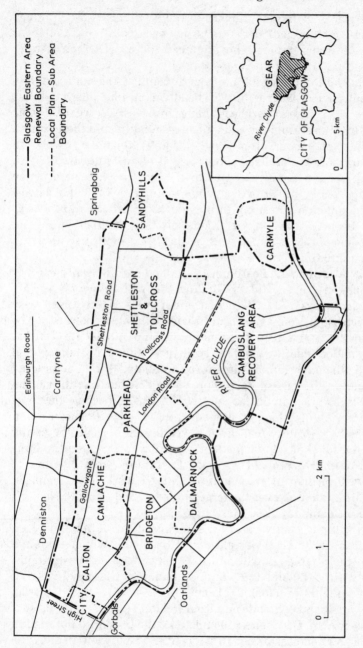

Figure 1.3 Glasgow and the GEAR area

17

the prices were much higher in the pit stores and the miners were maintained in a state of everlasting debt. It was Shettleston's miners who produced the coals which were to fire the Parkhead Forge.

In the middle of the nineteenth century, the main employment for non-weavers in Parkhead was in four pits in what is now the centre of Parkhead. Later, in the 1870s, weavers came to the village from the rural areas of Ayrshire and there was an influx of labour from England and Ireland to work in Beardmore's Parkhead Forge as it grew into the largest employer in the city of Glasgow. With the expansion of the Forge and the growth of the company into the largest conglomerate spreading throughout Clydeside, Parkhead was to become the engine room of the Scottish industrial revolution. As such, it was at the heart of British imperial accumulation.

The growth of Beardmore's and other nineteenth-century giants, however, did not follow the pattern which we are presently assured will save our inner cities. There was no easy progression from small firm to large capitalist enterprise. The growth of the British economy in the nineteenth century depended mainly on large-scale investment by commercial and financial capital already accumulated through imperial trade. In the case of Beardmore's, the first blacksmith who set up his workshop on the spot which was to become the forge went out of business very quickly. It was Robert Napier, already a wealthy man from a wealthy family and the owner of the forge at Camlachie since 1821, who acquired the forge in 1842. He brought William Beardmore from London to invest further in the venture and to work as a manager. Beardmore took over the forge and eventually bought Napier's parent company (Marwick, 1936, pp. 58-61).

During the early part of the industrial revolution, however, it was the villages of Calton and Bridgeton which exhibited the most rapid growth and experienced the greatest strains. Between 1780 and 1851, the population of Glasgow increased from 43,000 to 330,000 (Damer, 1976, p. 10). Migration from the Scottish Highlands and from Ireland accounted for most of this growth. Between 1819 and 1845, the proportion of Irish in Glasgow increased from 10 per cent to 15 per cent. In 1841 the weaving villages of Calton and Bridgeton had grown so fast that over half of the population of the former and 41 per cent of the latter came from outside Lanarkshire (Gibb, 1982, pp. 106-7). During the same period over thirty large factories were established in these suburban villages. The spread of industry into the suburbs is not therefore a new phenomenon. The 'sunrise' industries of the time – foundries, potteries, chemical and dye works, distilleries, brickworks and textile works – were situated on green field sites, attracting population, leading to the development of these villages and increasing the demand for housing.

Around the beginning of the nineteenth century, domestic outwork still dominated hand-loom weaving in Scotland but by the 1830s merchant and finance capital had developed a cotton industry from insignificance to industrial leadership. In 1819 hand-loom weavers constituted over 40 per cent of the labour forces of Calton and Bridgeton (Gibb, 1982, p. 105) but as industrial production developed in Glasgow, and in the east end in particular, their livelihood was threatened. They organised to protect their interests against the new industrialists who, in turn, set up a network of spies throughout the east end to identify the 'agitators'. On numerous occasions the army was called in to protect the masters' interests.

To cope with the rapid growth of population during this period, Glasgow, in common with other European cities but unlike England, built upwards. Glasgow's tenement housing goes back as far as 1760, but it was between 1780 and 1830 that the rapid expansion of tenemental building first took place in the city. The contrast between middle-class and working-class housing was stark. Although there is now a good deal of popular hostility towards planning, which is often thought of as a recent intrusion into our cities, vaguely intended to benefit the working class, it is quite clear that in the early expansion of our urban areas it was the middle classes who benefited from planning. In Glasgow, between 1780 and 1830, three middle-class 'new towns' were laid out in spacious grid-iron patterns to the south and west of the old town. These schemes were large, controlling about three-quarters of all the new building land added to the city in this period (Slaven, 1975, p. 148). As in other British cities of the time, the planning was exclusively directed towards middle- and upper-class needs and it was the growing working class who were left to the mercy of free market forces as the city tumbled eastwards.

The rapid increase in the working population led to speculative jerry-building in the backlands of existing tenements and anywhere else that space could be found close to the city centre. In these circumstances, the nearer east end villages of Calton and Bridgeton took most of the strain of a growing and poverty-stricken population (Slaven, 1975, pp. 148-9). The city rapidly expanded towards the east, filling in the space between the crowded core and the growing peripheral villages of Shettleston and Parkhead. Meanwhile, the centre of gravity of the main business district moved steadily westwards, and housing for the middle classes grew up further west and to the south of the Clyde. The overcrowding of working people in the old city centre brought increased incomes for slum landlords and reduced the motivation to demolish and redevelop.

Nevertheless, as occurred in London and other cities, the railway companies were involved in large-scale clearances of working-class housing before 1850 and in 1843 the Dean of Guild Court obtained powers to demolish dangerous slums. With no compensating construction of working-class housing, however, the clearances which did take place had the effect of increasing the misery and exacerbating the problem of overcrowding in the east end. The resulting squalor led to widespread ill-health and recurring epidemics. Dunghills of human and animal excrement were jealously guarded as a source of income, for sale to farmers. Life expectancy declined from 1821 and did not reach the same level again until the 1880s (Slaven, 1975, p. 151). Between 1840 and the 1870s, roughly half of the deaths in Glasgow were of children under five years of age. Outside the central areas, the worst affected districts were in the east end of the city.

The first action taken to improve the condition of working-class housing was prompted by the recurrence of the epidemic diseases of typhus and cholera. The ideology of the time placed the blame for these diseases squarely on the personal deficiencies of the impoverished masses, said to be sunk in drink and an irreligious proletarian culture (Damer, 1976). Cholera, however, was classless, paying little attention to the social boundaries between the well laid out avenues and the rickety slums. Fear of disease reduced resistance to the improvement of drainage, water supplies and working-class housing in the 1860s.

The City of Glasgow Improvement Act of 1866 established the City Improvement Trust, with the specific intent of attacking the slum problem. At the time when Templeton's carpet factory was winning two gold awards at the Paris exhibition of 1868, introducing the Axminster design, being lauded as a 'pioneer of artistic manufacture' and employing some of the most skilled workers in Europe, densities of over 1,000 persons per acre were to be found close to the factory in what is now the western section of the GEAR area, close to the High Street. With an initial life of fifteen years, the City Improvement Trust set about razing the central area at the same time as a building boom was pushing the city eastwards. Meanwhile, the growth of population had encouraged private contractors to start building tenements for the upper working classes around the end of the 1840s, and although the Trust had powers to build, the housing put up in the boom years of the 1860s and 1870s was built entirely by private builders.

But private investors tend to follow growing demands, not to overtake them, and by 1871 the overcrowding of the city was such that 79 per cent of households lived in one or two rooms and 23 per cent took in lodgers. Of these, 68 per cent were found in houses of one or two rooms (Slaven, 1975, p. 149). In Calton at this time, there was a population density of 388 persons per acre, a death rate of 37 per thousand and an infant mortality rate of 125 per thousand. Eighty-nine per cent of families were in houses of one or two rooms (Gibb, 1982, p. 131). This compared to a density of 37 per acre in Kelvin-haugh and Sandyford, where the death rates, infant mortality rates and congestion were around half of those in Calton. A system of lodging houses grew up, again mainly in the east end of the city, offering barrack-type accommodation to the poorest people of all. In 1876, it was estimated that there were 600-700 of these lodging houses in the city.

The ratepayers, who were mainly men of small capital, objected to the sixpenny rate which was imposed for the City Improvement Trust, which by 1877 had bought up seventy-seven acres of slums. In the same period, the private sector built houses for between 150,000 and 200,000 people. While

21

the Trust confined its efforts to the demolition of slums, the private sector was constructing for the top end of the working-class market and the middle classes. Thus the new housing which was built was not for the people affected by the slum clearance programmes.

The depression which began in the 1870s produced a crisis in the building industry and the market for land acquired and cleared by the Trust was reduced dramatically as the profitability of house-building collapsed. The working class was moving out of houses into single rooms and the builders, where active, were involved in 'making down' the bigger, old houses into single ends (one-room apartments) and rooming houses. Nineteenth-century conversion brought about a reduction in house size and an increase in congestion. In the City's first rehabilitation schemes, the Trust, in a preview of what was to happen one hundred years later, began patching up the substantial amounts of slum properties it found itself owning. From the 1880s it began to build artisan housing, in order to demonstrate to the private sector that the construction of small houses for the working class could be profitable. However, between 1866 and 1914, the Trust only built 2,199 houses and by the latter date the municipal lodging houses provided shelter for more people than the 10,000 who lived in the Trust Houses.

By the late 1870s the economy of the east end had begun to pick up again and in 1879 Beardmore added steel furnaces at his Parkhead forge, initiating the rapid growth of steel making in and around Glasgow (Slaven, 1975, p. 176). In order to secure an outlet for its production of large castings, plate bars and sections Beardmore's moved into shipbuilding, taking over Napier's yard in Govan in 1900 and laying a new yard at Dalmuir in 1906 (Mackinnon, 1921, p. 92; Hamilton, 1932, p. 188; Slaven, 1975, p. 178). They produced steel-making equipment and manufactured large rolling mills for steel and non-ferrous industries (Oakley, 1975, p. 118). Beardmore's became the most important conglomerate in Central Scotland. With an increasing demand for armour plating and naval warships as the First World War approached, they joined a UK arms cartel through which major firms divided up the industrial spoils of war (Checkland, 1976, p. 10). The fortunes of the east end were linked to those of the empire. In the period of rearmament before the world war which was waged in defence of Britain's imperial position, the industries of the Clyde were booming and none more so than those of this area. Nevertheless, huge numbers of east enders remained trapped in poverty and in brutal housing conditions.

By 1914, there were no less than 700,000 people – roughly the present population of the whole city – living in three square miles, making Glasgow the most heavily populated central area in Europe. The labour force was packed into its heart. In 1917, there were more than four persons per room in 11 per cent of Glasgow's houses, over three persons in 28 per cent and over two in 56 per cent. The figures for corresponding English cities were far lower – 0.8 per cent, 1.5 per cent and 9 per cent respectively (Checkland, 1976, pp. 19-20). This was despite the fact that Glasgow was one of the few cities in Britain to tackle the problems of slum housing and overcrowding at all. But the efforts of the City Improvement Trust had been overtaken by natural population growth and the immigration of impoverished Highlanders and Irishmen many of whom found the combination of work and crowded tenements to be an improvement on their conditions at home.

Co-existing with these horrendous living conditions was a flourishing economy which was expanding and diversifying. Beardmore's moved into the production of motor cars, buses and commercial vehicles on their 45-acre site at Parkhead and they also became involved in the production of aero-engines and aircraft, supplying no less than 650 planes during the war (Slaven, 1975, pp. 200-1). The manufacture of the finished product was carried out at their Dalmuir works, but the Parkhead forge was an integral part of the production process. In 1927-8 Beardmore's were to build what was the largest metal aeroplane and flying boat of its day and they also had considerable success with the construction of airships (Mac-Kinnon, 1921, p. 100). The period of diversification, however, soon gave way to contraction. Car production did not become an important aspect of Beardmore's work and they gradually withdrew from this. They also dropped out of the aircraft industry in the 1920s (Slaven, 1975, pp. 200-1). This withdrawal by Beardmore's from the new industries of the twentieth century was critical for the industrial future of the east end of Glasgow and the West of Scotland. Retrenchment,

rather than expansion into the new industries, meant disinvestment in the area and a lost opportunity for the growth of a
host of ancillary components industries. There was a commercial logic to this which was consistent with the tendency of
capital to become concentrated not only in a declining number of growing monopolies but also in a declining number of
growing cities. The possibility of restructuring the local economy was lost as Beardmore's retreated into steel production.

The community's response

By the end of the nineteenth century, people were becoming
less inclined to attribute poverty to the failings of the poor.
There was a growing recognition that slum dwellers were
trapped in their situation for reasons beyond their control, and
that the only way to house the working class was through
municipal enterprise. The municipalisation of water in
Glasgow in 1855 had initiated a process which incorporated
gas, electricity, trams and telephones by 1900. It was through
the issue of housing, however, that the communities of the
east end were beginning to produce leaders who were to take
up the fight against the brutalising effects of the free market.

Increasingly, from the 1880s onwards, local activists
promoted the ideas and philosophies of municipal socialism.
Much of the early impetus for legislative reform had come
from London, where the City Branch of the Independent
Labour Party (ILP) had, by 1900, drawn up a comprehensive
housing strategy which included provision for compulsory
purchase of land, directions to clear slum sites, government
loans and the rating and taxation of vacant land, the
introduction of a fair rents court, the public registration of all
land and house-owners, as well as the right of householders to
make representations about housing needs and to participate
in the administration of housing by local authorities.

Debates on these issues and demands that local authorities
should have power to acquire land for the construction of
municipal housing estates were increasingly informed by the
wider debate about the architecture and design of urban and
suburban estates associated with Patrick Geddes and Ebenezer
Howard (Melling, 1983, p. 37). Geddes's 'neotechnic' vision of
a new urban order characterised by electricity, hygiene, art
and efficient town planning encouraged academics, profes-

sionals and politicians to deal more scientifically and systematically with the deplorable social conditions associated
with housing need.

As a contribution to this general process, the east end
produced men who were to become the leading critics of the
free market economy and its effects on the living conditions of
working people. The Shettleston Branch of the ILP grew from
six people at the turn of the century to produce three of the
famous Red Clydeside MPs – John Wheatley, Jimmy Maxton
and Davie Kirkwood. During the period of rapid urban growth
before the outbreak of the First World War, there developed in
the east end of the city a community resistance to the
conditions created by the free operation of the market. This
carried through the war itself, with working people from all
over the city participating in rent strikes and industrial
stoppages which threatened the war effort.

It was the ILP and Wheatley in particular who were to lead
a process of working-class mobilisation in Glasgow which
directly contributed to the emergence of a new era of housing
provision in Britain. In the boom in shipbuilding and
engineering immediately prior to the First World War, there
was a rapid expansion of the population of the city, with
which the construction industry could not keep pace. In the
three years between 1912 and 1915 the population increased
by 65,000 people while only 1,500 houses were built (Castells,
1983, p. 28). In this situation the landlords began to raise the
rents of their houses dramatically. John Wheatley and the ILP
were in the forefront of the resistance to these moves and by
the summer of 1915 large sections of the east end had joined
with the working class of Partick, Govan and other areas of
Glasgow in a rent strike which was to force the government to
initiate a new housing policy in the face of opposition from
banking and property interests (Damer, 1980; Melling, 1980a
and 1983).

The Glasgow rent strike was dominated by the women of
the various working-class communities in the city and
provided a focal point which united different segments of the
industrial working class at the level of the local community. It
had the support of skilled workers and their trade unions and
the escalation of the conflict threatened industrial production
for the war. Communities in the east end became mobilised in

a struggle for municipal housing which combined industrial power and community-based action in a comprehensive social movement which led to the freezing of rents at a pre-war level and later to a series of Acts and legal decisions which, by restricting landlords' rents, ultimately compelled governments to build subsidised municipal housing.

The housing issue was at the root of the growth of the ILP in the city and it was this issue which helped bring the labour movement to power, both in Glasgow and nationally, in the 1920s. Elitist, technocratic interpretations of these events have explained the passing of housing legislation as a process of handing down benefits from the top. This would be to misconstrue the social and economic processes at work. The mobilisation of the people of the east end and elsewhere in Glasgow arose from a combination of grass roots rebellion and articulate political leadership. That mobilisation persuaded the state, which had captured a huge share of the national income through high war-time taxation, to use part of this increase in resources to bring about a substantial improvement in housing conditions. In the east end, radical movements for reform were particularly strong in Parkhead where, as in many other parts of Glasgow, cohesion as a workforce and loyalty to the local community were combined. Solidarity at the workplace was reinforced by people's shared experience of being powerless to do anything about intolerable housing conditions and the profiteering activities of landlords.

After the war these conflicts came to a head on Clydeside when Winston Churchill – acting in the shadow of the Russian revolution – sent tanks into George Square in 1919 to break up a mass demonstration and imprisoned its leaders. The fight to improve conditions did not end there. Opposition to the small capitalists who were landlords and demands for subsidised public housing gained a good deal of support from the owners of large-scale capital who needed a healthy, docile labour force willing to work for modest wages. But although bad housing left its mark on the health of the population – the concentration of one- and two-roomed housing correlating with high death rates – public building for working-class people during the interwar period was slow, and focused mainly upon the west and south of the city. Then, as happened again in the 1980s, one of the first casualties of the recession of the 1930s was the municipal house-building for general needs. At this time some tenements still had densities of 700 persons per acre. A boom in building for owner occupation in the Midlands and the south of Britain had little effect on Glasgow. There the stagnation in building for lower income groups and the continuation of nineteenth-century slum conditions appeared as aspects of the wider crisis of capitalism. By the 1930s, 58 per cent of Glasgow's workforce was in shipbuilding and mechanical engineering, but unemployment rates of around 30 per cent were sustained over a considerable period of time, and for shipbuilding workers the rate reached as high as 76 per cent in 1932 (Gibb, 1982, p. 149). Once again, it was rearmament which came to the rescue of the city.

The post-war decline of the east end

With the end of the Second World War, the Clyde Valley Regional Plan of 1946 and the Town and Country Planning Act of 1947 sought to reduce the spatial concentration of people and industry and led to an emphasis on regional centres of growth, the dispersal of industrial estates and the creation of the new towns of East Kilbride and Cumbernauld. In house-building, priority was given to providing houses for the needs of newly formed families. Meanwhile, the old east end of the city was neglected. Of seventeen new industrial estates in and around Glasgow, none was allocated to what was later to become the GEAR area. The new light industries of the post-war years went to more distant suburbs and as shipbuilding and engineering went into permanent decline, the east end lost thousands of jobs in metal manufacturing.

Housing problems persisted. In 1951 well over half of the houses in the east end were of one or two rooms, and in older, inner parts of the area such as Dalmarnock (see Figure 1.3) the level was 86 per cent. There were harsh, good reasons for this neglect. Priority was given to new building, which was not surprising in a city where 44 per cent of the houses were overcrowded, 50 per cent had no bath, and 38 per cent had only a shared WC. By 1961, despite a massive post-war municipal housing programme, 34 per cent of Glasgow's housing was still overcrowded, compared to 11 per cent in Birmingham and 6 per cent in Manchester. The industrial

27

triumphs of the empire's second city had been built on the bodies of its people, and subsequent generations were still paying that price – with fewer of the compensating rewards enjoyed by their predecessors.

But at last, as the shortages began to ease somewhat, attention turned to rebuilding the east end. Overspill agreements for rehousing were reached with the new towns and other existing local authorities. Meanwhile, many people were leaving the city to find jobs and houses elsewhere. The outflow of people leaving Glasgow moved towards 20,000 each year in the 1960s as Glasgow Corporation's redevelopment scheme gathered pace. Twenty-nine Comprehensive Development Areas (CDAs) were designated in 1957 and these included one in Bridgeton and Dalmarnock, and others at Parkhead, Tollcross, Shettleston, Townhead and Gallowgate (see Figure 1.3). Much of the increasingly derelict housing of the east end passed from private landlords to owner-occupiers, before being finally taken over by the local authority for demolition. Although this programme was a long-awaited triumph – the culmination of almost a century of struggle for the improvement of living conditions for the people of the east end – it hastened the flight of the young, the skilled and healthy who moved to the suburbs and other towns, leaving those who remained to contend with many years of blight and dereliction. Some of that was unavoidable, but they also had to suffer the effects of haphazard planning which owed more to housing subsidy policies and to the decisions of road engineers and other sectional bureaucratic interests than to any attempt to understand the needs of the people living in what were still amongst the worst slums in Europe.

The impact of clearance policies on the population of the east end was dramatic. In the thirty years between 1951 and 1981, the number of people in the GEAR area declined from around 145,000 to just under 41,000 (Table 1.8). Over the twenty years between 1951 and 1971, the population was already falling at rates of 21 per cent and 29 per cent in each decade, but it was after 1971 that the decline began to accelerate. Between 1971 and the end of 1977 the rate of population loss averaged around 7 per cent each year, leading to a 45 per cent loss in just over 6 years. During this period the population of the city and the Region was also declining, but at nothing like the same rates: the population of Glasgow fell by 1.4 per cent each year while the Region lost 1.1 per cent. In the east end, Bridgeton and Dalmarnock lost over 50 per cent of their populations, Camlachie lost 60 per cent and Calton 70 per cent. The residue of 45,000 which was left in the area at the beginning of the GEAR project meant a loss of 100,000 since 1951 and this decline continued through to the census in 1981.

Table 1.8: Population decline in the GEAR area

YEAR	POPULATION	% DECLINE
1951	145,000	–
1961	115,000	21
1971	82,000	29
1981	41,000	50

Source: Censi, 1951-81

In common with other inner areas, the population which was left contained large numbers of the elderly, the handicapped, the unemployed and people with lower than average educational attainment. Twenty per cent of the residents of the GEAR area were retired, compared to 15 per cent in the Strathclyde Region: the proportion of pensioner households had increased since 1971 because the younger married couples moved out. Compared with the Region, the east end had a lower proportion of married adults, a lower proportion of children under 16 and a higher proportion of widowed persons. Thirty per cent of its households included a physically or mentally handicapped person compared with 21 per cent in the Region, and more than half of these were over 60 years old (SDA, 1978b, p. 17). But the higher incidence of handicap was only partly explained by the higher proportion of elderly people in the area: the proportion of handicapped in all age groups was higher than in the Region. The majority of the disabled were blind or partially sighted, deaf or hard of hearing or people with heart conditions. Many were casualties of bad housing and working conditions.

By the end of the decade, the population statistics of the area resembled those of a country which had passed through a major war, with relatively few in the parental and working age

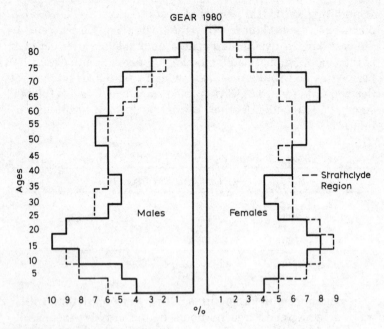

Figure 1.4 Population structure

groups (Donnison *et al.*, 1982, p. 22; see Figure 1.4). The huge emigration brought about by demolition must have weakened family and kinship networks which are crucial for the support of disadvantaged people in any working-class community, and depleted the groups – couples in their 30s and 40s – who play a large part in giving political leadership, helping the young into jobs and establishing standards of behaviour. Nevertheless, there was no evidence of a general breakdown of community in the pathological sense. Those left in the east end by 1977 were people with a long commitment to the area. Ninety per cent of households had a member who had lived in the area for more than ten years and 62 per cent had someone who had lived there for more than forty years. Despite the dispersal which had taken place, two-thirds of those who were left reported that they saw a relative not living with them frequently (i.e. at least once a fortnight) and 70 per cent of these saw relatives several times a week. That is, in spite of massive outward movements, there was still a high level of interaction amongst those who remained and between them and those members of their families who had moved away. This sense of community was still important in 1982, when our own survey showed that this was the main attraction of the east end for those who remained there. Some aspect of community relations was mentioned by half of the people who were asked to say what they liked about the part of the east end with which they identified (Donnison *et al.*, 1982, Appendix 2, p. 5).

In other respects, however, these communities were devastated. In 1977, the year after the GEAR scheme got under way, only 36 per cent of the adult population and 40 per cent of household heads were working, compared to 42 per cent and 60 per cent respectively (themselves low figures) in the Strathclyde Region. There was a very high proportion of households with low incomes and a rate of unemployment that was 50 per cent higher than the already high rate in the surrounding Region: male unemployment at the time stood at about 21 per cent – when that of Glasgow was 14 per cent and that of the Region 12 per cent. (In line with national trends, things are now much worse.) A higher proportion of the workforce continued to find employment in manufacturing than was the case in Strathclyde and, correspondingly, a lower proportion were in the service sector, but the continuing saga of manufacturing collapse was expressed in the fact that 60 per cent of unemployed males had been out of work for more than one year and 25 per cent had been out of work for more than three (SDA, 1978a, p. 50). The unemployment problem in the area, however, was to a large extent due to the skill profile of the labour force. The proportion of unskilled (20 per cent) was double that of the Region, while the proportion of employers and managers was half and that of professionals one-quarter of the Region's figure. Over three-quarters of adults had no formal school qualification and over two-thirds had no qualifications of any kind.

That does not mean that the people of the area were incapable of participating in the decisions which affected their future. On the contrary, the history of contentious and lively community participation lingers on and is expressed through community councils, tenants' and residents' groups and housing associations, which find their foci in the traditional villages of the area. That may not be appreciated by officials who work in the area. One senior police officer whom we met expressed a widely held view when he referred to those who remained in the GEAR area as 'dross' and asserted that 'all the good people have gone away'. For him the most pressing need of the area was to have two policemen on every corner. Although this was a rather extreme view, it represents the end of a spectrum which includes that of a Glasgow District planning official who complained that it was impossible to communicate with the people of the area, and who compared them unfavourably in this respect with the middle classes of the west end. The problem of communication is due partly to the fact that planners, like other officials and professionals, rarely live in the east end and do not base their offices there. It would not be so hard for them to understand what local people were saying if they did not have to make a cultural leap from the security of their middle-class suburbs to the very different life of the area they serve. These obstacles are themselves partly created by bad planning.

The approach of the Scottish Development Agency, which assumed leadership of the GEAR scheme, was rather different. They tried to make direct contact with the people of the area and they located an office within it. They sought out the views of the local people on issues that affected them and tried to act on these views in so far as their remit would allow. At first there were difficulties in communication but certain officers persevered until each side understood the other. This is not to say that a situation of consensus was reached. Rather, the relationship was based on a more realistic understanding of each other's position, and of what the state was and was not capable of delivering. Local people told us that whereas other authorities often sent different and rather junior people to different meetings – often held out of office hours and therefore an unattractive proposition – the SDA sent the same people every time and these included very senior officers. Despite the problems of the area, it remains populated by intelligent and articulate people who now have some understanding of how the state functions, who continue to make demands on that state and who have become fairly adept at playing according to the changing rules of the game.

We turn in the next chapters to the evolving framework for these rules. In this chapter we have tried to set the scene for the GEAR project by briefly tracing the experience of the people who have lived in the east end over the past two centuries: a 'bottom-upwards' view. In the next we turn to the politicians and officials in central and local government and their recent attempts to respond to the needs, problems and pressures of the area: a 'top-downwards' view of the same scene.

2 CONTINUITY, CHANGE AND CONTRADICTION IN URBAN POLICY

Ivan Turok

It is almost twenty years since the government first adopted an explicit urban policy, recognising that Britain's major cities were suffering disproportionately from poverty of various kinds – poverty which might have politically turbulent implications if nothing was done about it. Since then there have been elements of continuity in the way successive governments have responded. There have also been many modifications, leading to a large number of separate measures and an increase in the range of government interventions.

Yet despite the plethora of urban initiatives, conditions in the big cities have generally deteriorated throughout this period. Unemployment, poverty and social deprivation have become more acute, social inequalities and racial tensions have increased and in many places the physical environment has degenerated. Britain's inner cities and peripheral housing estates are often regarded as the most depressed 'regions' of the 1980s. In this chapter we examine the history of government policy towards the cities. We discuss the measures specifically directed at the inner areas as well as the urban implications of a number of wider national policies, some of which appear to be in conflict with the aims of urban policy. By examining the character and history of such initiatives we hope to place the GEAR scheme in a wider national context. We intend also to raise issues about national policies towards the cities which will be taken up and elaborated later in this book.

Three phases of national urban policy can be broadly distinguished, ignoring the long tradition of physically orientated programmes concerned with slum clearance, environmental decay, traffic congestion, etc.

Phase One: 1968-76
The urban initiatives introduced in the late 1960s had a more

explicit concern for people's economic and social welfare. They consisted of a number of separate, small-scale projects and programmes that offered some additional public resources for selected urban neighbourhoods where poverty and deprivation were considered to be particularly severe. The assisted areas were small, the resources were rather limited and the type of projects benefiting included family advice and community centres, nursery schools and improved educational facilities for ethnic minorities.

These early initiatives appear to have been based on the premise that urban poverty was largely a residual problem that resulted from certain characteristics of the poor themselves and of the areas in which they lived. People were poor because of their physical and mental shortcomings. Moreover, a debilitating 'culture of poverty' was considered to afflict the depressed neighbourhoods and an inter-generational 'cycle of deprivation' was reckoned to prevent the poor from raising their living standards. Policies offering special assistance in the form of improved educational facilities, enhanced family support services, etc. followed naturally from this basic premise and were intended to give deprived communities the capacity to solve their own problems.

By the mid-1970s, however, this perspective was being widely questioned. Unemployment had risen sharply and it was clear that the scale of financial hardship and bad living conditions in the inner cities could not simply be put down to the inadequacies of the poor. Emphasis was given instead to a much broader range of causes – national as well as local and individual, economic as well as social and environmental. Particular stress was laid on the crucial issues of employment and incomes, for it had become increasingly apparent that local wages were low, that many people could not find work at all and that pensioners and others dependent on social security were particularly impoverished. It was also clear that large numbers of the more successful people had been leaving the inner cities, thus aggravating the economic, social and physical decline of these areas. The clear implication was that tackling the root causes of urban deprivation would require much more than marginal adjustments to existing social policies.

Phase two: 1976-79

Official recognition of this was given in a major revision of urban policy in 1976-7, marked by an important White Paper, *Policy for the Inner Cities* (DoE, 1977a). This signalled much broader-based action on urban problems, combining economic, social and environmental programmes and involving new organisational arrangements between central and local government to provide a more co-ordinated and visible policy response.

The revised thinking acknowledged that the difficulties of the inner cities were more fundamental than had previously been assumed. The deterioration in housing conditions, inadequate community facilities, low levels of educational attainment, dereliction of land and buildings and so on were all symptoms of deep-seated processes. Underlying these problems was an erosion of the economic base of the inner cities, associated with a rapid decline in manufacturing employment and a large-scale exodus of people from inner areas to suburbs and smaller towns. This outward movement had been a selective one, taking the younger and more skilled people, and leaving the inner areas with a disproportionate number of residents particularly vulnerable to poverty and unemployment.

The new perception of the problem was associated with more ambitious objectives – to strengthen the economy of the inner cities, to improve their physical fabric, alleviate social deprivation and stem the ebb tide of population and jobs. It was also suggested that a comprehensive, area-based approach would be required. It would need to be comprehensive because physical, social and economic problems were thought to be interconnected, and area-based because of the intensity and apparent concentration of deprivation. Yet most of the extra public resources required would come from redirecting existing central and local government programmes towards the inner areas rather than from additional expenditure, although funds for the Urban Programme were increased at the same time. It was hoped that this public spending on basic services and the physical environment would attract further private investment from industry and from financial institutions, and thereby generate self-sustaining revival without a permanently enlarged public sector presence. Government would adopt an active enabling role.

Not all cities received the same level of support from the Urban Programme. Priorities were established on the basis of the severity of the problems in each district and this was reflected both in the powers available to the local authority under the Inner Urban Areas Act and in the allocations of Urban Programme funds.

In Scotland it was recognised that the scale and severity of Glasgow's problems were somewhat exceptional and demanded special attention. As in England, the Scottish Office made a general commitment to give priority to urban areas in its main capital expenditure programmes and in its distribution of the rate support grant to local authorities. In addition, the newly established Scottish Development Agency — set up by the government to promote economic development, create and safeguard employment, modernise industry and improve the physical environment — was required to give general emphasis to areas such as Glasgow which had suffered badly from industrial decline. More specifically, the GEAR scheme was embarked upon in 1976 to regenerate the east end of Glasgow. At the time this was a unique urban renewal programme involving the active participation of central government and its agencies as well as the local authorities. This administrative arrangement, with the Secretary of State playing a key role in overseeing the management of the project and co-ordinating the various agencies involved, was subsequently attempted for the 'Partnership Areas' in some of the English cities, but with altogether less effect. One of the obvious drawbacks there was the absence of powerful and resourceful bodies such as the Scottish Development Agency and the Scottish Special Housing Association whose involvement in GEAR has been so crucial.[1]

Probably the key objective of the government's new urban policy was to strengthen the economies of the inner cities, in particular to encourage the retention of people and jobs. There were several ways in which this was to be achieved. To begin with, existing regional industrial policies were to be modified to accommodate the inner urban emphasis, industrial development controls in London and the West Midlands would be relaxed and plans were made to wind down the New and

Expanded Towns outside the cities.[2] In addition, metropolitan authorities were encouraged to reorientate their mainstream policies towards assisting industry; for example, by processing planning applications more speedily, relaxing strict controls over mixed and nonconforming land uses, and providing improved roads and public transport services for industry. Their powers to assist industry more directly through the provision of land, buildings and financial aid were extended and the scope of the Urban Programme was broadened to include schemes for upgrading the environment, restoring buildings, clearing derelict land, landscaping, etc.

To fund these additional measures the Urban Programme was expanded. In the period between 1968 and 1977 a total of only £72 million had been allocated but in the financial year 1977/8 £29 million was provided in England and this was increased to £93 million in 1978/9 and £165 million in 1979/80. In Scotland the increase was from £6 million in 1977/8 to £20 million in 1980/1. Despite these increases, the Programmes remained only a fraction of overall local authority spending. Even in the Partnership Areas it was less than 1 per cent of total expenditure. Admittedly, the intention in 1977 had not been that the Urban Programme would be the sole mechanism of urban regeneration. Instead it had been made clear that the resources would have to come from a geographical reorientation of the government's main programmes. Programmes for housing, education, social services, transport, planning, industry, manpower and even the rate support grant were to be purposefully directed towards the inner areas. The deep-seated nature of the economic and social forces of decline would require nothing less.

In practice, however, the wide-ranging national and local assault on the problem failed by and large to materialise. There was little evidence of an urban dimension to wider national policies and the rate support grant provided little in the way of extra resources for even the most hard-pressed urban authorities. Indeed, the government's wider economic strategy meant that local authority spending was actually cut back. In this climate of retrenchment it was clearly difficult for authorities to redirect their own main programmes towards the inner areas, as they had been encouraged to do. Thus, most commentators have argued that very little of the intended 'bending' of existing programmes was actually achieved (Gibson and Langstaff, 1982; Lawless, 1981; Stewart, 1983).

So although 1976 was intended to be a watershed in government policy, refocusing the Urban Programme towards economic regeneration, the response was in practice more limited, at least in terms of the level of resources provided and the commitment shown by other government departments.

Phase three: 1979-86
Most of the initiatives begun by the Labour Government in the late 1970s were continued by the 1979 Conservative government, although modifications and many additions have subsequently been introduced. The incoming Conservative government was committed to radical change in the whole nature of the post-war welfare state. The intention was to reduce state intervention and enhance the role of the private sector. In the field of urban policy the broadly expressed objectives of the 1977 White Paper were accepted and the need for central government involvement was acknowledged but the complexion of the new policy measures was different. Thus, economic regeneration was reaffirmed as the principal objective but less emphasis was given to measures involving public spending and increased priority was given to involving private investors and the voluntary sector in urban renewal.

Initially the Conservative government had mixed feelings towards the Urban Programme and some key individuals and Ministries were opposed to it. Thus the funds provided in the first few years increased in cash terms but failed to keep pace with inflation. In England, for instance, £165 million had been committed by the previous Labour government for 1979/80 and this was increased by the Conservatives to £202 million in 1980/1 and £215 million in 1981/2. The riots of 1981 and the growing political significance of the 'urban problem' led to increased expenditure of £270 million in 1982/3 and £348 million in 1983/4. But even so, in real terms this increase was comparatively small, despite the deterioration in the economic situation and the dramatic rise in unemployment over these years. Since 1983/4 Urban Programme allocations once more failed to keep pace with inflation and in 1985/6, at £338 million, the programme 'again suffered a cut in its real value as part of the Treasury's long-running campaign to abolish it' (Pauley, 1985). Furthermore, the actual level of spending has been less than the allocation because of considerable under-spending. This is due to the inability of the inner cities to attract sufficient private investment to meet the requirements of a growing number of the government's urban initiatives (Committee of Public Accounts, 1986).

Since 1979 the character of the Urban Programme has also changed. Projects that can claim to be linked to economic regeneration and that involve one-off capital expenditure are much more likely to receive support than 'social' or commu-nity projects and those requiring continuing financial assis-tance. Greater emphasis is given to schemes that involve the private sector and that improve the physical environment: they should 'produce as great a visual impact as possible: tangible physical improvement will help to attract private investment' (DoE, 1981). Involving private industry and commerce in the formulation of local authority programmes of action is another requirement that has been imposed on them. These shifts of emphasis reflect the concern of the Conserva-tives that the Urban Programme was becoming for local authorities a means of compensating for shortfalls in their main spending programmes. The government wanted to impose their own priorities on local councils, to ensure that public funds were spent on basic infrastructure to attract private investors and middle-class households back to the inner cities, rather than on existing council activities. Indeed, while the Urban Programme was being expanded the govern-ment were actually cutting back on mainstream grants to local authorities as well as restricting the amount of money that they could raise themselves through local rates.

Besides these changes to existing policies and programmes, the scale of urban deprivation demanded that something new be done. **Enterprise Zones** were the most conspicuous of the new measures adopted. They were first mooted by Sir Geoffrey Howe in a speech on 'Liberating Free Enterprise' in June 1978, as an experiment 'designed to go further and more swiftly than the general policy changes we have been proposing to liberate enterprise throughout the country.' When eventually introduced in 1980, the scheme was less far-reaching than originally envisaged but did nevertheless include several elements which might provide a testing ground for the Conservatives' wider policies and philosophy. There were important financial incentives for the private sector and also elements of de-regulation and reduced state intervention. The incentives included exemption from Development Land Tax, exemption from rates on industrial and commercial property, and tax allowances for capital expenditure on industrial and commercial property. De-regulation took the form of simplified planning requirements, exemption from industrial training levies, faster processing of applications for customs facilities and fewer requests for statistical information.

The financial incentives in Enterprise Zones are geared towards property development, which is consistent with one of the short-term objectives of the scheme, to bring derelict land and buildings back into productive use. Many of the twenty-five zones that have been designated are in run-down parts of old industrial cities.[3] More importantly, however, it is clear that the zones have a wider remit, and that the physical development and improved supply of property in these areas are intended to stimulate activity in manufacturing industry and services, and to create new jobs. Preliminary evidence shows that after two years some of the zones have been reasonably successful at increasing the amount of property developed: a quarter of the land area that was not previously available for development has been reclaimed and serviced, and a total of 364,000 square metres of new floorspace has been completed (Roger Tym and Partners, 1984). Contrary to the laissez-faire ideology, a crucial factor underpinning these achievements has been heavy public investment. By mid-1983 rates relief is estimated to have cost £16.8 million; the value of tax relief on investment in industrial and commercial buildings was £38 million; and public expenditure on the acquisition, preparation and servicing of land and the construction of buildings amounted to £78 million. In Clydebank alone the Scottish Development Agency had spent £22 million by March 1985, mostly on factory construction (SDA, 1985). Given this level of state support, it is perhaps not surprising that a sizeable amount of physical development has occurred.

More important is the extent of new economic activity and

employment that Enterprise Zones have generated. During their first two years 725 firms and 8,065 jobs were attracted to the original eleven zones – in very crude terms a cost per job of £16,500, which would appear to compare favourably with regional policy. However, most of these jobs would have existed locally anyway: Enterprise Zones seem to have generated relatively little wholly new investment or employment. For instance, most firms relocating into the zones made short-distance moves: 92 per cent moved from within the same region and 86 per cent from the same county. Without the zones most would have stayed within the area. Of the new firms, over 90 per cent would have started up in any case. With existing firms, only 10 per cent achieved higher output and employment levels than they would otherwise have done. In other words, relatively few firms were able to use the Enterprise Zone subsidies to expand (Roger Tym and Partners, 1984).

Despite the rhetoric, therefore, Enterprise Zones had, by 1984 at least, stimulated little new economic activity. One of their limitations is that the measures brought to bear are primarily geared to increasing the supply of land and premises, but unless there is a particular local shortage or gap in the supply of property which acts as a constraint on the development of firms, one would not expect the provision of further property to bring about an increase in output, investment or employment. Instead the effect could simply be to attract enterprises which would otherwise be satisfactorily located elsewhere. There is little evidence that any systematic shortages exist now or existed at the time of designation, partly because of the depression and the falling demand for industrial floorspace it has brought about, but also because most zones are located in declining local economies where demand is particularly weak and where local authorities and regional agencies have already provided a great deal of industrial land, factories and workshops.

A second limitation is the tenuous link between physical redevelopment and wider economic growth. For individual firms, subsidies on property do little on their own to relax production, marketing or wider economic constraints on business expansion. Nor do such subsidies give any direct encouragement to firms to take on more labour. Instead the

Enterprise Zones' measures are blunt and indiscriminate. They benefit all kinds of firms, many of which serve only local or regional markets. Any improvement in the performance of these firms may cause offsetting reductions of output and employment among non-assisted competitors. For all these reasons neither the local nor the national economy may gain much benefit. Meanwhile, the abolition of development land tax in April 1985 and the simplification of planning procedures now taking place throughout the country are reducing the comparative benefits the zones offer and will therefore reduce their impact still further.

Thus, there are a number of question marks about who the ultimate beneficiaries of Enterprise Zones are likely to be. There is already evidence that the subsidies aimed at the firms occupying the factories, warehouses and offices are being passed on to the landowners who are able to push up rents and land prices as a result of the stronger demand for Enterprise Zone sites. Ironically some of these landowners are the very companies which closed down their plants and were responsible for the job losses and dereliction which the zones are intended to remedy. Property developers will also profit from any development that takes place. But the larger financial institutions have so far maintained a cautious attitude towards investing in Enterprise Zone property. They are concerned perhaps at the uncertainty involved because of their relatively unattractive locations and the short-term benefits offered: building allowances are a once-for-all windfall and rates relief lasts only for ten years. The zones do not provide 'prime' property of the sort that attracts the major institutional investors looking for security of income and rental growth (Cadman, 1982). Thus, all the evidence suggests that Enterprise Zones may help to bring about some physical redevelopment of derelict industrial neighbourhoods in larger cities, but they are unlikely to contribute much to the more important job of economic regeneration.

Urban Development Corporations (UDCs) were the second of the government's new urban measures. UDCs are bodies appointed by the government, modelled on the New Town development corporations with special powers and resources to promote land development. The official view is that UDCs -will bring singleminded management and industrial development expertise to the task of regenerating derelict dockland areas. Their powers and considerable resources give them a degree of control over land use and development that was previously denied to the local authorities. They are able to buy and sell land, to prepare sites for commercial, industrial and residential development, to lay down roads, water supply and other basic infrastructure, and to provide loans and grants for building work and more cosmetic environmental improvement. In 1981 two UDCs were set up in the Merseyside and London Docklands, effectively removing local planning and development powers from municipal councils.

The UDCs have been under pressure from the government to use their funds to attract as much private investment as possible. In London the Docklands Development Corporation (LDDC) appears to consider that the most realistic approach is to market the Docklands as an overspill area for the City of London. Thus it has sought to encourage speculative office development, luxury private housing, retail superstores, marinas and so forth. In order to lay the basis for attracting these prestigious and highly profitable forms of development the LDDC has had to bolster the property market with considerable expenditure on land acquisition and site development. By early 1985 £150 million had been spent in creating the right conditions to attract private investors to the area. In some cases pre-existing dockland firms occupying old and visually unattractive premises but providing valuable jobs for local residents have been induced to move out of the area in order to make way for more remunerative, 'confidence-boosting' developments. Elsewhere, large amounts of local authority-owned land, set aside for public housing programmes to accommodate people on council waiting lists and families needing homes with gardens, have been compulsorily purchased by the LDDC, and, after expensive servicing, sold to private house-builders to construct relatively high-priced houses for sale. In the first few years 'land was practically given away at £60,000 an acre' though the average price (for housing) land had risen to between £300,000 and £400,000 per acre by mid-1985 (Bevan, 1985).

These and other aspects of the UDCs' strategy have again raised questions about who is intended to benefit. Evidence suggests that local residents – and there are 40,000 in the

LDDC area – have so far benefited little by way of employment, suitable housing or social facilities. What is more, the
withdrawal within the UDC areas of powers and resources for
planning and development by local authorities has reduced
local accountability and deprived local people of a say in the
future development of their neighbourhoods. The LDDC has
been ignoring locally prepared statutory plans and hardly
consulting with local councils and local people. The emphasis
in its strategy is not on meeting local needs but on priming the
land market and promoting market-led development, almost
irrespective of its character.

There are questions too about how successful the LDDC's
strategy has so far been according even to its own narrow
objectives. Evidence suggests that major difficulties have been
experienced in generating interest from institutions responsible for industrial and commercial property development, in
spite of the extensive marketing and infrastructural investment that has been carried out. Developments and financial
institutions

> could see the attractions of docklands as a residential
> market but were very sceptical about its commercial
> potential . . . . Until recently, there have been virtually no
> signs that it [the LDDC] was succeeding, either in
> encouraging institutions to fund City-oriented projects or in
> convincing traditional City occupiers to move to the docks.
> (Cassell, 1985)

Cassell suggests, however, that the situation may be
changing because of large-scale restructuring by the financial
services sector which is creating a large demand for modern
floorspace capable of accommodating recent communications
technology; space which simply does not exist in the City of
London. The point then is that in encouraging the physical
development of this partly derelict location, the LDDC is in
the fortunate position of being located close to the buoyant
centre of London. Despite this, heavy public investment has
been necessary to bring about any development at all. Run
down areas in many other, more depressed parts of the
country such as Glasgow's east end have not had the same
advantages.

Derelict Land Grants and **Land Registers** are two further additions to urban policy. They are even more explicitly oriented toward land development and attracting private investment. Land Registers were introduced in 1980 as a way of making available publicly-owned land for development by the private sector. All public authorities are required to account for their current land holdings and register all vacant or underused land so as to provide information for potential purchasers. Much of this land is in inner urban areas. Along with measures to weaken planning controls, the aim of this policy is to encourage private development by removing alleged obstacles to it. This is a reversal of the previous government's attempt to call forth a larger public sector role in development through the Community Land Act. Already the new approach has run into difficulties. During the first two years of the scheme's operation less than 4 per cent (4,070 acres) of registered land was disposed of (Howes, 1984). This is a reflection of the limited nature of the initiative, and the weak interest of private investors in derelict and vacant urban sites which would be costly to develop.

Derelict Land Grants are a more active attempt to stimulate the development of this land. The subsidy is intended to attract private developers to sites that have previously been acquired by local authorities. Although it was originally introduced in the 1960s, the grant was reactivated in 1983 and the emphasis switched to *urban* land reclamation. Expenditure in 1984/5 amounted to £74 million. Only 12 per cent of this was spent on schemes in which a developer for the site was in firm prospect, reflecting once again the difficulties the government is facing in attracting private investment to derelict land (*Planning*, 1985). In view of the urgency of land reclamation in many depressed areas of the country, the level of spending on these grants seems derisory: the £2.4 million increase in the 1985/6 Derelict Land Grant budget did not even keep pace with inflation.

The principle behind **Urban Development Grants** (UDGs) is similar, except that they are aimed even more explicitly at the private sector. The scheme was introduced in 1982 following proposals from the Financial Institutions Group (FIG). This group was set up by the government after the 1981 riots to work in many of the big cities. It consisted of twenty-six managers seconded for a year from a variety of financial institutions. UDG was one of their proposals for increasing the effectiveness of the Urban Programme in attracting private capital. The grant is aimed at 'levering in' private investment to the inner city by making otherwise unprofitable developments profitable. It is attractive to investors because it can be incorporated 'up front' in the financing of the development project, rather than being just another weak enabling factor to be considered. The precise level of grant is dependent on the nature of the project concerned and on the amount required to give the developer a 'reasonable' return on capital invested.

A wide range of developments have so far been assisted, including the construction and refurbishment of factories, warehouses, shops and offices; the rehabilitation and building of private housing; improvement for sale of difficult-to-let council estates; provision of recreational and leisure facilities; hotel building and refurbishment. The budget for the UDG in 1983/4 was £60 millon and the ratio of public to private funding is said to have been 1:4. It is claimed that this 'leverage' ratio reflects the success of the UDG. However, this is obviously a narrow and partial assessment of the UDG because it says nothing about the wider effects, beneficial or otherwise, of UDG projects. Moreover, it is possible that the higher a project's leverage ratio, the less likely that public funds were genuinely needed in the first place (Alderton, 1984). There may be a real tension here between minimising public spending and maximising its impact, certainly in terms of its wider social benefits.

In Scotland UDG is administered by the Scottish Development Agency in a scheme known as LEG-UP (Local Enterprise Grants for Urban Projects). By March 1984, thirty-eight projects had received assistance amounting to nearly £6 million in total. Most of them involved the provision of new buildings or the conversion of older property for shops, flats for sale, recreation and leisure use, and industrial development. In one or two specific locations such as the 'Merchant City' in the centre of Glasgow, LEG-UP has helped bring about the successful conversion of older vacant property, significantly improving the physical appearance and level of commercial activity in the area. As with UDG in England, the projects tend, however, to be extremely diverse, suggesting perhaps that the rationale of the policy has not been developed beyond encouraging the physical redevelopment of urban land and the conversion of old buildings. One of the major operational problems of both schemes has been attracting sufficient private sector investment in developing inner city sites for whatever purpose. Between 1983/4 and 1985/6 only £47 million out of the total UDG allocation of £148 million was actually taken up (Committee of Public Accounts, 1986).

FIG also proposed that an agency be set up to put together development projects in inner city areas which could be offered to financial institutions for funding. In January 1983 **Inner City Enterprises Ltd** (ICE) was set up for this purpose with the backing of around fifty banks, pension funds, building societies and insurance companies. Two years later, however, it was having great difficulty in getting development projects funded and is making slow progress (*Town and Country Planning*, 1985). Once again the message seems to be that in the absence of heavy public investment and subsidies to underwrite the risk, the private sector appears to be pessimistic about the prospects of earning a profit from investments in the inner city.

ICE and UDG reflect the growing drive to minimise public spending while at the same time maximising the visibility of the money that is spent. This has had a number of consequences, including the emphasis placed on the physical development of land. Given the government's reliance on market mechanisms and its disinclination to intervene directly, private investors have by and large had a free hand to determine the pace and kind of development that has taken place. And as we have seen, this raises important questions about who the beneficiaries of urban policy are likely to be.

Looking back to the mid-1960s, British urban policy has undergone several shifts in direction. It focused in the early years on supplementing existing social programmes in order to improve the welfare of 'disadvantaged' individuals and communities. In the mid-1970s the emphasis shifted to restoring the industrial base of the inner cities through a mixture of public and private investment. Since 1979, through a variety of piecemeal initiatives, the government has endeavoured to minimise its involvement by putting the emphasis on private enterprise. This has often meant a weak, reactive role for the public sector – attracting and accommodating the requirements of private investors without substantially influencing the character of their development decisions.

Persistent features of national urban policy

In focusing on the shifts in policy there is a danger of exaggerating the changes that have taken place and of overlooking the underlying continuities. The first feature common to the different phases of policy has been the positive contribution made to a range of community-based groups and projects organised around social, educational and recreational issues. They have included schemes to support victims of crime, law centres, disability projects and community centres. Since its inception the Urban Programme has fulfilled a useful function in assisting such projects, many of which would not otherwise have received state support at all. Individually they have been extremely valuable though insufficient on their own to match the scale of urban decline. In 1979/80 a sizeable 51 per cent of Urban Programme resources in England were spent on 'social' projects, the heading under which most community schemes fell (Committee of Public Accounts, 1986). In Scotland the proportion is greater still. Here urban aid has served a useful purpose in supporting many community businesses, particularly in the Strathclyde Region (a development briefly discussed in Chapter 4). However, the situation has been changing and funds for community-oriented projects have recently been severely reduced. With capital expenditure and 'economic' projects receiving priority in a shrinking overall budget a major difficulty now faces many established community projects requiring continued support. An even greater problem confronts those now trying to get new projects started. Indeed a number of towns have also been excluded from applying for urban aid at all.

A second feature of urban policy has been the constant attention given to organisational and administrative considerations, over and above those concerned with policy itself. Many of the initiatives have appeared to concentrate on improving policy management and increasing co-ordination between public agencies. These priorities were apparent in the brief for the Community Development Projects (CDPs), in the reports of the Inner Area Studies, in the 1977 White Paper and in the designation of Partnership Authorities. Since 1979 further organisational steps have been taken, involving the setting up of groups, committees and joint working arrangements, ostensibly to increase policy effectiveness. More recently the Scarman Report on the Brixton disorders called once again for a concerted, better directed and better co-ordinated response to inner city problems. A subsequent House of Commons enquiry into urban policy also restricted itself to the 'problems of management' of urban renewal and, following Scarman, concentrated on the limitations of decision-making, implementation and co-ordination among agencies. Little interest was shown in how appropriate in themselves were the policies pursued by the agencies of renewal. Perhaps the most recent example was the establishment in 1985 of five new civil service City Action Teams to improve collaboration between central and local government in selected inner city areas. Central government departments (Environment and Manpower Services Commission) will lead the teams and will seek to work closely with local authorities and the voluntary sector. Organisational initiatives of this sort have arguably had at least two effects. They have acted as a substitute for more substantial changes in the content of urban policy and they have led to greater central government involvement in the affairs of urban authorities. There is little evidence that they have succeeded in improving the quality of civic leadership and decision-making or gone far to achieve the policy's wider objectives (though our study of the GEAR scheme suggests that, for a variety of reasons, experience there was something of an exception, as Chapter 13 indicates).

This is particularly clear in the case of the Urban Programme which was intended to be a focus for experimentation and innovation in local and central government policy-making. In practice, however, managerial considerations have been allowed to dominate, and administrative procedures and financial constraints have severely restricted the scope for the development of new initiatives. The programme has come to resemble any other local government programme, with the traditional relationship between local and central government, operating through local bids and central allocations, being used by the latter to control the type and level of expenditure by the former (Sills *et al.*, 1985; Stewart, 1983). Not surprisingly, most genuinely new initiatives in urban policy have been developed outside this framework.

Thirdly, urban policy has been characterised by a divergence between its aims and substance. The policy has always been a response to poor social, economic and environmental conditions in inner urban areas. The principal expressed objective has been to improve the social and economic welfare of local residents. Yet the substance of urban policy has not been consistent with these broad aspirations. For example, a serious commitment from a number of key government departments was required to support the inner city as a priority area but in practice this has not been forthcoming. Discrepancies have also been apparent between the nature of the policies and their intended beneficiaries. Many of the measures have been directed at physical development and renewal, through environmental improvement, land assembly, factory building, commercial development and new residential development, relying increasingly on private enterprise. They have on the whole made limited impact on the level of local employment opportunities and local incomes, on the vitality of the local economic base and on the stability and security of inner city communities.

Specific policy measures have been mainly designed to attract private investment. Improving the basic physical infrastructure of older inner city areas has been one element of this and is obviously an important preliminary measure, but pursued half-heartedly and without the support of other policies it has not brought about the major economic and social changes that were and are required. Similarly, the reliance on market forces and private initiative has meant that commercial imperatives have been uppermost in determining the pattern of development, and that the needs of the community for appropriate jobs, homes and social facilities have only been incidental to this process.

A fourth feature of urban policy has been the consistent emphasis on small areas. This dates back to the Educational Priority Areas and the CDPs of the late 1960s. More recent examples are the industrial and commercial improvement areas, the designated districts under the Urban Programme and the Enterprise Zones. The intention appears to have been to target resources on the worst-affected parts of cities in the hope that spatially focused assistance will produce a more substantial aggregate effect than the equivalent amount of assistance spread thinly over a larger area. This approach may have some justification where problems are restricted to the physical fabric. But where the problems are more deep-seated the approach has major limitations. For instance, arbitrary boundaries drawn around particular areas do not isolate them from the wider urban economy and this form of assistance may have adverse repercussions elsewhere. Jobs may be displaced from surrounding areas as a result of competition with assisted firms and as a result of plant relocations. Jobs created locally may be taken by more qualified workers commuting in from elsewhere. Additional public resources spent in the targeted areas may also have been diverted at a direct cost to other areas. The net result of this redistribution of activity may simply be to encourage division and competition between communities for jobs and resources. Instead, deep-seated social and economic problems would be more effectively tackled by a combination of purposeful national economic policies intended to get more people back into work, national social policies aimed at helping poor and deprived sections of society unable to earn an adequate living from paid work, and more detailed urban-level interventions with public authorities playing a leading role.

Conflicting national policies

In the early years at least, the government publicly acknowledged that inner city problems required a concerted response across a wide range of policy fields. It suggested, for instance, that the public resources for urban development should come from directing its main policies and programmes towards the cities as well as from specific urban initiatives. Yet there is considerable evidence that these intentions have not been adhered to in practice. To begin with, many mainstream programmes have suffered overall cut-backs and controls, often in excess of any Urban Programme compensation that local authorities may have received. Government expenditure on housing has been the most seriously affected programme, being reduced from £5,803 million in 1978/9 to £2,264 million in 1984/5 (at 1982/3 prices), a cut in real terms of 61 per cent. This has had a major impact on the building of new public sector housing and on the amount of improvement work carried out, which has been particularly serious in inner urban areas where the housing stock is often oldest and in greatest need of repair and renewal. According to the Department of the Environment there has been a slight shift in the balance of spending in favour of the inner city (DoE, 1982), but this has been far outweighed by the size of the overall cut-back. Moreover, the shift in the balance of government subsidies towards owner occupation (via increased mortgage tax relief) and away from council housing has had a disproportionately negative effect on the inner cities, where there is so little owner occupied housing.

Similar points could be made about the government's policy towards the rate support grant – the principal source of local authority resources. In England, for instance, the total RSG suffered a 25 per cent cut in real terms between 1977/8 and 1984/5 (Church of England, 1985). Between 1977 and 1979 some emphasis was given to channelling greater help to inner city areas, but since then this has not happened. Thus, urban authorities have not been specially protected from the national cuts in RSG, which means that grants to the inner city Partnership and Programme authorities declined in real terms by 16 per cent between 1981/2 and 1984/5 (Church of England, 1985). In constant prices this reduction was nearly ten times greater than the increase in Urban Programme funding that these authorities received over the same period. These large reductions in central government support created serious difficulties for local authorities and led initially to substantial rate rises to protect the existing level of local services. The reaction of central government was to introduce highly controversial legislation enabling the Environment Secretary to impose penalties and to restrict the rate increases that local authorities felt it necessary to make in order to maintain services meeting growing needs. Curiously, many of the authorities that were ratecapped are the same ones that are recognised as in need of special assistance from urban policy.

Central government's wider industrial policies are also of obvious relevance to the prospects for urban economic development and job creation. However, evidence suggests that here too national policy has done little to improve the position of the inner cities. One of the principal objectives of the government's industrial policy has been to improve the international competitiveness of British manufacturing industry. In the late 1960s and 1970s a relatively active policy was pursued towards this end, attempting in the 1960s to promote efficiency through company mergers and rationalisations, and in the mid-1970s to increase exports and reduce imports by concentrating support on key companies and industries. In both cases geographical considerations were not permitted to impinge on the policies' wider objectives and the cities failed to secure their share of new investment (Lawless, 1981; Massey and Meegan, 1979). Between 1960 and 1981 major conurbations lost 1.7 million of the 2.1 million manufacturing jobs lost in Britain as a whole.

Developments in industrial policy since 1979 have had more serious effects on the cities. Most forms of direct state support for industry have been cut back, particularly for the older basic industries such as steel, shipbuilding and motor vehicles which have historically received substantial assistance. Government policies, together with increasingly competitive external conditions, have led to the closure of capacity and widespread redundancies. At a broader level restrictive macro-economic policies contributed substantially to the collapse of output in the economy in the early 1980s and to the sudden rise in unemployment: 1.2 million jobs were lost in manufacturing between 1980 and 1982 alone.

One of the few fields in which the government has extended support is in advanced technology, where a variety of schemes have been set up to promote industrial modernisation by encouraging the development and application of new products and processes. Most of these programmes have consisted of subsidies to companies for new investment and have been kept insulated from deliberate geographical influence – certainly no attempts have been made to direct investment to particular locations. For a variety of reasons, including questions of amenity, operating costs and traditions of labour organisation, the newer industries have generally shied away from the inner cities and shown a preference for the suburbs and smaller towns. This is clear, for example, in the case of the electronics industry in Scotland, where the major employers have avoided the strongly unionised labour markets of the large cities in preference for dispersed locations such as the planned New Towns of Livingston, Glenrothes and East Kilbride, towns such as Dunfermline and Greenock, and other smaller towns in the central lowlands. Many of these firms have, incidentally, benefited as much if not more from regional industrial policy as from new technology programmes, reinforcing the point that the whole gamut of the government's industrial measures has been poorly integrated with, if not contradictory to, its urban policies.

Interestingly, in Scotland the latent tension between urban development and wider economic objectives has been allowed to persist within a single agency – the Scottish Development Agency – and has to some extent been accommodated by an institutional separation into different divisions. By having a distinct area development division, many of the SDA's other mainstream activities, including its direct investments in industry, its attempts to attract inward investment and, increasingly, its provision of industrial sites and factories can be pursued without regard to the problems of particular localities. But within the area development division projects have a more clearly defined geographical basis and most are aimed at the older industrial towns. The SDA's programme of area-based activities began with the GEAR project in 1976 and was extended when crises arising from large-scale industrial closures in the Garnock Valley, Ayrshire, in 1979 (Glengarnock steelworks) and in Clydebank in 1980 (the Singer factory) demanded a major government response. The 'Task Forces' that were established involved the SDA in clearing and improving derelict land, building factories and offering advice and some financial support for industry. In 1981 the SDA tried to develop a more formalised area policy enabling it to plan ahead its interventions instead of responding at short notice to problems defined by others. The new approach was partly intended to allow the SDA to select localities which had better prospects of attracting private investment rather than being pressured into the worst-off problem areas in which it would be more difficult to achieve anything.

In practice a mixture of areas has been selected, reflecting the balance between political pressures for agency involvement (e.g. the Motherwell and Dundee projects) and the search for areas with more 'potential' (e.g. Leith). By March 1985 the SDA had spent a sizeable £141 million in its eight largest area projects. The GEAR scheme alone had taken £58 million of this (SDA, 1984a; 1985). In the rest of the Strathclyde Region, area projects and more informal agreements with local authorities have been established in Clydebank, Coatbridge, Port Dundas, Govan/Kinning Park and Finnieston. With the gradual reorientation of the SDA's approach in recent years, associated with the change in national government, area-based projects now include some smaller towns and rural areas as well as the traditional declining urban areas. The scope of these projects has changed too – they have become more short term, more narrowly focused, more interested in attracting private investment of whatever character, and less concerned with the wider social and economic development of each locality.

There are a number of possible reasons why the area approach has proved attractive (Boyle and Wannop, 1982; Keating and Midwinter, 1984). From the point of view of central government, area projects are highly visible, certainly more so than isolated, one-off investments. They are also less politically controversial and financially risky than providing long-term loans or acquiring shares in individual companies, because the public sector is simply providing the external conditions for private investment to take place rather than intervening more directly. Area projects also act as convenient shock-absorbers enabling government to accommodate and defuse local political pressures while nevertheless reducing local authority expenditure and pursuing avowedly business-oriented policies in tune with current Conservative thinking. For the SDA itself area projects provide a way of generating complementary programmes from local government. For local authorities they provide a welcome, albeit limited, addition to resources for promoting industrial development and environmental improvement in an increasingly stringent financial context.

Most of the area projects reflect the physical emphasis of the national urban initiatives referred to earlier. In the later projects in particular, the SDA concentrated on land development and factory construction, complemented by local authority road building and environmental improvement programmes. Relatively little direct investment in industry has taken place in these areas. This is partly because the main investment programmes of the SDA have been kept separate from the area projects but also because the SDA as a whole currently invests only a small amount directly in industry.[4] It has been forced increasingly to adopt a strictly commercial policy with clear requirements that it reduces the element of risk in its investments and earns a reasonable rate of return. This is a constraint that has increased since 1979 and limited the SDA's capacity to pursue a broader development strategy and a more active, strategic approach to investment guided by considerations other than short-term commercial viability. Other changes in the remit of the SDA, together with general restraints on expenditure, have, as indicated earlier, led it to adopt a lower profile in urban regeneration and to pursue a policy of maximising private investment at the expense of wider social and economic considerations. The emphasis increasingly is on marketing, image-building, providing advice and other selective activities which require less public sector involvement but which maximise its apparent impact.

Conclusion

In this wide-ranging survey of recent developments in Scottish and British urban policy we have set the context for our more detailed study of the GEAR experience. By way of a conclusion we can reflect briefly on some of the lessons that a study of the GEAR project may have for urban policy more generally. There is, for instance, an important question about the size of government resources committed to urban regeneration. During the 1980s there have been substantial reductions in public spending in the cities, both in urban initiatives themselves, and in more conventional local services, such as housing, education, transport and environmental programmes, for which the old industrial cities have particularly urgent needs. The GEAR scheme must be assessed within that larger context.

Questions must also be posed about the form and objectives of public spending. Using a series of very simple contrasts, it is possible to detect in urban policy in recent years a series of shifts in concern towards places rather than people, wealth creation rather than job creation, development *in* the inner cities rather than development *of* them, the favouring of incoming residents rather than existing inhabitants, and initia-

57

tives being imposed from central government rather than responding to the needs of local people and being developed in consultation with them. In the GEAR scheme the situation has been different in many respects, as we show in Chapter 12. Local people were consulted more extensively, local and central agencies worked more closely together, greater interest was taken in the living conditions of existing residents and development programmes were more wide-ranging and broadly based. Thus the experience gained here may offer useful lessons which challenge the directions in which national urban policy has been evolving.

Notes

1 See Chapters 3, 5, 6 and 12 for a fuller discussion of these issues.

2 In Scotland support for the growth of already established New Towns was not affected to the same extent except that the newly designated New Town at Stonehouse was cancelled.

3 There are three Enterprise Zones in Scotland, in Clydebank, Tayside and Invergordon.

4 At the end of March 1985 direct investment (shares and loans) stood at only 10.6 per cent of total capital employed whereas investment in land and buildings was 85 per cent (SDA, 1985).

PLATES

Some Images of GEAR
Shiela T. McDonald

GEAR used to house major employers in the engineering field like Beardmore and the Clyde Iron works. In the past few years these factories have been swept away, feeding the huge scrapyards in the process, and offering sites for other uses on reclamation.

1a Part of the giant Beardmore complex

1b The former Clyde Iron Works. The site is now part of Cambuslang Investment Park

2a Templeton's carpet factory, known as the Doge's Palace

2b Factory units at Broad Street

The fate of all the large factories has not been demolition. The spendid Templeton's carpet factory of 1889 on the edge of Glasgow Green is now restored to new life as the Templeton Business Centre. It has offices, workshops and studios for small businesses, as well as a specialist advice service.

New accommodation for small firms has also been provided on several sites using 'secure' designs. Workers in existing firms have found new opportunities for a lunchtime game on sites which, instead of being left in a derelict state, have been temporarily grassed over as part of the environmental improvement programme in GEAR.

3   A new urban landscape is there to be enjoyed

Most of the housing in the east end was in stone-built tenement blocks. The poor living conditions were not confined to GEAR, and throughout the city programmes of modernisation and backcourt improvement have been vigorously pursued with the help of community-based housing associations. The size of the buildings means that scaffolding is required, and a great deal of inconvenience can be suffered before change is accomplished. Cleaning of the tenement facades, especially on main road frontages, has done a great deal to enhance the image presented to the world.

4a Backcourt at Bridgeton in 1977

4b Scaffolding on a tenement at Tollcross Road undergoing refurbishment by a housing association

5a Blackened frontages at Parkhead Cross in days gone by

5b The centre property in 5a now modernised, and cleaned to bring
out the pinkish colour of the sandstone

6a A management co-operative has been set up in this street. Window replacement is in progress

6b Houses have been re-roofed but the environment is poor and an initiative is under way

6c A dovecot: typically any vacant site is colonised by a local 'doo fancier'

Not all the housing in GEAR is in tenement blocks. The area has a rich variety of house types, including high rise flats and four-in-a-block dwellings with gardens. Unimaginative layout in some existing local authority developments has prompted new approaches in recent public housing developments.

7 A little over half a mile away the landscaping is looked after by a management co-operative in this Scottish Special Housing Association development

The Scottish Special Housing Association gave identity to another scheme by incorporating one of the city's oldest tenements. The tenement dates from 1771, and several bodies contributed to its restoration.

8a The street frontage of the old tenement on the Gallowgate which was restored in 1983 after many vicissitudes

8b Rear view before restoration

8c Rear view of the restored building incorporated into a new development

9a New private housing near Glasgow Green, approached here by a path created as part of an environmental improvement scheme

9b A private refurbishment at Shettleston

The early evidence of improvements in GEAR quickly encouraged private developers to take up the opportunity of building new houses or of refurbishing old ones.

The scale of the change in GEAR is not always appreciated by people coming to the area today. Much clearance took place in the 1960s and early 1970s and vast derelict sites covered 20 per cent of the area when GEAR started in 1976. The vastness of the space and the depressing effect of blighted properties is already beginning to be forgotten as schemes transform the appearance of the area and the opportunities it offers.

10a Part of Crownpoint Road twenty years ago. Ten years ago it was vacant ground in Planning Committee ownership

10b The sports complex which opened to the public in 1985 has a wide range of facilities and is linked to adjoining schools

11a Will it bring new opportunities to youngsters like these?

11b One place in GEAR where minimal change is desirable is this natural laboratory in a loop of the River Clyde

The need to retain and reinforce the focal points within the area to maintain continuity and preserve identity has led to much attention being given to environmental schemes at traditional centres.

12a The Bridgeton 'Umbrella' was built as a night shelter for the destitute in the nineteenth century. It retains a place in the affections of local people following redecoration and creation of an environmental scheme for local traffic. There is even talk of floodlighting here . . .

12b An open sitting area close to a new supermarket has been well received by local people

13 Parkhead continues to be a meeting place. The carving and detail on significant corner buildings has been revealed anew by cleaning, in this case of a light sandstone

14a The police service has moved into extensive new offices in London Road where maintaining local contacts could be harder, despite the efforts of the community involvement branch

14b Modest community flats in the area have become a focus of local activity

Sites and premises, large and small, have been taken up by public authorities participating in GEAR, including Greater Glasgow Health Board, the Regional Council and the District Council.

15 Refurbishment of the Winter Garden of the People's Palace at Glasgow Green brings events into the locality, in this case Glasgow Senior Citizens' Orchestra

Glasgow's weekend market has been given a facelift and now has an Enterprise Trust to continue the development and management of the market area. It stands as a symbol of the revitalisation of Glasgow's east end, continuing a local tradition in the inner part of the area which draws many people from further afield into GEAR.

16 One of the new gateways to the Barras seen from a pedestrian route

With acknowledgments to the people of GEAR, and to the Glasgow Herald (1a, 4a, 5a), John Hume (8a, 10a), Keith Kintrea (4b, 5b, 6a, 6b, 9b), the People's Palace (15), the Scottish Development Agency (1b, 2b, 11b), the Scottish Special Housing Association (8b) and Leslie Whitefield (2a, 11a, 14a).

PART II
The GEAR Project

3 URBAN RENEWAL AND THE ORIGINS OF GEAR

Urlan Wannop and Roger Leclerc

Urban renewal: provision or promotion?

Urban renewal managed by public enterprise is not new in the United Kingdom. The first civic improvement commissions and trusts were set up considerably more than a century ago. The GEAR project came more than a century after Glasgow's City Improvement Trust was established in 1866, empowered to acquire and clear unfit and overcrowded housing and to make new streets. Within a decade, the Trust had built Alexandra Park but had failed to find private builders prepared to redevelop sites in the old city, from which 25,000 people had been displaced by clearance (Slaven, 1975). Trying itself to build where the private sector had failed, the Trust had by 1914 replaced only 2,000 of the many more houses it had demolished (Butt, 1971). The long delays before housing demolished in renewal schemes is replaced are still a familiar problem three-quarters of a century later. Thus the GEAR scheme is only an episode in a longer and larger story of urban renewal, running far back in time and still unfolding, and involving many agencies besides those principally responsible for the project. This chapter introduces the project and places it in that wider context.

The United Kingdom's experience has provoked four important criticisms of the management of renewal. By the 1970s it was being said that local authorities had organised their programmes badly – particularly in allowing clearance to precede rebuilding by many years, thereby wreaking social havoc and wasting resources on a colossal scale. It was held that the quality of design of the new houses and their environment often lacked the domestic humanity of the buildings demolished. It was asserted that the comprehensive development areas which had been declared under planning legislation from the 1950s onwards were brutally insensitive, not only in their impact on the mature communities which Willmott and Young (1957) described, but also in destroying the local economy and the social and economic value of much

61

of the housing and the surrounding urban structure. Finally, it was claimed that renewal often made little improvement in the care which families gave to their new environment, or in their new public landlord's willingness to involve them in planning and managing this environment. These failings were not confined to public authorities nor to Britain. While some of the criticism directed at the management of British renewal schemes derived from well-researched British cases (Davies, 1972; Dennis, 1971), much was inspired by experience in the United States (Goodman, 1972) which was less relevant to British conditions.

Many of Glasgow's problems of large-scale clearance and population dispersal were clearly foreseen. Right at the outset of Glasgow's programme of comprehensive renewal, Brennan (1959) had foreseen that because overcrowding of the inner city had been so much reduced since the Clyde Valley Regional Plan of 1946 (Abercrombie and Matthew, 1949), the need for overspill had already so declined that the impending policy of clearance might lead to abandonment of inner areas. Twenty-five years later, Brennan's warning of 'the consequence of pursuing the official policy and ignoring or postponing for another decade the renovation of existing property' (1959, p. 199) had become a commonplace criticism of what went wrong with renewal in the 1960s and early 1970s. He prescribed that

> for the majority the obvious solution, if it could be managed, would be to make available to them the components for a better life – not in a new town in ten or twenty years' time, but in Govan now . . . It should not be necessary, however, for the same agency – the local authority – to be planner, developer, owner, operator and social guardian of the scheme. (1959, p. 200)

Brennan went on to suggest

> that what is needed is a fillip to redevelopment and the reorganisation of affairs so that individual decisions and actions towards improvement can become cumulative. What is needed is a promoter rather than a provider (p. 201)

His proposition was that

The road and footpaths could be repaired, the lighting improved, a little extra care taken in street cleaning, and so on. The planning powers which the local authority already possesses could also be used to improve the appearance of shop fronts and commercial premises. Above all, the Corporation could let it be known that these areas were not being allowed to deteriorate until they joined the list of places awaiting demolition. It should be made clear as forcefully as possible that, on the contrary, they are to be reconstructed and repaired; that they would be profitable districts in which to consolidate or expand business, that because their future was assured they would be good districts in which to try out new kinds of services or establish new ventures, and that they would be very pleasant places in which to live. They should be publicised as centres of a new 'Brighten up the City' campaign. (p. 202)

Brennan's perceptions – formulated a quarter of a century before the 'Glasgow's Miles Better' campaign – were neglected for many years, not only in Glasgow, but up and down the United Kingdom – in Bute in Cardiff, in the Kite in Cambridge, on the Scotland Road in Liverpool, at Rye Hill in Newcastle, on the Shankhill in Belfast and in other less publicised renewal projects.

Provision rather than promotion continued as the policy for Glasgow throughout the 1960s, against Brennan's prescription. When Glasgow's planners and its Medical Officer of Health took stock of the City's housing problems in the late 1950s (Corporation of the City of Glasgow, 1960), 85,000 of a total of 114,000 houses in twenty-nine separate areas of inner Glasgow were considered to be left with only a 'short life'. Clearance before 1980 was assumed appropriate for all these houses, although it would

involve the demolition of almost 90,000 houses or nearly five times the number cleared in the 20 years between the wars. To this total must, however, be added the thousands of equally poor houses throughout the city which are not contained in the areas of major redevelopment.

The planners knew that the intended renewal programme

was of unprecedented size, just as they noted the failure of pre-war slum clearance to provide open space, playgrounds and other community facilities to accompany fit, new houses. Consequently, it was argued that the twenty-nine comprehensive development areas (CDAs) should be larger than slum clearance normally required, so that the general urban environment as well as the houses could be improved.

The practical difficulties of managing Glasgow's unprecedented programme of urban renewal were soon evident, apart from any social and economic problems which the City shared with others. Hart (1968) closely studied the way in which the Corporation mounted the CDA programme. Although he saw that the old slum clearance would have been inadequate, his account shows how complex and protracted the comprehensive approach could be. He noted that while the lower-status Planning Committee produced the outline plans for use of land in the CDAs, the higher-status Housing Committee was able to clear and redevelop for housing in advance of detailed plans. Two difficulties arose in particular. In inner parts of the City, houses were being cleared much faster than the Corporation was replacing them. New building was mostly confined to remote suburban fields. Also, legal and purchasing procedures were cumbersome and the outline form of the CDA plans brought uncertainty and blight to local owners and firms. The CDAs were intended to provide a total approach, but implementation was fragmented and painstaking. This was not all the Corporation's fault; the Scottish Office was sometimes equivocal in its support for the CDAs.

Hart's independent view of the early years of the CDA programme saw continuing problems. Though progress had been made, it was questionable whether it matched Glasgow's housing and industrial needs. Hart thought it right that there should be firmer and more systematic supervision of each project. He considered legal procedures to be adequate, but that political will and local administration were diffuse and insufficiently co-ordinated.

The road to GEAR
Into the 1970s, however, the climate for urban renewal changed, and GEAR emerged not directly from the foresight of Brennan and Hart, but from the convergence of various

motives. In Britain, there was accelerating intervention by central government in local government's responsibilities for urban management, a reduced need for extra space in new towns coupled with growing concern about the 'inner cities' and, in Scotland, there was a history of rising tension between the Scottish Office and Glasgow Corporation over the quality of the City's renewal and the future to which it was leading the City.

Early in 1972, a memorandum by the Scottish Development Department was forthright about 'Glasgow Planning: Present Problems and Their Implications for Policy'. As the basis for pressure on the Corporation to change its approach, the memorandum took a total view of the City. It pointed out that the population was falling faster than assumed by the Development Plan which enshrined the CDA programme, but it was less concerned about the size than about the structure of population. It was the rising proportion of the very young and the very elderly which was worrying, and the high number of dependants associated with a diminishing proportion of people of working age. Similarly, unskilled workers were becoming a progressively larger proportion of the population, associated with the failure of the City to attract new industry and to put enough effort into improving the range and number of jobs. The problem was suspected to be partly allied to the limited choice of housing tenure in Glasgow, and to the form of much housing. 'In general Glasgow is becoming more and more a City in which the family seeking accommodation has very little choice other than a Corporation house, which is likely to be in a multi-storey block or walk-up tenement block, or an old and probably sub-standard private house.'

The way out of Glasgow's descending spiral of social and economic decline seen from the Scottish Office in Edinburgh was by co-ordinated action. A government assisted pro-gramme of environmental recovery was about to begin – 'Too much of the City appears bleak and has a look of present or imminent dereliction.' The social as well as the physical environment required treatment:

Until then those from elsewhere who might have a
contribution to make to Glasgow's social and economic

65

well-being will generally be unwilling to come to the City and many residents who could also do much for the City will consider that life is better elsewhere and act accordingly.

The memorandum sought to show that there was a case not so much for revision of Glasgow's Development Plan as for a fresh start. It said that there was immediate need to suspend development which was making the City's position worse. The CDAs, including even those already approved in detail, should be examined first, with readiness to change drastically where not irretrievably committed. It was suggested that no purpose would be served by the Corporation submitting further CDA proposals based on the then Development Plan, or by the Scottish Office issuing further approvals for housing schemes already before the Scottish Development Department.

This was the troubled road to GEAR, routed across the whole face of the City and not just the east end of Glasgow, where CDAs were particularly extensive including the proposals for the Bridgeton-Dalmarnock CDA in the early 1970s which crystallised the issues that concerned the Scottish Office. As an area approach to regeneration, GEAR descended from this local history as well as from the lineage of the Inner Area Studies carried out for the Department of the Environment (1977c) in Liverpool, Birmingham and Lambeth, together with the earlier Urban Guidelines (Department of the Environment, 1973). Representing the Department of the Environment's claim to co-ordinate policy for inner city regeneration, these studies carried over some of the lessons learnt from the early Community Development Projects (1974), launched by the Home Office in 1969 and financed by the Urban Programme announced the previous year, particularly their emphasis on the regeneration of the economy. Arising between these initiatives and the Labour Government's 1977 White Paper on Policy for the Inner Cities (Department of the Environment, 1977a), from which flowed the Partnership and Programme projects for English and Welsh cities, GEAR incorporated central government intervention in urban renewal on a scale unequalled in England until the Conservative government introduced Urban Development Corporations six years later in the London and Merseyside Docklands, under the powers of the Local Government, Planning and Land Act, 1980.

Although an independent study (Forbes and McBain, 1967) had been made of the problems of Springburn – an old, inner district of Glasgow – Scotland lay outside the field for which the Department of the Environment and Home Office were responsible; the one exception was the Community Development Project in Paisley. Eric Gillett (1983), who headed the Scottish Development Department as GEAR was launched, has referred to urban aid as

> the only government policy specifically directed towards helping inner urban areas. Both Labour and Tory administrations have been anxious to see this employed more widely, in other cities as well as Glasgow, but it is not a policy specifically designed for Scotland, and changes in it have to a large extent followed the line taken in England. Scotland's distinctive contribution to inner city policy was the measures adopted for eastern Glasgow. (Gillett, 1983, p. 118)

The GEAR project accordingly coincided less with the rising tide of experiments in urban renewal and area management taking place in England, but was perhaps most impelled by the hardened dissatisfaction in the Scottish Office with the quality of Glasgow's comprehensive development projects and their management. Ministers of both Labour and Conservative governments appear to have shared these concerns, reinforced as they compared the deteriorating condition of Glasgow with what they regarded as successful planning policies in the new towns, for which they were themselves responsible. The challenges of Ministers to Glasgow's councillors over the slow pace and drab quality of rebuilding in comprehensive development areas, had been answered by the Corporation's (1972) calculations of their city-wide deficiency of recreation space and of social facilities, to which were attached assessments of massive financial needs based upon abstract target standards. Ministers never quite reached the point of rejecting any of the Corporation's proposals despite the encouragement of their civil servants' memoranda, although they came close to doing so with the Bridgeton-Dalmarnock CDA.

When announced by the Secretary of State for Scotland in May 1976, he said that the Glasgow Eastern Area Renewal project had emerged from talks about mounting a major attack on urban deprivation in West Central Scotland, supported by Strathclyde Regional Council, Glasgow District Council, the Scottish Development Agency and the Scottish Special Housing Association – a housing authority funded and directed by central government to operate all over Scotland, in agreement with local housing authorities. Funds for the project were to be found primarily by diverting existing resources to areas of severe multiple deprivation, with additions from the resources of the Scottish Development Agency, the Housing Association and the Urban Programme. The Secretary of State noted that the project was to achieve 'the comprehensive rehabilitation of a major sector of the City' within a wider programme, co-ordinating

> the application of resources to a single large area, without making any additional call on the ratepayers or reducing the resources available for the redevelopment of the rest of the City. The remit will cover the planning and development of the social, environmental and industrial life of the area. The management and co-ordination of the project was to be the responsibility of the Scottish Development Agency. The Agency would also contribute by carrying out its own functions of derelict land clearance and environmental improvement, by building factories and helping to fill them with employment-creating projects, and by supporting appropriate commercial developments. For the purpose of this project, the Agency would build up a specialist staff. In doing this it would hope to be able to call on staff who would have worked on Stonehouse, in addition to drawing on its present staff resources.

Stonehouse was the latest Scottish new town on which work was about to start, but which had been cancelled a few days earlier.

One feature of the management of the project was revealed in the Secretary of State's declaration that the Scottish Special Housing Association was to carry the main burden of house-building, while building for owner-occupation and renovation were to be given greater emphasis. This was a clear change of direction in policies for the east end which was steadily becoming a huge council estate. But uncertainties remained: the first task would be to prepare a new comprehensive plan, while the District and Regional Councils would retain their full statutory powers in the area, including planning and the provision of infrastructure. Such planning procedures could be workable only with exceptional tolerance by Glasgow District Council, whose responsibilities had to be tacitly if not formally suspended, allowing the SDA's team to take over the lead, reassessing priorities and opportunities in the light of the new resources to be devoted to the GEAR area.

These arrangements presaged a real but not inevitable hiatus, while the Agency team learned to undertake political and technical tasks for which neither they nor anyone else in the United Kingdom had much experience. Meanwhile, the District Council had to adjust not only to the fact that since the creation of Strathclyde Regional Council in 1975 it was a minority shareholder in its own City's government, but to the GEAR project's further reduction of its powers over a part of the City which had great political significance – as we showed in Chapter 1. This hiatus persisted for at least two years while the two local authorities reconciled themselves to the Agency's role in the project and learnt to work together. Key officials in central government and in policy planning sections of the Agency felt, as we did in making our review (Wannop, 1982), that the Agency's GEAR team was less assertive in reviewing planning strategy in the east end than was justified. Certainly economic changes on Clydeside, changes in the conurbation's housing market, and the collapse in the demand for land in certain parts of the city together called for a major rethinking of urban strategies.

Later on, central government tried to resolve many of these problems in England by creating the London and Merseyside Urban Development Corporations, which were given full powers for the development of land in their areas – much like a new town development corporation. But the Secretary of State for Scotland did not persist with the proposition of a Development Corporation for GEAR when his suggestion was rejected by the Regional and District Councils (Gillett, 1983), and in Scotland the divided planning responsibilities of the GEAR project persisted in the Leith, Dundee, Motherwell and

other subsequent SDA projects. The SDA tried to resolve the
resulting difficulties, and avoid the initial hiatus at the start of
such projects, by preparing for these later schemes a more
rigorous Project Agreement, based on more assertive use of the
Agency's financial bargaining power.

Why did Scotland act so early?

Why was GEAR launched when it was, so soon after the
creation of a new system of local government which included
a strategic authority like the Strathclyde Regional Council,
uniquely extensive and resourced amongst metropolitan
authorities in the United Kingdom and designed primarily to
tackle Clydeside's historic planning problems? And why did
another five years have to pass before comparable government
interventions in England created the two Docklands Development Corporations and the Department of the Environment's
Task Force for Merseyside? The explanations lie in circumstances peculiar to Scotland. Until the mid-1970s Glasgow
was regarded by the Cabinet as being itself an exception – the
most striking example of metropolitan decline in the United
Kingdom. It was some years after GEAR was launched that the
comparable plight of English conurbations was recognised as
they were hit by economic disaster which was highlighted by
the riots of 1981.

Because Clydeside is the only conurbation within the
Scottish Office's responsibility, it received the kind of
attention which the Department of the Environment has to
divide between seven metropolitan areas in England. Moreover, Scotland is a smaller country. Since the Clyde Valley
Regional Plan of 1946 and earlier, the Scottish Office has been
able to give much closer attention to local affairs than is
possible for Ministries in England. That was reflected in a
remarkable continuity of Scottish regional planning policies,
expressed not only in strategic plans but in determined action.
Government drew local authorities into the preparation of the
West Central Scotland Plan, presented in 1974, whose major
proposals included not only the fullest analytical case for
what was to become the Scottish Development Agency – a
case wholly welcome to the Scottish Office – but also a
recommendation – unwelcome to government – that the
recently designated new town at Stonehouse should be

deferred. The following year, the new Strathclyde Regional Council, as one of their strategic initiatives, pressed not for the mere deferral of Stonehouse, but for its abandonment. Government came to concur, and GEAR followed immediately.

Why did major local authorities accept what they might have regarded as an unprecedented displacement of their status within a major British conurbation? To Strathclyde Regional Council, success in persuading the government to abandon Stonehouse may have given them the confidence to accept the SDA's shared responsibility for the GEAR project. It may also have been that the Scottish Office's sceptical view of the capacities of Glasgow's management of its renewal programme was shared by the councillors from Lanarkshire, Ayrshire and other former authorities outside the City, who dominated the leadership of the Regional Council. To Glasgow District Council, which had acquired a lot of new members in the course of local government reorganisation, it may have seemed that the invasion of the city by the SDA was more a criticism of its predecessor's capacities than of its own; or it may simply have been glad of the extra funds which this central government intervention promised for the City.

Moreover, for a recently elected central government and two new local authorities, 1976 was also a time of hope, encouraged by the control which the Labour Party had secured at all three levels. Coupled to the longer history of central government intervention in Scottish affairs, conditions in Glasgow were ripe for something like the GEAR project to a degree not reached in English conurbations until the riots of 1981.

4 JOBS AND INCOMES
Andrew A. McArthur

Prosperous cities renew themselves, generating new investment that replaces obsolete buildings and finding new uses for
vacant land. The first priority of the GEAR scheme, led by an
industrial development agency, was to revive the failing east
end economy. A substantial proportion of the funds channelled through the scheme have been used to construct and
rehabilitate premises for small enterprises and to improve the
industrial environment. This partly reflects a popular view
that an important cause of the economic decline of large cities
has been the lack of small factories and workshops in areas
long dominated by large enterprises and the generally low
priority given to small enterprises in programmes for urban
renewal. These problems have been exacerbated by large-scale
redevelopment programmes which demolish so many small
shops and factories. Our own main concern with factory
building policies was to assess how far they have achieved
their main objective of replacing lost jobs, and to consider
how they could be made more effective and what other locally
initiated policies might be available.

We made a survey of small firms in premises provided by
the Scottish Development Agency (SDA) in the Clydeside
conurbation. Our sample of enterprises was drawn from the
GEAR area in Glasgow's east end and from Clydebank, a
neighbouring town on the north-western fringe of Glasgow
with a population of about 50,000. These are the two main
areas of the Clydeside conurbation where large-scale policies
of this sort have been brought to bear. In the GEAR area, by
March 1984, £9.6 million had been spent on land assembly
and site preparation, £17.8 million on factory building and
£12.8 million on environmental improvements – some of
which was designed to make the small factories more
attractive (Leclerc and Draffan, 1984). In Clydebank, the
financial commitment of the SDA totals £19 million of which
£10.5 million had been spent by March 1982 (SDA, 1982).

An emerging tradition

Government policies for Glasgow's east end were described in Chapter 1. Only a brief reminder of their evolution is needed here. As the numbers out of work have risen, central and local authorities have increasingly resorted to locally-based strategies concerned wtih economic development, the training of the unemployed and other steps to reduce the numbers out of work. The GEAR scheme marked the beginning of the new urban policy in Scotland, and the SDA had ambitious economic objectives for this initiative. These were to retain and create jobs in the area, to help local residents secure work, and to involve the community in the process.

Area development policies have been taken further by the Conservatives since 1979. Clydebank was the new administration's first Scottish initiative of this sort, introduced in response to the closure of the world-famous Singer sewing machine factory in the town. Part of central Clydebank was designated as one of the first enterprise zones in 1980. Here firms received 100 per cent rates relief and a 100 per cent allowance for tax purposes on new building works. Compared with the objectives outlined in the GEAR scheme, the stated aims in Clydebank and subsequent area projects have been less ambitious, involving little discussion of community issues. They have been confined to vaguer notions about improving the health of the local economy and creating the conditions for generating wealth. The Clydebank enterprise zone is, however, very much a 'planned' environment, quite different from the early free market conceptions of enterprise zones which gave rise to fears that they would lead to a return of nineteenth-century squalor. It has provided yet another marketing tool and an additional layer of financial incentives to support a national development agency's expensive strategy for creating an attractive, modern, well-serviced environment for business. The consultants commissioned by the Department of the Environment to monitor enterprise zones throughout the country found that this zone had received the second largest amount of public expenditure by May 1982 (Roger Tym and Partners, 1983).

Tackling a legacy of decline

As we showed in Chapter 1, Glasgow's east end has suffered a steady erosion of its industrial base with decline becoming catastrophic during the 1970s. Clydebank has had a similar experience. Since 1961 the GEAR area has lost over 24,000 manufacturing jobs and Clydebank over 27,000. Some small growth in employment has taken place in both places in the service sector of the economy, but when compared to the collapse in manufacturing this contribution pales into insignificance. This poor performance is largely a consequence of having a very high proportion of jobs in manufacturing industry – particularly in its more vulnerable sectors. As a result the national decline has been magnified at the local scale. The loss of jobs has come mainly through the contraction or closure of the larger and longer established local employers, many of whom had become household names – firms such as Singer Sewing Machines and John Brown's shipyard in Clydebank, and Beardmore's, the Clyde Iron Works and Templeton's carpets in the GEAR area.

These losses struck at training as well as jobs, being concentrated in the larger firms which used to recruit a lot of apprentices. At the time of my survey in 1982, the ten largest manufacturing firms in the GEAR area – though they still accounted for around two-thirds of the total workers – had reduced their workforces by 30 per cent or 3,200 jobs since 1977. In Clydebank the collapse of employment in large firms was even more pronounced. Four firms had accounted for 60 per cent of employment in local manufacturing industry in 1978. By 1982 two of these – including Singer which had employed 5,600 in 1976 – had closed, and the remaining two had drastically reduced their workforces.

The erosion of an area's industrial base has many consequences for the community. As jobs decline many people leave in search of work. These migrants tend to be the most mobile, with better skills and prospects of securing work. They leave behind the poorer and less able. Both areas have lost a lot of people. Strathclyde Regional Council expect Clydebank's population to have fallen from 58,727 in 1971 to around 49,500 by 1985, a decline of almost 16 per cent. In the GEAR area, where industrial decline has been combined with a massive slum clearance programme, the loss was catastrophic. Population fell from 81,900 to 45,000 (−45 per cent) between 1971 and 1978. Meanwhile unemployment rates rose. In the summer of 1982, 17.2 per cent of Clydebank's workforce (6,265 people) were out of work and, in the same year, in the GEAR area, male unemployment averaged around 30 per cent. The relationship between unemployment and the number of jobs in an area is not a simple one. It must be understood before better employment strategies can be formulated. Clydebank has a workforce of around 24,500 but had only approximately 17,250 jobs in 1981. It may, therefore, seem surprising that unemployment is not higher. Part of the explanation lies in the fact that Clydebank is closely integrated with the surrounding urban economy. Large numbers of workers travel in and out, cushioning the town somewhat from the impact of adverse changes in the local economy. Approximately two-thirds of those working in Clydeside commute to the town, mainly from north-west Glasgow, and from Dumbarton a few miles to the west. A similar proportion of workers living in Clydebank have jobs outside the town. Furthermore, the local workforce is relatively highly skilled. When jobs are lost, skilled workers are generally more mobile and have better chances of finding work than unskilled labour.

The GEAR area is different. Although here too there is a large interchange of labour with the wider conurbation, it is less pronounced than in Clydebank. Almost half the resident workforce appeared to hold jobs outside the area in 1982. The relationship between jobs and the proportion of residents who are economically active is the reverse of that in Clydebank. The east end is 'job rich'. Despite having an unemployment rate which is about 10 per cent higher than Clydebank's, there are around 40,000 local jobs for a local labour force of about 16,000. Put another way, while in Clydebank there are approximately 0.7 jobs for every worker living in the town, in the GEAR area there are over three and a half times as many − about 2.5 jobs per worker.

The reason why unemployment in the GEAR area is so high, despite this apparent abundance of jobs, is that the area houses higher concentrations of workers of the types who are most vulnerable to unemployment − particularly the unqualified young, the unskilled and redundant workers from industries with a long history of decline. Most young people in the east end leave school without any qualifications and unemployment in the under 18 age group is twice the level reached by the whole of Glasgow. At the time of our study, over one-third of the jobless had been out of work for over a year, many for much longer. Those particularly affected by long-term unemployment were the young adults under 24, in what should be the first decade of their working lives, and older workers under 45 who may never get a job again. Almost one-quarter of the long-term unemployed in 1982 had been out of work for over three years. Therefore, despite a gross surplus of jobs, large numbers of local people were effectively excluded from the plentiful opportunities for work available locally.

If economic policies operating solely in a particular locality are to be effective in reversing such an industrial collapse and helping those who suffer from it they must provide opportunities for the young and the older workers, the poorer and the less skilled groups, and particularly for people who are tied to, or trapped in, the area. In fact the area-based strategies operating in Clydebank and the east end take no account of those needs. They are based on the hope that, by expanding the stock of small premises in the area, tidying up the industrial environment and providing a range of financial and other incentives particularly geared to the small firm, a wave of new entrepreneurs will come forward and set up new businesses. Some of these people, it is hoped – previously employed in contracting local industries – will set up new firms (possibly using their redundancy money for such purposes) and provide jobs for local people on the unemployment register. The role of the state is to support, advise and encourage entrepreneurs. Collapsing large-scale manufacturing industries will be replaced by dynamic small firms with a strong potential for growth.

Some policy-makers privately express doubts about this scenario. Others support it partly for lack of any convincing alternative. But notions of this sort underlie most area-based policies for generating jobs, and, on the basis of statistics showing overall totals of firms setting up and jobs created, frequently quoted by public agencies, many people believe these policies are already succeeding. In the GEAR area, for example, the SDA expected to create up to 4,865 jobs by 1983 as a result of its factory and workshop development. In Clydebank, the SDA reported in April 1984 that projected total employment among the 170 firms occupying their premises at the time was around 2,098 jobs but gave no time-scale for this estimate (SDA, 1984b).

These are impressive claims. However, before such policies can be evaluated we need to know what is genuinely new among the enterprises and jobs attracted, and how much of this activity is attributable to the policies concerned. We must also consider redistributive effects which may not be immediately obvious if we look only at one area in isolation. These effects may be positive and negative. A firm which moves to an SDA factory may release premises, which, being older and cheaper, may be filled by a new firm, thereby giving a hidden boost to a new enterprise (Valente and Leigh, 1982). In other cases such redistributive effects may be damaging if firms simply switch jobs from other areas and – by operating within a relatively subsidised environment – increase unemployment elsewhere.

'Softer' and more qualitative issues are also important. In an area like Glasgow's east end many workers are virtually excluded from the formal economy. We should therefore ask who is gaining and who is losing from the employment generated, and consider not only the numbers previously unemployed who are securing jobs, but the types of unemployed people they represent, how they found out about and secured a place in work, and where they live. Similar questions can be directed towards the entrepreneurs by considering the extent to which local people, particularly from among the unemployed, are moving into self-employment. We should also consider the costs of the whole operation and think about other ways in which the millions of pounds poured into depressed localities might be more effectively used.

We explored these issues in the GEAR area and Clydebank. One hundred interviews with managers or owners of firms were carried out which amounted to 80 per cent of firms occupying SDA premises in these two places at that time. Total employment among the firms interviewed amounted to

Andrew A. McArthur

1,175 people which was about 2 per cent of all those working in the GEAR area and 1.8 per cent of those working in Clydebank. It was possible to learn a good deal about these employees because their firms were small independent concerns run by people who knew their workers well.

Generating new enterprise
The main impact of providing small factories in the GEAR area and Clydebank seems to have been a redistribution of existing enterprises within the Glasgow conurbation, rather than the emergence of new economic activity. The majority of the firms, three-fifths, had previously occupied other premises from which they had moved part or all of their business activity. The remaining two-fifths were new, their business activity not previously having taken place elsewhere on a full-time commercial basis. The two areas differed in this respect: in the GEAR area only one-quarter of the firms were new enterprises, whereas in Clydebank the figure was more than twice as high (58 per cent).

A more detailed knowledge of these movements is needed to assess what has happened to the total stock of enterprise, both in these areas and in the wider urban economy. Of those firms which had moved, the overwhelming majority (88 per cent) had come from premises situated elsewhere in the Glasgow area. Indeed, in the GEAR area, approximately two-thirds of the moves took place within the east end itself. Incoming investment from outside the conurbation was small. Only two firms moving in from outside the Strathclyde Region had set up in these premises (Table 4.1).

New firms may have emerged elsewhere to work in premises left by those moving to SDA workshops. The moving

Table 4.1: Origins of moving firms

	Local	Elsewhere in Glasgow	Elsewhere in Strathclyde Region	Other	Total
GEAR	25	11	3	–	39
Clydebank	7	10	2	2	21
Total moving	32	21	5	2	60

firms were therefore asked if they knew the current use of their old premises, and fifty-three of these sixty firms did know. Eighteen of their old premises were occupied by another firm which moved in after they had left, and thirteen were still occupied either by the respondent firm or by another with which it had shared the premises. The remaining twenty-nine were either demolished, vacant or had been based in the entrepreneur's home. Thus about half the old premises were occupied and providing work, though not necessarily in new firms. This figure will probably be higher when seven of the premises which were known to be vacant are used again for another purpose. Thus, at one step back in the chain reaction, slightly more than half of the original premises were either housing a second tier of new enterprise and employment or providing a better basis for the expansion of existing business. If half the new premises and a similar proportion of premises involved in subsequent links of the chain have these multiplier effects, then the total number of enterprises affected will be double the number of new premises initially provided.

It seems unlikely that many of the firms in SDA premises would have been lost to the Regional economy without these new factories. Although about one-third had considered an alternative location, for seven firms this was a local one, for seventeen a location elsewhere in Glasgow, and for ten elsewhere in Strathclyde. Therefore, had they not set up in their location most would probably have looked for another location within the city. The government's official monitoring study of the enterprise zone in Clydebank confirmed this finding by concluding that had firms not located in the area where the special policy was operating, most would have remained in the region with only 15 per cent locating elsewhere (Roger Tym and Partners, 1983). Further information about the markets of the firms surveyed confirms their close association with the Clydeside economy: 53 per cent of them purchased their main supplies from within the conurbation while over half the firms' main customers lay within Strathclyde Region and were centred mainly on the Glasgow conurbation.

Self-employment
Changing the focus from firms to people, we must ask next

whether local people, particularly the unemployed, gain opportunities to enter self-employment and set up new businesses. The home addresses of entrepreneurs in the new firms show that there were few people from the local area among them. Only twelve people or 18 per cent of those in new firms lived locally, while a further sixteen lived elsewhere in the City. Over half of the new entrepreneurs lived outwith Glasgow, possibly preferring the more affluent and attractive townships outside the urban area (Table 4.2).

Table 4.2: Residence of entrepreneurs
(percentage of total)

	Local	Glasgow	Strathclyde Region	Other	Total
Moving firms	16	37	37	10	100
New firms	18	25	35	22	100
Total	17	32	36	15	100

Information is for 163 individuals in 91 firms

The extent to which people have moved from unemployment into self-employment has also been small. Only about 8 per cent of all entrepreneurs or one in five of those in new firms, claim to have been previously unemployed before setting up in their premises. The previously unemployed entrepreneurs (fourteen in all) were responsible for nine firms employing a further sixteen workers. Their enterprises were mainly service concerns (like the motor trade, printing and bicycle repair) and jobbing manufacturing (like joining and shopfitting, and the manufacture of nameplates). Only one of these entrepreneurs lived locally. Most came from elsewhere in the City or Region. All but one of these firms were based on an activity in which the owners were skilled and had previously worked. In the sole non-conforming case two young men had started a business out of an existing bicycle repair hobby. Furthermore, five of the previously unemployed entrepreneurs had previous experience of self-employment.

Although these fourteen people had previously been unemployed, the length of time spent out of work was overwhelmingly of short duration. In only one case was the businessman out of work for over six months, and this was a peculiar case caused by an unexpectedly long delay in finding an alternative location for a firm forced to move by the compulsory purchase of its old premises in the City centre. The owners of four of the nine firms with previously unemployed entrepreneurs had already decided to become self-employed while working as employees in another firm and in three of the cases the individuals chose to quit their jobs or accept voluntary redundancy to realise their aspirations.

There was little evidence to support the assertion that the provision of small premises and other incentives had significantly widened the possibility of self-employment as a realisable option for unemployed people. In the small number of cases where self-employment had been taken up by people previously out of work, these were either individuals who had already selected self-employment as their aim, or who on being made redundant demonstrated their greater aptitude to escape unemployment by setting up their own firm. The essentially transitory nature of the unemployment experienced can perhaps best be regarded as a short holiday – either chosen or forced – filling the interim period between leaving paid employment and starting their own enterprise.

Unskilled adults and the long-term unemployed are not found among the 'enterprising unemployed'. Our 1982 survey of a sample of all GEAR households found that only about 4 per cent of all residents had ever considered self-employment as an option open to them. These findings are not surprising. For many workers in areas like the east end and Clydebank their experience of employment has been unvaried, unskilled and in large firms in declining sectors of the economy. Even when they have skills these are often difficult to transfer to independent small-scale production.

The types of people going into business for themselves are precisely those one might expect to do so. On the whole, the new entrepreneurs were skilled males with a solid working experience as employees in their line of business and its markets, frequently with sales and marketing experience. In short, they were fairly well equipped by their experience to go into self-employment and survive without special 'hand-holding' support. To give other workers in the local community similar opportunities new forms of education, training and support will be needed.

Andrew A. McArthur

Job creation

How many people will these firms employ? Since setting up in their new premises about two-thirds of them had taken on more workers, adding a gross total of 404 jobs, or slightly over six persons per expanding firm. More than half of this boost in employment, however, had been eaten away in job losses – concentrated in the GEAR area – among a smaller group of firms whose labour force had declined. In the GEAR area, after subtracting the number of jobs lost from those added, the net increase in jobs since the firms set up in their premises was only thirty-nine. Employment growth was only sufficient to offset decline by a small margin, and contributed very little to the total stock of jobs in the local labour market (Table 4.3).

Table 4.3: Employment changes since setting up in current premises

| | GEAR | | CLYDEBANK | | TOTAL | |
	Firms	Jobs	Firms	Jobs	Firms	Jobs
Increase	39	246	26	158	65	404
Decrease	7	207	1	13	8	220
No change	7	–	20	–	27	–
TOTAL	53	+ 39	47	+145	100	+184

In both areas a large proportion of people found out about jobs through word of mouth (Table 4.4). Entrepreneurs tended to hire friends, relatives or others known to them. Over half of the firms used personal contacts of this sort as the main method of recruiting labour and hired 46 per cent of their recent recruits by these means. Jobcentres were used to a lesser extent. One in three of the firms used the jobcentre as their main recruitment method. The importance of this personal contact in the hiring process is endorsed by the household survey of GEAR residents: 32 per cent of workers in that survey claimed to have found their present or last job through word of mouth compared to 14 per cent who had found work through the jobcentre.

New enterprises setting up in the premises appeared to be even more dependent on personal contacts in the hiring process than moving firms. Eighty per cent of the employees hired by new firms were previously known to the entrepre-

Table 4.4: Method of recruitment
(percentage of recruits)

Proportion of recently hired workers hired through:

	Personal Contact	Job Centre	Advertisement	Other	Total
All firms	46	34	14	6	100
Moving firms	35	41	18	6	100
New firms	80	12	3	5	100

Information for 396 recruits

neurs in some way. These patterns are not surprising: one would expect small firms, particularly new starts, to select their workers very carefully, choosing people known to be trustworthy and efficient and in whom the owners have confidence. There was also another factor to explain the previous associations between entrepreneurs and their employees. It seems that some of the 'new firms' could better be described as 'phoenix enterprises' because they comprise, in some part, a regrouping of old workforces shed by local firms which had either closed or cut back on employment. Although this process was not examined systematically during the study, entrepreneurs in five of the firms in the GEAR factories had established their business in a salvageable portion of their old firms' market and employed a number of their previous colleagues. Useful though it may be, this is perhaps a reflection of industrial restructuring and the contraction of employment rather than the emergence of new enterprise and may deserve more systematic study.

To test the effectiveness of these policies for the local community we asked three questions: Where did the workers in these firms live? How many of them had previously been unemployed? And how long had they been out of work? While 86 per cent of the employees lived somewhere in the city, less than half of them lived locally; and even among the new firms, which might be expected to recruit from the local area to a greater degree, the situation was virtually the same (see Table 4.5). At face value, the policies seem to have been more successful in generating jobs for the unemployed generally than they have been in directing them to local people. Information was obtained on the previous employment situation of 396 workers, and 72 per cent of them had been out of work immediately before starting their present jobs. Among the new firms the proportion previously unemployed was lower at 64 per cent (Table 4.6). There was a slightly different pattern in the two areas in this respect. In the GEAR area almost three-quarters of the employees had previously been unemployed and among new firms the proportion was 80 per cent. In Clydebank the corresponding figures were lower at two-thirds and 64 per cent respectively, which may reflect a higher degree of labour 'poaching' among firms coming to the enterprise zone, or the more skilled workforce of the Clydebank area.

Table 4.5: Residence of employees
(percentage of employees)

	Local	Glasgow	Strathclyde Region	Other	Total
All firms	42	44	13	1	100
Moving firms	42	44	13	1	100
New firms	41	44	14	1	100

Information for 1,095 employees

Table 4.6: Previous employment state of recent recruits
(percentage of recruits)

	Unemployed	Employed	Other	Total
All firms	69	31	1	100
Moving firms	71	28	1	100
New firms	64	36	–	100

Information for 396 recruits

Where a recruit moves from another job, this may provide a vacancy which could be filled by someone out of work. Thus, in a similar fashion to the filtering process in the industrial premises market described above, jobs filled by previously employed people may have some hidden impact on local unemployment rates through a chain reaction in the labour market. Assuming that the ratio of employed to unemployed observed among the recent recruits (i.e. 31:69) in the sample firms holds throughout the labour market, and that all the jobs vacated by workers leaving other firms were subsequently filled, then we might expect the results shown in Table 4.7.

Table 4.7: Job filtering effects

			Number of jobs going to employed	Number of jobs going to unemployed
Total number of jobs generated in firms surveyed			124 (31%)	276 (69%)
Indirect job generation during filtering	Stage	(i)	38	86
		(ii)	12	26
		(iii)	4	8
		(iv)	1	3
		(v)	–	1
Total indirect effects			55	124

Assuming a gross total of 400 jobs generated

If the assumptions above hold, then the direct generation of 400 jobs will have an indirect employment effect on a further 179 workers in other firms. Of these, fifty-five will already have been in work and will have changed their employer, while 124 unemployed people will have moved into jobs. Hence the number of unemployed people moving into paid employment following the firms setting up in their new premises would have been not 276 but 400, an addition of nearly 45 per cent. Furthermore, assuming the same ratio for the residential spread of employees as identified in Table 4.5, fifty-two of these 124 extra unemployed people finding work will live in the local area.

This is not a rigorously precise treatment of the area. The 404 extra jobs we identified have been generated directly by the firms surveyed in both areas and are a gross figure. In the GEAR area job losses in other firms working from SDA premises offset most of this increase, as we have explained. But such calculations should remind us that the jobs generated among the firms surveyed create further ripples in the labour market. How large these are we cannot be sure, but the total number of unemployed people finding work as a consequence of the factory building policy must exceed those employed by the sample firms alone.

The duration of unemployment experienced by these

workers is known in almost three-quarters of the cases. When this is considered, the attack on unemployment appears much less profound. Of those previously unemployed, only 10 per cent in the GEAR area and 14 per cent in Clydebank had been out of work for over six months. The vast majority had been jobless for a matter of weeks or at the most a few months. A large proportion of the workers either seem to have known that another job was imminent or were quickly snapped up by employers known to them. Their unemployment can possibly be regarded as frictional. Having been out of work for a short period between jobs they form quite a distinct group from the long-term unemployed.

When asked about future employment prospects, sixteen firms said they had existing vacancies with an average of two per firm. Many more (almost three-quarters) hoped to increase their workforce, mainly in the skilled category, over the following two years. If their expectations are borne out they should lead to a gross increase of almost 350 jobs, or an average of 6 per expanding firm. These predictions should probably be regarded as rather optimistic because respondents tended to give upper-level estimates – the chances of these forecasts being borne out often depending on the success of a certain product or a significant improvement in the economy.

Employment predictions are also made by the SDA. When allocating premises, the Agency note both 'existing' employment within the firm and the 'additional' increase expected above this. The sum of the two across all firms represents the number of 'new' jobs the Agency 'expect' to provide in an area. This is a somewhat arbitrary way of evaluating the likely impact on jobs of this policy and could lead to an over-optimistic estimate of its results. The whole concept of a 'new' job is a complex one and the simplistic way it is often interpreted by public authorities, who have strong reasons for being seen to be successful, can exaggerate the real employment effects.

In the GEAR area, for example, by 1983 the SDA expected to have created up to 4,865 jobs as a result of their factory and workshop development. By breaking this figure down to the level of individual firms it is possible to compare directly, for the firms surveyed, the possible future employment as perceived by the owners with the predictions of the SDA. Of the Agency's predicted jobs in the factories surveyed, 43 per cent, or over 500 in total, had still to materialise. Among the new firms alone the shortfall was 33 per cent which meant that employment needed to increase by 50 per cent to reach the SDA's estimates. Even on the basis of optimistic forecasts by the firms, future employment growth will probably fall substantially below the Agency's predictions. Meanwhile the owners of firms themselves did not consider more jobs to be the main impact of the scheme. When asked about their perceptions of the GEAR project and what it would do for the local area, only one respondent suggested new employment opportunities for local people. Overwhelmingly, businessmen felt the scheme's main contribution to be the improvement of the physical environment and the general image of the area and an expansion of the opportunities open to small firms.

Summing up

What then have regeneration policies really achieved? Most of the emerging industry and employment attracted to these areas by the SDA's small factories is not new but would probably have existed anyway, if not in the study areas then elsewhere in the same conurbation. The provision of these units appears to have redirected a number of existing firms and attracted some new enterprises into each area, and it has retained in these areas a certain amount of business which might have left the locality had suitable premises and other incentives not been available. As a result, a large proportion of the economic benefits enjoyed by the GEAR area and Clydebank have probably been won at the expense of other areas, not far off, where a degree of disinvestment and job loss and a diminished ability to attract industry will have been experienced.

These policies have treated each area as a separate entity and ignored their effects on the wider economy. That is a criticism which does not dispute that local regeneration policies of this sort confer considerable benefits, but suggests that the selection of areas should perhaps be carried out more carefully, with an eye to probable effects all over the conurbation and its surrounding region. Help might then be given to selected firms on a more carefully targeted basis.

The direct impact on jobs made by this programme have

been very modest, and the cost per job is certain to be high, although this study has not attempted a full costing. Assuming that the firms surveyed in the GEAR area were typical of all those in local SDA premises at the time, and allowing for the indirect job creation effects, the factory building policy had, by the spring of 1982, brought a gross increase of 445 jobs, of which 187 would have gone to local people – a tiny contribution when compared to the 4,000 unemployed residents in this area. Similarly, in Clydebank, on the basis of the average size of firm surveyed, 650 genuine enterprises of an equivalent size would have been needed to replace the local jobs lost by the Singer closure alone since 1978.

These policies also seem to be ineffective in reaching the disadvantaged and marginal workers. In 1984, for example, male unemployment figures in the inner, Bridgeton-Dalmarnock part of the east end were the highest area rates in Strathclyde. Although unemployed people were getting jobs in the new factories, they were not the kind of workers who find themselves repeatedly out of work or jobless for long periods. They were the better-off groups among the unemployed, those best equipped to find work through a network of informal contacts with employers, colleagues and friends. In seeking to generate work and incomes for disadvantaged workers in depressed communities, locally-based strategies should recognise the social impacts of unemployment which serve to break up social networks and exclude people from activities in the community which they would have participated in had they been in work. They should also recognise that apparently similar areas like GEAR and Clydebank may have a widely different reservoir of skills, entrepreneurial capacity and so on. Each will call for rather different policies.

Despite many weaknesses in these policies, they have had some other good effects besides their modest impact on jobs. The morale of the local business community will have been boosted and a lot of derelict industrial neighbourhoods which no-one would otherwise have touched have been cleaned up and well landscaped. This achievement was not the main objective but it is still a significant gain, and, if a major industrial revival does come eventually, then these places may be in a position to secure more benefits from it than they otherwise would have done.

Towards more effective local action
These comments conclude our discussion on the local employment impact of factory provision for small firms in GEAR and Clydebank. Looking to the future, we can identify a number of related themes around which expenditure targeted towards communities faced with economic collapse may be made more effective in tackling the problems of local disadvantage. It may be possible to do even better with small factory policies through better planning and closer integration of public services to ensure that the demand generated by public investment is used to boost local production of goods and services. By a planned allocation of contract work on construction, housing, the environment and so on, the health of the local business community can be improved by giving greater priority to firms in the area. Positive discrimination could be extended further with better co-ordinated economic, employment and training strategies. Where the skills required do not already exist locally, training programmes and other developmental work and support could be initiated to establish them within new business structures in a bid to ensure that the community, particularly the more disadvantaged, benefit to a greater degree.

With conventional small enterprise apparently unlikely to recruit from the ranks of the long-term unemployed, other strategies which generate work and incomes for this group are desperately needed. A new form of enterprise which may offer some help here is the community business. Originating out of voluntary sector initiatives, these are trading organisations, owned and controlled by the local community, which aim to create jobs for local people, particularly the long-term unemployed, and retain and recycle any profits made for community purposes. So far community business innovation has been particularly focused on Strathclyde and a small number of other areas in central Scotland where local authorities have shown an interest in their development. The present reality is, however, a good way removed from the ideals upon which the movement is built. Most community businesses – which totalled around thirty-five in central Scotland at the close of 1984 – are struggling, under-capitalised and dependent on public subsidy in the form of urban aid, or help from the Manpower Services Commission or the European Social Fund. The difficulties they face are not surprising. Being focused on communities where there is often low demand, employing people who may take a lengthy period to readjust into working life following the damaging effects of unemployment, of the difficulty in getting people with entrepreneurial talent and working with others with a strong sense of social purpose makes them hard to manage and difficult commercial propositions. But although the movement is in its infancy, it already shows some hopeful signs. A recent survey of community businesses found that only 7 per cent of their workers had previously held normal jobs. Almost 79 per cent had been out of work at least once during the previous four years and around a third had a recent history of repeated unemployment, having two or more spells over the four year period (McArthur, 1986).

The further development of unconventional forms of economic activity like community businesses will depend on strong public support which, in some cases, may involve subsidising an initiative for several years. Support for commercial organisations whose objectives are to work for the benefit of the local community and retain and recycle surplus profits for community purposes, would be a radical departure from the current use of public expenditure to subsidise the accumulation of wealth in small firms. It might even mean that public money would develop entrepreneurial activities which undermined small-scale capitalism. It might nevertheless be a more effective way of providing the type of services and productive activities which are often lacking in deprived areas and ensuring that local people gain from the work and incomes generated as a result.

Attempts to generate economic activity for poorer groups need not be restricted to the formal economy or even to collective enterprises, of whatever form. Funds spent on some public services could make a more direct impact on the incomes of local families. Municipal housing, for example, demands a huge amount of expenditure. Where the work required essentially concerns individual households, such as the repair and maintenance of homes and their sites, residents could be given greater opportunity to administer or carry out this work themselves. Through its tenants' grants improvement scheme and through housing associations, Glasgow District Council has gone some way in pioneering the use of public expenditure to boost household income directly in this fashion, as we point out in the following chapters. The education services for adults can make an important contribution to the success of such projects, as we show in Chapter 14.

Attempts to put together better integrated local development strategies will face many difficulties. Training programmes for new entrepreneurs, for example, tend to cater for those already on the verge of self-employment. These will have to be redesigned to encourage an interest in self-employment. Temporary wage subsidies for the unemployed (such as that already provided on a modest scale by the Manpower Service Commission's [MSC] Enterprise Allowance Scheme) may be needed, linked with the provision of workshops and the loan of tools. Present manpower initiatives operate outside mainstream regeneration strategies. There is no formal link between the training and temporary employment which takes place under MSC schemes and the employment generated by small firms. Instead of merely increasing people's 'employability', then releasing them into the labour market where they probably continue at a competitive disadvantage, training centres could become bases for the animation of new enterprise where people could be supported (collectively or individually) to embark on productive activity which would meet needs and provide services which are lacking in the community. Alternatively, those subject to a training initiative could be offered better chances of getting jobs if public agencies entered into 'local planning agreements' with firms who occupy their premises and enjoy other forms of subsidy. Under these agreements, businesses might be committed to directing a proportion of their future job expansion towards those facing particularly acute disadvantage in the local labour market. Although not targeted in this way, local planning agreements are being used innovatively in some areas. In Sheffield and the West Midlands, for example, they are being used to try to ensure that firms receiving public assistance give priority to the local area in their future investment decisions. We say more about these possibilities in Chapter 13.

Andrew A. McArthur

If locally-based strategies are to become more effective as agents of economic and community regeneration, integrated local economic programmes will be needed which pull together available resources and policies to a greater degree than at present, and use these partly to expand the informal economy and support the development of unconventional forms of economic activity. To make this possible, local authorities and other public agencies will have to adopt attitudes and policies which break from established accounting practice. Projects directed to the unemployed often bring social benefits as well as economic ones, even if they cost more and call for long-term subsidy. Community businesses may be one example of such projects. This has direct implications for public expenditure at a time when those who allocate public resources are largely concerned with keeping the level of expenditure down and demonstrating a short-run cost-effectiveness in the projects supported. In 1980 it was estimated that the annual cost to the Exchequer when a married man with two children on average weekly earnings became unemployed was £6,006 (House of Commons Library Research Division, 1981, p. 22). This calculation was based totally on the revenue losses associated with the non-payment of income taxes, taxes on the consumption of goods and services, and national insurance contributions, and on the payments government makes to the unemployed through the social security system. It did not include other financial costs, such as those associated with lost production, increased ill-health, declining morale and stresses within families. On this basis it should be possible to demonstrate that some projects which involve people who would otherwise be unemployed and which appear to involve public subsidy might actually operate on terms which give a financial surplus to the state.

Meanwhile there will probably be other indirect financial gains from reducing unemployment and poverty, such as a fall in the costs incurred by certain public services like health, police and social work. Although such 'economic' justifications will be an important ingredient in justifying a case for new attitudes and approaches by policy-makers, they should not exclude less quantifiable social considerations: a reduction in poverty and despair, and a heightening of local morale and self-confidence may be sufficient justification for support.

92

5 PUBLIC HOUSING
David Clapham and Keith Kintrea

The GEAR project may be judged ultimately by its success in attracting and creating jobs and reducing unemployment in the east end of Glasgow. The fundamental importance of economic opportunities in depressed urban areas was the main lesson of the Community Development Project of the 1970s and the government's Inner Areas Studies which led to the White Paper of 1977 (DoE, 1977a) and subsequent legislation. Nevertheless, for many people in the east end housing is more important than jobs. In the GEAR area 34 per cent of heads of households are retired and many others are disabled or have to stay at home to care for children or elderly relatives. They are not in the job market but their housing conditions are highly important in determining their quality of life. Furthermore, housing is of importance even when job creation is the main objective because it influences who is attracted to, or excluded from, the area. Housing is also a major component of the built environment, and influences its appearance. In fact, the importance of housing seems to be recognised in that more than half the capital invested in the GEAR area by central and local government since the project began has gone into housing. Along with the landscaping, improvement of the area's housing is one of the most obvious physical changes since the inception of the GEAR project.

Three chapters of this book are devoted to housing issues. This one deals with public housing, while the next deals with the rehabilitation of older private sector housing which, in the GEAR area, has largely been carried out by housing associations. The third deals with new housing built for owner-occupation. Each of these chapters leads to some conclusions and at the end of the third some broader reflections on the role of housing policy in the regeneration of inner city areas are presented.

Housing in the GEAR area
Much of the GEAR area was once covered with privately rented tenements. Slum clearance has eliminated most of

them and the remainder have been largely acquired by housing associations or sold to owner-occupiers. Only 3 per cent of the households in the area now rent their homes from private landlords and further investment in privately rented housing now seems unlikely. The remaining demand for it, which comes largely from students and other transient groups who are excluded from house purchase and council housing, is supplied in the west end of the city closer to educational institutions and entertainment facilities.

Public housing now accounts for 76 per cent of the total stock, 63 per cent of which is owned by Glasgow District Council Housing Department and is mainly administered from the Gallowgate Aea Office situated in Parkhead in the heart of the GEAR area.[1] The rest of the public housing belongs to the Scottish Special Housing Association (SSHA), a central government agency which has performed a variety of roles in the provision of housing in Scotland. The proportion of public housing in the GEAR area is more than double the British national average and higher than the figure for Glasgow as a whole (63 per cent), which is itself unusually large.[2] Very little of the public sector stock has been sold to tenants under the 'right to buy'. By 1984 only 1.25 per cent of council stock in the Gallowgate area had been sold. In comparisons with other inner city areas such as the inner London boroughs, the dominance of the public sector in the GEAR area is striking. In Hackney the public sector accounts for 56 per cent of the stock and in Lambeth only 40 per cent. Tower Hamlets, which was heavily bombed during the war and massively rebuilt afterwards, has a public sector amounting to 80 per cent of the stock and is the only inner city local authority which exceeds the GEAR area in its proportion of public sector housing (DoE, 1979).

The social characteristics of the GEAR area are in many ways similar to those of other inner city areas. There are many old, sick and unemployed people and lone parents. This is a residual population: many of the economically active have moved away to other parts of Glasgow or to new towns further afield. Within the GEAR area economically inactive households and those with low incomes are heavily concentrated in the public sector. For example, in the 1982 household survey it was found that 86 per cent of households with incomes of

£40 per week or less live in the public sector. Similarly 80 per cent of the heads of households who are unemployed, 86 per cent of those who are permanently sick and 82 per cent of those who are retired are public sector tenants. Only 18 per cent of heads of households in the public sector are in full-time work compared with 35 per cent of those in the private sector.

In contrast to many other inner city areas the huge dispersal of the more affluent white population from the GEAR area has not been followed by an influx of ethnic minorities. There are no significant ethnic minority groups here; therefore the problems of racial discrimination and access by minority groups to public housing are not on our agenda. In this respect the GEAR area is very different from many other inner city areas in Britain. The GEAR area is also quite different from many other British inner city areas in the type of housing that is found there. Paul Harrison (1983) has characterised inner areas in this way:

> These are areas of particularly bad housing, a mixture of old Victorian terraces often built specifically to house manual workers and now reaching the end of their useful life, and more modern council estates, frequently of the worst possible design; an environment . . . full of dereliction and dehumanized concrete. (p. 23)

The nineteenth-century tenements still left in the GEAR area are perhaps the Scottish equivalent to the terraced housing that Harrison refers to but the public sector stock is quite dissimilar. It is partly for this reason that the area has avoided many of the problems typical of inner city housing.

The public housing in the GEAR area is very varied in type and age. The predominant dwelling type is the tenement which has the advantage over most other types of flatted housing of being built on a relatively human scale, usually three or four storeys high with six or eight households sharing one common stair. There were more tenements built in the inter-war period in the GEAR area than in other parts of Glasgow but these schemes appear to have mostly escaped the stigma and unpopularity often associated with estates of that era (Damer, 1974). Furthermore, the housing estates are generally small and most of them offer good access to social and recreational facilities and to the city centre. The GEAR area is also fortunate in that most of its public housing was built either before or after the period when systems-building was in vogue. Five Comprehensive Development Areas were declared in the 1950s within the GEAR area but none of these had progressed further than haphazard demolition and widespread planning blight when the programme was halted in 1975 (Gibb, 1983). In other inner city areas and in other parts of Glasgow nineteenth-century housing was replaced by tower blocks and deck access flats which now commonly present an inhospitable and inhuman environment which is often exacerbated by structural faults and dampness. There are a few multi-storey blocks and deck access complexes in the GEAR area but they neither dominate the stock nor present serious fabric problems.

In the context of the City of Glasgow, which both historically and currently has suffered appalling housing problems, the characteristics of the public sector in the GEAR area mean that, as a whole, the area's housing is not unpopular or difficult to let. While the GEAR area is not as desirable as the early cottage estates of Mosspark and Knightswood, for example, it is spared the severe problems of the peripheral estates.

Nevertheless the council has declared GEAR a 'Geographical Priority Area' along with the peripheral estates of Castlemilk, Drumchapel, Easterhouse and Pollok and the inner city area of the Maryhill Corridor. In designating these areas the council was seeking to direct capital spending to the areas where it was most urgently required. However, priority area status is only one criterion for the allocation of capital resources for housing. Others include the location of a 'special initiative' in the area, and the rating which it gets in the Housing Department's 'stress area categorisation'.

Special initiatives take a variety of forms but are basically intensive management projects in difficult-to-let estates. Only one of the thirteen in Glasgow is in the GEAR area: this is the Barrowfield initiative which will be discussed later. Stress area categorisation is a five-point scale based on three main variables derived from lettings information. These are vacancies, turnover and demand for transfers out: the higher these figures, the higher the stress rating accorded to the area. In total, the peripheral estates have 77 per cent of all their property in the two worst stress categories. In contrast, the Gallowgate office has only 38 per cent of properties in these categories, which is marginally better than the figure for the whole city which is 40 per cent. At the other end of the stress scale Gallowgate has a greater proportion of properties in category 5 (least stress) than the popular suburban area of Anniesland and the city as a whole.

The 1982 household survey confirmed that this is a reasonably popular area: 88 per cent of those interviewed claimed they were either 'very satisfied' or 'fairly satisfied' with the neighbourhoods in which they lived. Very few in the public sector wanted to move and, of those who were seriously thinking of moving, 72 per cent wanted to stay in the east end. Together, these opinions demonstrate a very high level of contentment.

The GEAR area's housing, then, does not fit many of the widely held assumptions about inner cities. It is clear that it does not present the difficulties that are often associated with public housing in inner city areas and is unproblematic compared with the peripheral estates in Glasgow. Nevertheless there are some exceedingly unpopular neighbourhoods in the east end including a housing scheme which contains two of Glasgow's worst ten census enumeration districts in terms of social deprivation. This scheme will be considered towards the end of this chapter following a broad review of the important issues facing public housing in the GEAR area and how they relate to the objectives of the GEAR project.

Public housing objectives
A major difficulty in the evaluation of the GEAR project is the lack of clear and meaningful objectives. This difficulty is not only confined to housing and is considered more fully at the end of the book. However, in terms of housing it is difficult to discover any authoritative statements at all. The project started in 1976 and in 1978 some 'key issues' and 'objectives' were laid down (SDA, 1978a). Two years later another document was published containing 'basic objectives' supported by 'strategies' (SDA, 1980a). These two documents share some common themes but are not closely related and differ on important details. Of the two documents, the latter

seems to be the more authoritative because it is referred to in later material. However, none of the objectives refers directly to housing. Further confusion ensues from GEAR publicity material (SDA, no date) where the objectives of the 1980 document take on a different form of wording, including the specific objective of 'creating better housing'.

None of these documents suggests that public housing can be considered to be a major concern of the GEAR project. Nevertheless, several of the 'strategies' which support the 'basic objectives' in the 1980 document have implications for public housing. There are four major areas of interest: the condition of the housing stock, the promotion of demographic change, environmental improvement and the involvement of residents in the future of their area. Progress on these issues is now explored.

Condition of the stock
Improving the condition of the existing housing stock in the GEAR area was seen as central to the objectives of stemming population decline and improving the quality of life for residents. Attempts to improve the stock in the public sector have, however, been severely affected by the imposition of cuts in capital allocations by central government. Capital investment which falls on the Housing Revenue Account has, in Glasgow as a whole, been reduced from £90.8 million in 1979/80 to an estimated £46.7 million in 1984/5 at current prices, even when capital receipts from recent sales of land and houses are taken into account. This contrasts with an estimate of £85 million per annum over five years which the District Council estimates is necessary merely to keep existing property in a safe, weatherproof condition. As a result, the Council is now doing no new building in the GEAR area and expenditure on modernisation and major items of repair, which are also funded out of the capital budget, has been reduced.

In spite of pressure on spending, the modernisation of the inter-war stock of housing can be regarded as a moderate success, partly due to the Scottish Special Housing Association (SSHA) and its Redevelopment Assistance Programme (RAP). Since the SSHA was set up in 1937 as an agency of central government it has performed a variety of roles as government priorities have changed. In 1975, after a period spent in helping local authorities to meet general needs and provide for economic expansion, its role was revised and the SSHA turned to urban renewal. The Redevelopment Assistance Programme enabled it to build new housing in depressed inner areas and to relieve the burden on local authorities by acquiring dwellings from them for modernisation.

The SSHA's investment in the GEAR area has been considerable. During the course of the GEAR project it has built over 1,000 new houses for rent, including more than 200 sheltered units, and over the same period it has modernised over 1,500 houses acquired from Glasgow District Council. Its commitments under RAP have not yet been completed although progress has slowed. In the early 1980s the SSHA was devoting about 70 per cent of its annual capital spending in Glasgow to the GEAR area. More recently the overall level of spending in the city has tailed off and area priorities have changed. New building programmes have slowed down and the Redevelopment Assistance Programme is being wound up, with the result that projects in the GEAR area now account for 32 per cent of the SSHA's expenditure in Glasgow, of which half is devoted to modernisation.

The District Council's progress on improvement programmes for its own stock has been comparatively modest. By 1983, 2,363 inter-war houses, representing 32 per cent of the stock of that age, had been fully modernised. Considering that more than 1,500 houses had been sold to the SSHA to be modernised under RAP this was not a particularly great achievement, since the city-wide figure for the modernisation of inter-war houses was 41 per cent. Since 1983 the modernisation programme has been curtailed: instead a more limited Improvement and Repair Programme (IRP) supported by tenants' grants for interior improvements has been instigated. By 1984, 1,949 inter-war dwellings (27 per cent of the stock) had received IRP, so that, taking the two programmes together, the Gallowgate area, with 59 per cent of its inter-war council housing either modernised or treated under IRP, has slightly surpassed the city-wide average of 55 per cent.

So, although the GEAR area is a Geographical Priority Area and improving the condition of the stock was stated as being central to the strategy of the project, there was less activity here than in the rest of the city and only recently has the level of improvement risen to surpass the city average. In the Anniesland area, the division of the city which scores lowest overall in terms of stress rating and which has no special priority for resources, 68 per cent of dwellings have been fully modernised and a further 7 per cent have received IRP. Overall, capital expenditure on housing in the GEAR area by the council has fallen from £8.7 million in 1979/80 to £3.3 million in 1984/5, which represents 16 per cent and 12 per cent of capital expenditure respectively. Clearly, there is still a considerable investment required to bring the GEAR area's older public sector stock up to modern standards: at the same time much of the post-war stock, of which only 436 non-traditional houses have been modernised, is beginning to become obsolete too.

The priority of the GEAR project has been on modernisation and improvement. However, it is also proving difficult to maintain the stock in good repair. The maintenance and repair of the stock is as vital to insure good house conditions as its improvement and modernisation, but this is not an area where the GEAR project has had any influence. Like many authorities, Glasgow District Council has a repair policy rather than a maintenance policy in that it reacts to problems as they are brought to its attention rather than positively setting out to keep all of its stock in good condition. The intention is to start a planned maintenance programme to halt the deterioration of the stock but financial cuts make this increasingly difficult in the near future. The SSHA already operates a type of planned maintenance but this is not confined to the GEAR area.

At present the repairs system for the council's stock is inadequate, as it is for other authorities in Scotland (Stanforth *et al.*, 1986). Within the GEAR area and across Glasgow the repairs service is a major source of dissatisfaction among tenants. In a recent poll (Mori, 1986) 62 per cent of tenants were dissatisfied with the service. A new repairs system which is based on a centralised computer record has been operating since 1983. Repairs are divided into three categories depending on urgency, and routine repairs are meant to be carried out in each area according to a five-weekly cycle. Operational problems mean that housing assistants can spend as much as half their working time administering repairs. There is also a lack of understanding of the system by the public, difficulties in accurately identifying and categorising repairs and there is no system of appointments to allow access for workmen. Nor are there sufficient resources to cope with the demand for repairs: the council has had to transfer £11.5 million from its capital account in its 1985/6 programme to cover outstanding repair work normally funded from the Housing Revenue Account. Moreover, the deteriorating condition of the stock means that the demand for repairs is increasing by 5 per cent per annum. As a consequence, in some months of the year up to 33 per cent of repairs are not carried out within the period specified for their completion (ten weeks for non-urgent repairs) which means that in the Gallowgate area, in any one month, 900 individual repairs may be overdue.

In summary, in spite of its bold statements, the GEAR project appears to have made little difference to the condition of the public sector stock in the area. Considerable progress has been made in the modernisation of some of the older council housing, but no more than was to be expected in the absence of the project. Although some additional resources have been channelled into the area's public housing through the SSHA it is abundantly clear that the promotion of the GEAR project has been given second priority by the government to the reduction of spending on public housing. Virtually since the start of the GEAR project, Glasgow District Council, in common with other authorities, has had to operate in a highly restrictive and unpredictable financial environment and has had its Housing Revenue Account capital allocation repeatedly reduced. Inevitably this has restricted the Council's ability to invest in the stock in the GEAR area.

No effect has resulted from the GEAR project on the inadequate systems of repair and maintenance and, although the Council has made changes to its systems and is attempting further improvements, these are part of a city-wide policy and owe nothing to the GEAR project.

Demographic change
It is an objective of the GEAR project to increase the proportion of economically active households in the area and

to attract and retain young families. Apart from attempting to improve the condition of public housing, this has been pursued also by building new private housing for sale, which is discussed in Chapter 7.

Two features of public housing in this area make it difficult to achieve these demographic objectives. The first is the size of the dwellings in the stock; there is a surplus of units with two and three rooms in addition to kitchen and bathroom, but a great shortage of larger family houses. Over 80 per cent of council housing in the Gallowgate area has three rooms or less, while less than 3 per cent has five rooms or more. A limited 'opportunity conversion' programme has been devised whereby small dwellings are amalgamated but it moves slowly because suitable adjacent houses rarely become vacant at the same time. Only twenty-three converted dwellings were created in the period 1980-4 in the whole Gallowgate area. Other areas of Glasgow, where changing the demographic profile was not a concern of a major urban renewal scheme, have achieved greater rates of conversion.

The second difficulty is the Council's allocation scheme which also covers the SSHA's stock. This operates on a city-wide basis and does little to promote the demographic aims of the GEAR project. The allocation scheme was revised in 1981 to include, among other things, an element of 'local connection' which awards extra points to people wanting to remain in, or return to, their home area. This is not specific to the GEAR area, since the intention of the policy was largely to stabilise the communities in the peripheral estates and reduce turnover there, and neither is it an important component of the points scheme. Local connection points may help to retain existing residents but they do not encourage inward moves from people who have not lived in the area before. Furthermore, the letting sub-areas, which are the basis of local connection and of the area choices which applicants for rehousing can make, are not co-ordinated with the boundaries of the GEAR area.

In practice, the allocation system makes it hard for young people to get a house in popular areas. The heavily time-weighted nature of the points system means that elderly people have an advantage in gaining access to public housing in the GEAR area, which often commands a fairly high number of points because of its popularity. In most cases young families with relatively few points are able to be housed faster in other parts of the city and as a result a large dependent population of elderly people is retained in the GEAR area as a whole by new allocations. Where less popular estates do exist in the GEAR area lettings tend to be made to younger rather than older people. The result is the segregation of social groups within the GEAR area and not the achievement of a balanced population in particular neighbourhoods (Clapham and Kintrea, 1986). This suggests there should be a special allocations policy for the GEAR area to achieve the project's demographic objectives. Indeed, this was recommended in 1976, but it does not appear to have been considered by the council in subsequent reviews of the points system. In any case, a special allocation scheme for the whole GEAR area could not deal satisfactorily with the needs of all the smaller neighbourhoods within the east end. For example, the Whiterose Co-operative has a preponderance of elderly tenants and, therefore, its committee feel that it needs younger households. In contrast, Barrowfield has a high proportion of young families with children and the need is to reduce the child density.

To secure the demographic objectives of the GEAR project what is required is an allocation scheme for the GEAR area within which local allocation policies based on the needs of individual estates could be developed. But the opportunity for a fundamental reappraisal of policy was lost and the current allocation scheme is making no contribution towards the objectives of the GEAR project.

Apart from amending the allocation system for existing houses, young, economically active people could be attracted to the GEAR area by new building in the public sector. Two thousand new public sector dwellings were built between 1977 and 1984, although it should be noted most of these were planned prior to the GEAR project. However, given the allocation system, it is unlikely that these new houses served to change the population balance. To achieve this, any future new building (when spending constraints are lifted) would have to be aimed at a particular population. Given the increasing attraction of owner-occupation for young, economically active people a better strategy might be to build for sale.

Public housing has been seen as a means of providing for the existing population rather than being used to encourage immigration. In the GEAR area, with a high proportion of elderly and chronically sick and disabled people, this means that a high priority has been given to 'special needs' housing, the major component of which has been sheltered housing for the elderly. Since the inception of the GEAR project more than 200 sheltered units have been provided by the council, by housing associations and by the SSHA. These have been either newly built or conversions of existing property, either in private tenements as part of a housing association rehabilitation programme or in multi-storey blocks. As a result the Gallowgate area has 40 per cent of its estimated need for sheltered housing satisfied, which, although undesirably low, is the highest of any area in Glasgow. It is likely that sheltered housing provision will continue to expand in the future because the SSHA still retains an 'Assistance with Special Needs Programme'. At present, sites for the development of a further 122 units are actively being considered. However, it is ironical that the GEAR area leads the city in one aspect of public housing provision which directly contradicts the demographic objectives of the GEAR project.

The environment
Residents in the GEAR area consider their environment to be very important. In the 1978 household survey it came second only to 'crime and vandalism' as a problem. Largely because of the huge sums of money poured into the area by the SDA, the general environment has been improved enormously and this problem had sunk to ninth place in the list in the 1982 survey. Much of the derelict land that has been landscaped and converted to recreational use is close to public housing schemes and the tenants in the 1982 survey seemed to be at least as satisfied with the physical appearance of their neighbourhood as private households were. Environmental issues are dealt with more fully in Chapter 8, but there are some important developments which relate specifically to public housing.

Although the SDA has devoted considerable resources over the course of the project to environmental improvements in housing areas, particularly backcourt improvements and stonecleaning, these have been almost wholly confined to the private sector. Only recently has the agency become involved in major environmental improvements in two public sector neighbourhoods: Millarfield and Barrowfield. Millarfield is a cluster of unattractive multi-storey flats, whereas Barrowfield is an estate of tenements which is divided into two by a wide road. The road was once planned as a major highway but is now a cul-de-sac; it looks bleak and splits the community. Millarfield has undergone environmental upgrading, and the Barrowfield scheme, after discussions lasting many years and the threat of cancellation as a result of a reassessment of priorities by the SDA is now going ahead.

Generally, environmental improvements within public housing areas must come from the capital budgets of the SSHA or the Council, but according to the Housing Plan, Glasgow District Council only spent £1,600 on this in the period 1981-5. There are some small-scale environmental maintenance projects which were started by tenants themselves. For example, as part of the Barrowfield project, an amenity cleansing squad was set up, funded from Urban Aid and employing local residents to remove rubbish and maintain the common areas. Some tenants' associations have also set up schemes to maintain front gardens and communal areas, particularly for those residents unable to do the work themselves.

These schemes go a little way to improve the environment of public housing and to give residents a stake in the upkeep of their estates. There are often formidable problems, created by the initial design of the housing schemes, which make it difficult to control common areas and establish 'defensible space' for which people can gain a sense of responsibility. Some neighbourhoods are clearly suffering from many years of poor maintenance. This is due sometimes to trade union action; for example, the Council's Parks Department refused to enter Barrowfield and its common areas were left without maintenance. But more often neglect is a consequence of an inadequate or inefficient service.

Environmental problems may ultimately reflect a breakdown of human relationships and a lack of sense of community which no amount of investment by an urban renewal project can by itself alleviate. However, in public housing estates in the GEAR area it is very clear that this aspect has been given a very low priority.

Involving the residents

There are three ways in which housing authorities have attempted to involve their tenants in public housing in the GEAR area. First, on a city-wide basis, the District Council has begun a limited programme of administrative decentralisation and area management. In this the GEAR area is not treated any differently from other parts of the city and the boundaries for decentralisation and area management do not fit with the boundaries of the GEAR project. Most of the routine management tasks, such as estate management, housing allocations and rent collection and arrears control have been decentralised to the Gallowgate Area Office which is responsible for 13,500 properties including most of the public housing in the GEAR area. This office has very little freedom to depart from city-wide policies.

Below this level there are four neighbourhood offices which provide a base from which housing assistants work. In most cases these have not been created as an act of policy but have resulted from the pressures on space at the area office. The neighbourhood offices are readily accessible to the public for enquiries, but they do not provide facilities to deal with the most common enquiries about repairs and allocations which have to be referred to the area office.

Gallowgate Area Office and the adjoining Mid East Area Office together form the East District which covers 24,000 council houses and is the unit on which a decentralised system of area management is based.[3] The East District is a very large unit which is bigger in population and in the size of its stock than many local authorities elsewhere in Britain. An Area Management Committee has been introduced for the East District consisting of District and Regional Councillors and MPs, supported by an Area Management Team of Council Officers. The Committee formulates priorities for capital spending within the East District and supervises a small local budget for special projects. It is also given the responsibility of seeking Urban Aid funding for projects within the District. Its purpose is to provide local input and accountability but, unlike most other districts in Glasgow, local residents are not directly represented on it. Furthermore there is little co-ordination between the system of area management and the management of the GEAR project. Although several individuals are engaged with both, the two area management projects share neither territory nor objectives.

In contrast to some other housing authorities, such as Islington and Walsall, where decentralisation is based in very small areas, Glasgow's attempt at decentralisation is proceeding cautiously. The basic units of management are so large that residents have little more control than they would have if the city was managed as one unit. Indeed, it is partly the size of the areas that makes it difficult to select residents to represent the East District because of the wide range of interests to be found there. Meanwhile, policy and resource allocation is still decided at the centre and the small area budget (£305,000 1984-5) does not compensate for the lack of general autonomy. There is no local allocations policy, no local repairs team and the neighbourhood offices are merely bases for the Housing Department's field staff. Decentralisation in Glasgow will have to go much further if it is to make any impact on residents' involvement.

As a second type of programme involving local people, the council and the SSHA have both fostered tenants' organisations. The council is committed to involving residents in general local management issues and, in particular, in the improvement of housing schemes, but its support is limited and haphazard. In the GEAR area it employs a community development worker, part of whose remit is to encourage the tenants' movement, and it has also provided five tenants' halls and eighteen 'community flats' which can be used by a wide range of community groups, including tenants' associations. In this respect the area is much better provided for than other areas of the city, but it is doubtful whether the GEAR project has had much influence on this.

Tenants' groups work best when they are established by tenants themselves and when financial and administrative support is available. The Drumover Tenants' Association is one example of a tenants' group in the GEAR area; it was formed at the beginning of 1984 by tenants who were frustrated with the repairs system. The Council provided speakers to explain the workings of the housing department, supplied headed notepaper and gave a grant towards the purchase of a typewriter and a filing cabinet. The Association negotiates with the Council over repairs and attends meetings of the Repairs Monitoring Group, which is a group set up by the Council to consider problems experienced by tenants with the new cyclical repairs system.

The three tenants' co-operatives which have been established recently within the GEAR area constitute a third initiative. These are Whiterose, which is a Council scheme, and Claythorn and Fairbridge, which are both SSHA schemes. Whiterose is a management co-operative, covering a scheme of 1920s sandstone tenements at Parkhead which, so far, remain unmodernised. The impetus for it came from the residents themselves who recognised that their area was declining and were determined to reverse the trend. In particular they were dissatisfied with the standard of repair of their houses and the outcome of the allocation system on their estate. After two years of negotiation, an agency agreement was signed in 1983 which gave the co-operative responsibility for most housing repairs but not major investment programmes. The co-operative is given a management and maintenance allowance by the Council which is used to put repairs contracts out to tender to the private sector. Once a tender is accepted the contractor maintains a presence on the scheme which means that there is a fairly close relationship between his staff, the co-operative's administrator and the tenants. The steering committee is very happy with the new repairs system and has even managed to underspend the allowance, using the savings to decorate the common entrances and stairways to their homes.

The co-operative has also developed its own allocation policy, the form of which is influenced by the fact that 70 per cent of the existing tenants are pensioners. In an attempt to allow young people into the area in order to correct the population imbalance and to provide social support for the elderly residents, 70 per cent of lettings now go to people with an immediate family connection with an existing resident. A further 20 per cent are made to people with some other local connection while 10 per cent of lettings go to people with no previous connection with the area. All applicants are taken from the Council's waiting list and priority within each group is decided according to the priorities of the Council system. Demographic change, however, is likely to be slow because of a relatively low turnover of people in the area.

It is too early to assess the success of the Whiterose co-operative although the commitment of residents and the high level of community spirit are obvious. Progress to date has been speeded by the untiring efforts of two very able members of the management committee who, on being made unemployed, have devoted all their time to the estate. Future co-operatives may not be so fortunate. It is clear, however, that the formation of a co-operative cannot circumvent all the problems of traditionally organised Council housing. At Whiterose the houses have yet to be modernised fully and the residents are putting pressure on the Council, which remains responsible for capital investment, to upgrade both the exterior and the interior of the properties. The back-courts and other communal areas are also in urgent need of upgrading.

The recently formed Claythorn co-operative of forty houses in Calton was an attempt to get potential tenants involved in the design of their new homes. Nine families were nominated to the SSHA by the council some two years in advance of the first house being completed, and these prospective tenants had some influence in the design of the houses. These pioneers were joined by others and gradually the co-operative took shape. The houses were completed in late 1982 and the co-operative formally signed the agency agreement in March 1984.

Fairbridge in Bridgetown is now four years old and is a small co-operative in newly built housing. One of three co-operatives, Fairbridge seems to have encountered the most problems although this may be due to the fact that the problems have had longer to surface. From the start, major problems were encountered with construction defects in the houses and relationships between the co-operative and the SSHA became strained. Arguments over financial matters made things worse. There have also been problems with the participation of members in the co-operative and it has proved difficult to keep them interested enough to attend meetings and work for the co-operative.

All three of these co-operatives are at an early stage of development and will require time to mature. Each group had different motives for co-operation so it is difficult to generalise about them because they were trying to achieve different things. Together they involve only a very small percentage of the residents of the GEAR area and it is clear that each of them has developed in rather special circumstances. Co-operatives will not be a panacea for all public housing.

These three aspects of residents' involvement show that, in the GEAR area, there is a desire to involve tenants in the management of public housing and other issues, and a desire by some residents to get involved. However, they only affect a minority of tenants and all are in a fairly early stage of development. We cannot say what their long-term impact will be and can only recommend careful monitoring.

The Barrowfield Project

Barrowfield has been mentioned several times in this chapter: this is because it is a scheme where many of the issues discussed here arise in a heightened form and where the strategy adopted illustrates the general strategy for public housing in the GEAR area as a whole.

The Barrowfield Project is a special initiative intended to turn round a difficult-to-let estate. Barrowfield is an estate of 600 tenement flats surrounded by major roads, derelict industry and a football stadium. The estate was planned in the 1930s but not completed until after the war. It has been stigmatised since it was built and it now has a poor reputation which was exacerbated at the outset of the project by adverse coverage on BBC television. Its problems could be listed but it is probably more helpful to say that, as a very unpopular scheme, it has for years taken those who had nowhere else to go. Although the houses themselves were modernised in 1977 this did not improve morale on the estate. Now, at last, it is realised that a comprehensive approach is required.

The Barrowfield Project started in 1981 as a working party of relevant officials from Glasgow District Council and Strathclyde Regional Council. In early 1984 a neighbourhood co-ordinator, funded by Urban Aid, was appointed and a management office was established on the estate for housing and social work staff who work together as part of a corporate approach to the needs of the estate. In this respect the project differs from the Priority Estates Project, sponsored in England and Wales by the Department of the Environment, which is solely housing based. Barrowfield's objectives include improving the economy of the area and increasing access to public services as well as the improvement of the physical environment and the popularity of the area. A considerable period was spent establishing and seeking approval for these objectives in consultation with residents. Getting tenants involved is not easy because of the complexity of social networks on the scheme and the scepticism of many residents who have seen concerned officials come and go with other initiatives in the past. However, their spirit is evident in the fact that a group of residents made their own film to counteract the BBC's.

The neighbourhood housing office provides a very important point of contact between housing staff and residents. Most major functions, however, are still controlled from the area office which is about one mile away. The Priority Estates Project has shown the importance of estate-based allocation of houses and a local repairs team. The Barrowfield tenants, in conjunction with the project workers, have set up a repairs co-operative in an effort to improve maintenance and make it more responsive to tenants' needs. Progress on estate-based allocation policy is slower. The intentions are that vacant houses will be let more quickly and a more balanced demographic and social structure for the estate will be achieved.

A major objective of the social work team is to ensure that tenants receive advice on welfare benefits and the management of expenditure and, with this in mind, it is hoped to set up a credit union and a consumer protection office. Questions of income are extremely important in an area with unemployment nearing 50 per cent. Environmental problems are also important and some backcourt areas are now being improved.

The strategy for Barrowfield is, therefore, a mixed one with the emphasis on a co-ordinated approach to the estate. This strategy may appear comprehensive but in reality it is quite limited. While physical improvements and a localised repairs service may change the living conditions of some of the people there, a major difficulty is to alter the social composition of the community. Experience from elsewhere

(Lyon, 1984) indicates that local allocation schemes will not achieve this unless there is a demand from households who can exercise some degree of choice in where they live to come to the area. It is unlikely that the present initiative on its own will be enough to create this demand and something more radical will have to be done to improve the scheme.

Barrowfield's problems are immediate and serious but to a large extent they represent an extreme version of the problems facing much of public housing. A combination of the attraction of owner-occupation and the lack of good quality, readily available public housing has dissuaded economically active young people from entering the public sector. Many better-off council tenants have been persuaded by rising rents and discounted prices that their best interests also lie outside the sector. Those with no option but to rent are left in a sector where housing quality is decreasing, where services are often inefficient and where restrictions on public investment are tight. Those with the least choice live in areas where these negative aspects are intensified. Although these trends have been evident for some time (Robinson and O'Sullivan, 1983) they have been reinforced by policy changes since 1979 (Malpass, 1983). In the longer term part of the answer to the problems of the least popular housing estates must be a move towards equalising the advantages associated with the two major housing tenures. Nevertheless, housing authorities are faced with tackling the problems that exist now.

Central government has proposed two approaches to run-down housing estates. One is the intensive management developed in the Priority Estates Project (Power, 1982) which has been adopted in large measure in Barrowfield. Although this approach has not been independently evaluated it does appear to have had some success in improving management and maintenance services, reducing turnover and raising morale. But in Barrowfield improved management on its own may not be sufficient to remove the bad reputation of the area.

The government's second answer to such problems is the Urban Housing Renewal Unit (DoE, 1985) which exists to encourage local authorities to co-operate with the private sector to renew run-down Council estates. Primarily this means selling estates to developers for improvement for sale but also the encouragement of private trusts on the model of

Stockbridge Village (near Liverpool) and tenant management and ownership co-operatives. In other parts of Glasgow some empty public housing has been sold to developers for renewal. 'Homesteading', when unimproved flats are sold to individual households to improve, has also been tried in order to encourage more economically active people to move into run-down areas. Not only are these initiatives politically unpopular in Glasgow at present, they would result in the existing residents being moved out. Experience has shown that a considerable area of houses would have to be taken out of council ownership to give incoming owners sufficient confidence. Many of the residents of Barrowfield have enough difficulties without having to start life over again in a new neighbourhood. More positive options should therefore be considered, in close consultation with the residents, which should aim at substantial investment and gradual social change.

In a bolder extension of the initiatives already taken, Glasgow District Council is attempting to involve private investors while retaining resident control by proposing schemes of 'Community Ownership' (City of Glasgow, 1985b). These are to be housing co-operatives managed by the residents who would collectively buy the property from the Council with a mortgage supplied by a financial institution, and then rent individual flats to themselves. The co-operative will thus be able to modernise their houses with the help of improvement grants, still available to private owners, while tenants retain their right to housing benefits. Such an initiative has a clear advantage over private trusts because the residents have greater control of the renewal process and the subsequent management of their houses. These proposals were rejected by the Secretary of State for Scotland whose approval was required for the schemes to go ahead. However, three pilot co-operatives in estates outside the GEAR area are still to be formed. Although they are now to be funded and monitored by the Housing Corporation, the council has not abandoned the prospect of private funding for future co-operatives. A co-operative of this kind might eventually offer another way of tackling the problems of areas such as Barrowfield.

Conclusion

It is difficult to judge whether the GEAR project has made any difference to public housing in the east end. This is partly because the project defined no strong and consistent objectives in this field, and partly because it is hard to assess what would have happened without the project. Council housing has borne the brunt of the government's attempts to reduce public expenditure. Meanwhile central agencies such as the SDA, the SSHA and the Housing Corporation have been more generously treated. Thus some of the housing department's more ambitious plans have had to be shelved. Progress was made in improving public housing, mainly because of the involvement of the SSHA, in improving the surrounding environment, thanks to the SDA, and in the provision of sheltered housing for existing elderly residents. Progress on other fronts has been more limited and appears to have been largely due to city-wide policies pursued by the housing department. Meanwhile it must be remembered that council housing in this area is not particularly bad by Glasgow's standards, nor is the east end as a whole an unpopular area in which to live. It would, therefore, be surprising and perhaps unjustifiable if it had received overwhelmingly more resources than other parts of the city.

The views of people living and working in the area are interesting. Officials consider that the GEAR project has made a difference to public housing in the area and point mainly to the widespread progress achieved in modernising houses. Tenants agree that housing conditions have improved but more sceptically point to similar improvements elsewhere in the city.

Meanwhile the contribution which housing could make to the larger aims of the GEAR project has been ignored. The powers of the housing authorities were not used to the greatest effect in bringing about economic and social renewal and many major opportunities have been missed. For example, public housing could have been used to achieve the demographic objectives of the GEAR scheme, rather than obstructing them. Those responsible were neither prepared to develop flexible, varied, community-based local strategies for recruiting and retaining the kinds of people they want in the area, nor prepared to back the private sector wholeheartedly to achieve some of the same aims. They went a little way in each direction, but inconsistently and hesitantly. If repairs and improvements for housing and the surrounding environment had been designed in collaboration with the Manpower Services Commission and its training schemes to employ more local labour, this kind of investment might have helped to create more economic opportunities. Similarly, if tenants can get together to manage their own houses they may be able to tackle other economic enterprises and should be encouraged to do so. As soon as resources are available, more emphasis should be placed on improving the housing of existing residents. In many parts of the east end, the housing authorities are failing in their responsibility even to maintain their houses. The Council appears to be taking the first tentative steps towards monitoring the condition of its housing, and better procedures for organising repairs are being developed. There is still much to do.

The next major priority is to involve tenants more effectively in housing decisions. Both the council and the SSHA have taken some steps in this direction on a city-wide basis by launching a decentralisation plan, by supporting management co-operatives and by fostering tenants' associations. They hope to go further by setting up the Community Ownership scheme. More widespread improvements have been achieved in a community-based fashion through the housing associations described in the next chapter.

Before these developments go much further, hard thought must be given to the question of the relevant scale at which management, decision-making and public participation are to operate. Clearly the appropriate scale must vary with the function to be performed. On the one hand, even the scale of the whole GEAR area is thought by many to be too small to provide a basis for economic regeneration, a sphere in which the problems are regional or national in scope. On the other hand, public participation on housing issues generally develops most effectively on a very small scale amongst neighbours in a few streets. At present the scale at which effective decisions can be made about the management of a significant volume of resources in the public housing sector lies at the city-wide level. The housing authority's decision to decentralise much of its administration to the level of a District so large that it contains more Council houses than many housing authorities in Britain owes more to administrative convenience than to a sensitive understanding of these issues.

If housing conditions in the GEAR area are to be improved, the fact that 76 per cent of the housing stock is in public ownership and that within public housing the proportions of the elderly, the unemployed and other vulnerable groups are even larger, means that the major emphasis must be placed on that sector. Central government has in recent years turned its back on public housing and the main flow of public funds has been switched to tax reliefs, price discounts and improvement grants which benefit the house buyer. But in the GEAR area Council housing is not going to fade away; very few council tenants have bought their homes under the 'right to buy' policies. Thus in the east end the long-term future of public, rented housing must also be respected. To avoid steady deterioration the government must soon develop a positive policy of investment aimed at securing a better future for council housing and the people who live in it.

Notes

1 Although most of the properties in the GEAR area are administered from the Gallowgate Office the boundaries do not coincide exactly. Much of the information quoted in this chapter is for the Gallowgate area.

2 Unless otherwise stated figures in the text have been taken from Housing Plans 7 and 8 and Annual Reviews 1983 and 1984, published by Glasgow District Council.

3 At present area management boundaries are being changed so that Gallowgate will be combined with Balillieston to form a new, somewhat smaller East District.

6 REHABILITATING OLDER HOUSING

Duncan Maclennan

The context

At the turn of the century, Glasgow's east end consisted of stone tenements usually standing in long rows four storeys high and containing eight or twelve small flats in each 'close' or stairway. The City Council started clearing away this dreadful housing and rehousing its tenants in the 1930s resuming the task in the 1950s and completing it in the 1970s. In all, about 100,000 people, some seventy per cent of east end households, were rehoused between 1950 and 1980. Together with similar projects in the Gorbals, Maryhill and other parts of the city, these were the biggest slum clearance schemes in the world. Most of this housing was intolerably obsolete and ill-equipped. Some of it was overcrowded (Gibb, 1983). Most of the tenants and their political representatives were determined that it should be demolished and the Council was under constant pressure to get on with the job as quickly as possible. But many now recognise that the better tenements had a dignity and grace, and preserved a sense of history of their neighbourhoods, and the people who live there, which should not be lost. Thus in the 1970s attention turned increasingly to rehabilitating those which were left.

The scale of Glasgow's housing problems has often been so daunting that the city's drive to surmount them has had to take equally epic proportions, thereby exerting an influence on housing policy throughout Scotland and sometimes in the rest of Britain too. The first steps towards rent control, the first building of good public housing on a massive scale for working-class families, and the campaign to abolish the slums all bear the marks of Glasgow's experience. The city has also produced some of the bleakest and most poorly-serviced neighbourhoods to be seen in Britain. But it is again playing an innovative part, particularly in the rehabilitation of older housing. Partly because it is ahead of many others in this task,

117

its programmes – often owing more to political commitments and the funding arrangements they have generated than to sensitive or efficient planning – show failures as well as success. Other cities can learn from both. Often there has been a failure to recognise that housing investment must be part of a broader strategy concerned with other sectors of the economy and the spatial arrangement of the activities and resources involved.

In Britain some academics have been dismissive of the importance of rehabilitation policies, believing that their impact has been minimal and largely restricted to helping upper- and middle-income households to gentrify working-class neighbourhoods (Bassett and Short, 1981). But in Glasgow rehabilitation has, since 1974, operated on a large and complex scale in many working-class neighbourhoods. The GEAR scheme might have developed a suitable framework for planning this housing investment, but although an important range of benefits has been achieved for residents since 1976 they are no greater (and for some sub-programmes they are less) than those achieved in other old, run-down neighbourhoods of the city. The GEAR area's experience shows how national policy can be 'bent' to help particular neighbourhoods. But it also shows that many of the potential benefits of this 'bending' have so far been lost.

This chapter falls into four main sections. In the first section the conditions for housing rehabilitation in GEAR are outlined. In the next, policy instruments are discussed. The penultimate section examines the impact of rehabilitation spending in GEAR. Finally, some broad conclusions are offered.

Older housing in the GEAR area

The major phases of housing policy designed to cope with Glasgow's, and GEAR's, most obvious problems were directed at housing built between 1860 and 1910. In the east end, as in other older neighbourhoods, these buildings still reflect the land economics of the period when they were erected: the need to develop large volumes of housing for low and middle-income families, initially at work sites and then later along public transport routes. In the rush for space, residential units were juxtaposed with industrial and commercial land uses;

Table 6.1: Size distribution of dwellings by tenure
in GEAR and Glasgow, 1977
(percentages)

Dwelling size (rooms)	Rest of Glasgow			GEAR		
	Owner-occupied %	Private¹ rental %	Local authority %	Owner-occupied %	Private rental %	Local authority %
1	1.1	3.0	3.8	9.2	9.0	5.1
2	20.0	37.8	9.7	47.6	55.5	23.5
3	25.5	34.1	56.1	25.1	30.8	56.5
4	25.6	19.3	27.0	11.7	3.6	13.6
5	16.3	3.8	3.1	4.4	0.8	1.3
6	5.2	1.8	0.3	1.4	0.2	–
7	6.3	0.7	–	0.7	0.1	–
Total units (100%)	58,752	30,516	144,913	3,579	3,181	17,732
Per cent of units	25.1	13.0	61.9	20.2	17.9	61.9

Source: Valuation Roll

1 Includes Housing Associations except Scottish Special Housing Association which appears in LA column.

indeed the ground floor spaces of tenement dwellings were often designed to contain commercial and workshop spaces. The small backcourts were often colonised by workshops.

The sizes and tenures of dwelling units in the GEAR area in 1977, as shown in Table 6.1, reflect this history. These figures overstate the size of dwellings in earlier times because pre-1977 demolition selectively removed smaller units. Even in the owner-occupied sector, 57 per cent of GEAR owners lived in one or two rooms, compared with 21 per cent for the city as a whole. The surviving privately rented houses are even smaller, only one-third having more than two rooms. On a national scale Glasgow's housing is distinctively small, reflecting the difficulties of extending or converting stone tenements, and within Glasgow the GEAR area has a particular concentration of small units.

Subject to strict rent controls and discriminated against by tax and subsidy policies since 1915, private landlords did few repairs and made no improvements. A survey in the GEAR area of 300 properties, now let by housing associations,

showed their previous owners had made no major improvements and done only minimal maintenance from 1970 to
1980. Indeed, from 1960 onwards there had been a progressive
transfer of units to low-income residents, either via cash
purchases or rental purchase agreements. The GEAR area is a
British example, par excellence, of the way in which landlords have tried to shed their investments in older property
in central cities. This results in the growth of low-value, low-
quality owner-occupation.

Research on property values in various parts of Glasgow for
the period 1972-84 (Maclennan et al., 1984) shows dwelling
prices in the GEAR area always averaging less than 40 per cent
of average house prices in Glasgow. This reflects not only the
poor quality and small size of GEAR housing but a range of
other factors associated with past growth and decline. The
earlier rush to build had sited tenements upon old 'stoop and
room' mineworkings, as in the Tollcross area, and this created
problems of dwelling settlement and instability. In turn,
financial institutions and the local authority had avoided
lending for house purchase in a number of GEAR neighbourhoods. In such locations cash purchase or unconventional
loan sources had commonly funded 80 per cent of the local
housing market. Such patterns were reinforced by the fact that
in the 1970s the GEAR area had come to constitute a
distinctive, indeed isolated, submarket within the city's
housing system. In 1977 a representative sample of first time
home-buyers in Glasgow systematically rejected the GEAR
area as a place where they would consider looking for houses.
Even with the prospect of a major public regeneration
programme only 14 per cent of households, often on lower
incomes, would have considered living there. Their reasons
for rejecting inner areas such as the east end, are set out in
Table 6.2. Clearly there was little prospect in 1977 of bringing
about much residential improvement by attracting inmovers to
GEAR.

The reasons why people reject areas like this are not
surprising. Those most frequently cited deal with appear-
ances, disorder and dereliction – much of it created by the
renewal process itself – rather than the quality of housing. It
may be that citizens, town planners, and academics too, form
unduly negative expectations about such areas during and

Table 6.2: Rank order of inner area problems perceived by first-time buyers in Glasgow, 1976

Factor	Frequence of mention rank	
	New households	All
Poor general appearance	1	2
Violence and crime	2	3
Derelict buildings and sites	3	1
Declining property values	4	4
Absence of suitable houses	5	5
Inaccessible to job	6	6
Absence of similar industry	7	8
Absence of good schools	8	7
Too many council houses	9	9
Atmospheric pollution	10	10
Low property prices	11	12
Unattractive jobs in area	12	14
Too many rental houses	13	13
Absence of low price properties	14	11
Number of respondents	298	504

Source:The Cheaper End of the Glasgow Housing Market Study, 1979

soon after periods of clearance.

The rehabilitation of east end housing had therefore to be aimed at a distinctive, low-quality segment of the Glasgow housing market – much of it owner-occupied. The properties were small, run-down and structurally defective. The residents were largely of local origin; they had low incomes, and in many instances they had already been displaced by the renewal programme and left out of the public sector housing programme. The rented sector and its tenants were much the same, their houses predominantly unfurnished. Young professionals and students who moved into the inner west end were not prepared to live in the east end. This context clearly influenced the range of costs and possible revitalisation strategies for the GEAR area.

In detailed analyses we made of housing conditions, tenures, prices, price trends, etc., for small areas made of up 100 and 500 metre square grids for the whole of Glasgow, we found that housing conditions varied sharply within short distances and that housing values did not have a simple monocentric pattern or smooth gradients. Owing to past patterns of growth along the highways, gradually incorporating previously freestanding suburbs, and their varying rates of decline and demolition, housing decay is scattered patchily throughout the city. Moreover the GEAR area has no monopoly of run-down tenements. Indeed, it contains only 8 per cent of stock classified by the authorities as 'below tolerable standard' (see below). Other wards of the city have higher concentrations of disrepair and none of the GEAR wards is amongst the city's five worst housing wards, as measured by lack of housing amenities within the private sector. Within the area there are marked variations in the quality of housing. These variations in observed market values are reflected in, and no doubt reinforced by, the existence of well-defined communities and activity centres within the east end, such as Parkhead, Tollcross, Bridgeton, etc. Thus, in the private sector, as in the public sector, there are no clear reasons why the GEAR area should have become a special focus of housing policy. The reasons for this situation are best explained by considering the policy context for rehabilitation in Glasgow.

The development of a rehabilitation policy

The vigour and scale of Glasgow's post-war slum clearance programme, noted above, is well known in western Europe. In the east end, between 1950 and 1970, population losses were not due primarily to individual moves prompted by market mechanisms, as in most US cities. Rather they reflected a combined programme of demolition of small, older, privately rented units and their planned replacement by peripheral public housing which was largely allocated on 'needs' criteria. The state called the tune and changes in population tenure and housing standards followed. In the GEAR area (see Figure 6.1) there were major urban renewal schemes, called comprehensive development areas (CDAs) at Wellpark, Gallowgate, Tollcross, Bridgeton and Parkhead.

The CDAs were 'comprehensive' only in the sense that the demolitions they brought about were comprehensive. They were largely driven by simple conceptions of what constituted good and bad housing and there was no attempt to foresee and provide for other needs. This kind of urban renewal destroyed what have been called 'incubator spaces' for new industrial and commercial developments (McKean, 1975). Rehousing

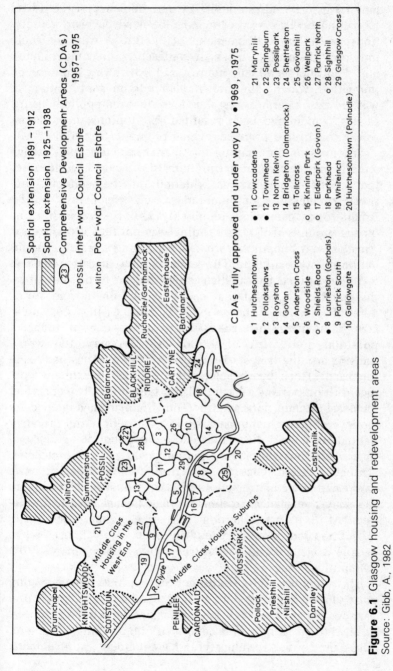

Figure 6.1 Glasgow housing and redevelopment areas
Source: Gibb, A., 1982

may have distorted the flexibility and efficiency of the urban labour market by disregarding people's needs for work and for transport to work (Engleman, 1977). But it was not such important distortions, themselves reflecting the compartment-alised and non-economic approach to British city planning of the period, which called the strategy into question. Rather, it was growing awareness, by the 1970s, that the public housing estates, which had been regarded as solutions, now them-selves constituted problems which prompted a rethink.

When plans for shaping the spatial structure of Glasgow were being formulated shortly after the Second World War, the notions of housing rehabilitation and the economic and social regeneration of older areas were given short shrift. Bright young planners were quickly disabused of such ideas on the grounds that new building was politically preferable. Anyone who remembers what the old inner areas and their landlords were like can understand why their spokesmen were determined to tear them down and move people out to the suburbs. Rehabilitation began to take on new meaning when the decline of the peripheral estates set in, when inner area home-ownership grew, when smoke control reduced pollution and when demolition had removed the worst housing and the largest, most overcrowded families had been rehoused. Thus, by the close of the 1960s, neighbourhood regeneration became a local political possibility. The critics of wholesale demolition, such as Tom Brennan, had helped to erode unthinking confidence in the past policy, and growing national economic difficulties had led national policy-makers to consider whether rehabilitation might not be a cheaper strategy. Within Glasgow, interest in rehabilitation was sharpened by the 'great storm' of January 1968 which seriously damaged an estimated 40,000 older houses in the city. At first, rehabilitation was seen as an adjunct to demolition, designed to extend the lives of old houses for a decade or so until they could be cleared (Maclennan et al., 1983).

The attempt to improve older housing, first translated into policy following the 1969 Housing (Scotland) Act, adopted a narrow conception of the role of housing investment. Houses deemed to be 'unfit' could be formed into Housing Treatment Areas by the local authority and grant-aided improvements made to those with an expected life of at least ten years. Grant aid was confined to housing, even within buildings which contained mixed uses. Scottish legislation did not embrace (and still has not) the wider conception of improvement embodied in English legislation. Although concerns were expressed about the displacement of existing residents, little was done to enable people to participate in project design or implementation.

Improvement under this procedure was slow in Glasgow, as elsewhere in Scotland. The city council placed responsibility for developing the rehabilitation programme in the Town Clerk's Office, not in housing or planning departments. In the east end a single and abortive Housing Treatment Area scheme emerged in Tollcross. In 1974, however, a new framework for housing rehabilitation developed which in the next decade brought about in Glasgow some of the most intensive rehabilitation in western Europe.

The basis of the Scottish framework for rehabilitation is the Below Tolerable Standard (BTS) house. Tolerability is assessed, as a statutory responsibility of the local authority, on a nine-point scale of dwelling quality. Where more than 50 per cent of dwellings in an area (usually of between 40 and 400 houses) are declared to be BTS, with at least one dwelling BTS in each included tenement, then a Housing Action Area (HAA) may be declared. The Action Area may be for demolition, improvement or a combination of both processes. The Action Area status allows preferential grant aid rates for improvement and repair (up to 90 per cent of costs) and also gives the local authority additional powers of compulsory purchase in relation to unwilling improvers. These powers were provided by the Housing (Scotland) Act of 1974.

In formulating its strategy the local authority, which is responsible for declaring Action Areas, may choose a number of agents to do the work of improvement. Glasgow's choices have been different from those of most English cities. The authority can declare HAAs and then await applications for grant aid from individual owner-occupiers and landlords. Such a strategy, led by the private sector, may be feasible in neighbourhoods where individual incomes give investors the confidence which generates a pervasive commitment to rehabilitation. But in tenements with common as well as individual repair and improvement obligations, with mixed tenures and multiple ownership, very high levels of private sector interest will be needed before much money is spent. In the GEAR area between 1970 and 1980 there was little interest in such grant aid (even at a 90 per cent rate), and this was still true in 1982/3. Poor response to inducements for 'spontaneous' grant-aided improvement aroused concern, not only for the GEAR area. The poorest private sector neighbourhoods missed the boom in improvement grants which occurred in many well-organised housing authorities after 1980. Glasgow tried to target resources to lower-income neighbourhoods. In various ways compulsory repair notices increased statutory repair spending in selected privately rented housing areas, but the GEAR area was not a major beneficiary of these innovations in policy.

A second alternative open to the local authority was to purchase run-down tenements and do the job themselves. Between 1970 and 1980, Glasgow rehabilitated 1,200 units in this way but with minimal impact in the east end (aside from one prestigious scheme in the centre of town). Then, after 1980, centrally imposed spending constraints put an effective end to this programme. But more than a decade earlier the Council had decided that their procedures were not sufficiently sensitive for rehabilitation work and had, instead, focused upon housing associations as the agents of change.

Housing associations operate under the supervision of the Housing Corporation, a central government agency. The operational form of housing associations varies considerably in scale and structure throughout the United Kingdom but there is a distinctive Glasgow model which has been used to deal with the main regeneration activities in the east end. The Corporation has concentrated its resources upon locally-based associations with defined territories of between 1,000 and 2,000 pre-improvement housing units. In Glasgow there are now twenty-one territorially based associations, four of which work in the GEAR area, namely in Tollcross, Shettleston, Parkhead, and Bridgeton and Dalmarnock. The designation of territories for comprehensive rehabilitation emerges in a complex and variable fashion. At Tollcross and Bridgeton, for instance, well-defined and active groups of residents (focused respectively on previous Housing Treatment Areas and demolition plans of the Council) were in place at the onset of the 1974 programme and capable of putting pressure on the Council. Meanwhile, at Parkhead, an association arose not from local pressure but because the Corporation, in conjunction with the District, identified major areas of housing suitable for association-based improvement. This was part of a city-wide process which occurred between 1977 and 1979.

The project areas for housing association activity were thus largely planned before the GEAR scheme began. The selection was conducted on a relatively crude basis and evaluation was based upon the likely financial costs of improvement. No attention was paid either to the costs of rehabilitation required for non-housing land uses (even when it occurred within the area occupied by tenements) and there was no detailed planning of how investment should progress within project areas which might take as long as twenty years to complete. That is, within the project area resources were not focused on the worst houses or on blocks where the maximum impact might be made. Progress was largely opportunistic. The main aim of the programme was simply to improve housing conditions.

From the start, however, the programme was also intended to mobilise citizen participation. The Housing Corporation sought not only to make housing associations locally operational but also locally accountable. They were to be run by management committees elected by local people. In the east end committee members now consist entirely of residents within the project areas named. In conjunction with a sensitive development process, this organisation gave citizens an important channel for their views and energies.

After project areas were declared and management committees elected or co-opted, rehabilitation proceeded through a series of phases. Development staff, appointed by the committee, would first undertake a survey of residents, eliciting attitudes to improvement. The staff, helped by management committee members, would formally and informally disseminate information about rehabilitation intentions and processes. Development officers would then identify pockets of willing improvers and, more importantly, concentrations of landlords willing to sell properties. Given the shared character

127

of comprehensive repair and improvement, all owners in a close had to agree to improve or sell (compulsory acquisition being a cumbersome and slow process). Preferably a block of from three to eight adjacent closes was required to generate economies of scale in organisation and construction. Thus the detailed pattern of improvement did not progress in serried ranks of improved tenements but developed opportunistically. Commercial property owners in tenements, who expected few benefits from rehabilitation and common repairs, resisted incorporation in projects and in 1981-2 the number of improved commercial properties in tenements was falling seriously behind the proportions improved in Housing Action Areas. This was not surprising. Because the programme was focused on improving houses there was no grant aid for commercial owners. Neither, unfortunately, was there any plan to convert surplus or marginally surviving commercial units into housing. The provision required for shopping and other commercial activities had simply not been thought out in such a detailed fashion.

After feasible blocks of closes had been identified as potential contracts, initial and then revised plans would be submitted to the Housing Corporation and the Scottish Development Department for approval to proceed and seek loan finance. Contract specifications were discussed in detail with residents and preferences were explored for various internal flat designs, the possibility of amalgamating small dwellings and transfers to other flats in the improvement area. The scope of choices must not be exaggerated, however, for they were severely restricted by the physical structure of the units and the cost-limit system of project control.

The financial evaluation of specific projects forwarded for approval remains mysterious. Approval was almost invariably granted, even when projects exceeded cost criteria by as much as a third. Either the central government had little faith in its cost indicators, or it had a commitment to rehabilitate as much of GEAR and older Glasgow as possible. As we shall show, a more wide-ranging perception of the benefits of the programme could, in the 1970s at least, have provided a stronger defence of the subsidy and spending levels in the GEAR programme. These were high. Comprehensive rehabilitation costs around £25,000 per unit in 1984 prices. The housing association programme in the GEAR has so far cost around £70 million (for housing rehabilitation alone) and about 90 per cent of these project costs are met by public subsidy.

Tenders were invited for contracts through competitive bidding and then contractors were engaged. There is no evidence to suggest that east end firms or employees were favoured in this process although the firms hired were all based in Glasgow. Before work commenced, residents were moved out into the most suitable local vacancies available. After reconstruction flats were re-let to the original residents at 'fair rents'. If there were any surplus units they were assigned to people qualified by present or past residence in the area. Allocation decisions were taken by the management committees and the association managed and maintained the flats thereafter. The District Council has nomination rights to this housing but has never used them.

A lot of progress has been made under this system, as can be seen in Table 6.3. But the table also shows that resources were not disproportionately focused upon the GEAR area. This is unsurprising. Prior to 1980, the volume of capital secured by an association was not rationed by the Housing Corporation but depended on the flow of feasible projects which the associations could generate, and there were more funds than projects available. Since 1981 the growth of projects has exceeded the growth of Housing Corporation funds. The capital allocation criteria of the Corporation are not open to analysis but there does not appear to have been a pro-GEAR bias in post-1980 allocations.

Table 6.3: Housing association progress in GEAR

	Shettleston	Tollcross	Bridgeton & Dalmarnock	Parkhead	All Glasgow
Tenders Approved 1982-3	171	102	171	113	2,501
Completions 1982-3	106	13	100	70	1,286
Total Unimproved Stock, March 1983	199	72	229	250	3,928
Total Improved Stock, March 1983	337	494	342	283	7,334

Source: Housing Corporation

Staff and management committees of associations whom we interviewed in 1980 and 1981 appreciated the work of the SDA in the area, but felt that GEAR status had not helped them in housing rehabilitation to any great extent. The Housing Corporation and District Council were seen as the major agents of change. This judgment is perhaps a little harsh on the SDA, which was clearly spending a lot on environmental improvements and other projects.

Notwithstanding this broader assistance from the SDA, the overall strategy for revitalisation failed in a number of ways to make the fullest possible use of the housing rehabilitation programme. Housing was never thought of as a 'lead sector' in the local economy, capable of generating jobs and incomes. The role was thought to be social rather than economic.

Potential spillover effects of rehabilitation were not recognised. The enormous amount of work done, and the networks of contracts established, by housing committees were never perceived to be a base on which complementary components of revitalisation could be grafted. There was no coherent multisectoral strategy for different parts of the local economy. Shops, schools, transport and other services required by the changing population of residents were not considered in these programmes.

These are not new thoughts. During the late 1970s the Department of Housing and Building for the city of Berlin developed a strategy for the revitalisation of the decayed tenements of Kreuzberg – in many respects West Berlin's equivalent of GEAR. The plan was thorough and imaginative and it suggested an integrated approach to regeneration at the neighbourhood scale which contained the following proposals:

- Technical and social surveys to predate improvement;
- rehabilitation and new construction to be jointly planned at the project scale;
- an integrated approach to be adopted for different land uses within tenements and backcourts;
- environmental redesign to be given a high priority;
- traffic management schemes to be considered;
- centres for training young unemployed residents to work in revitalisation trades to be developed; and
- a community council of up to sixty residents and other land users to be established.

It is only fair to add that by 1982 the Kreuzberg proposals remained no more than proposals. The GEAR machine may have been crude, but it got a lot done, at least in the field of house improvement. There is no reason, however, why it should stop there. More imaginative and comprehensive approaches may yet evolve from this starting point.

Assessing the impact of the programme

The period covered by our research was one in which public spending on every aspect of inner area improvement was growing – in Britain, in Glasgow and in the GEAR area. Now all that has changed: local authority funds for the rehabilitation of private property, improvement grants from the central government and the Housing Corporation's budget have all been cut back. Even to defend the programme – let alone to mobilise new private sources of finance which may come to its rescue – we need a clearer understanding of the impact of rehabilitation.

'Rehabilitation' is itself too vague a concept for rigorous analysis. It covers too many different processes: improvements inside the house, outside, or in the surrounding environment, operating at every scale from minimal to massive, from heavily concentrated to widely scattered, with correspondingly varied effects. Rehabilitation in the GEAR area has followed a mixture of these policies. To illustrate the way in which they work three scenarios can be contrasted.

First, substantial investment in the improvement of housing, whatever form it takes, will demand materials and labour from the local construction industry and its suppliers. In a city like Glasgow, with high unemployment, this is an unquestionable benefit – although that benefit may not come to rest within the GEAR area itself. The housing association's programmes in this area generate, somewhere, about 250 jobs directly, and this effect may be doubled when other jobs generated indirectly by this expenditure are taken into account.

Second, improving the inside of the houses – their equipment, appearance and general quality – will benefit residents and may be welcomed by the taxpayers who subsidise the work. Better housing costs more, so either rents and prices will rise, or subsidies must be increased to prevent

131

that happening. If higher costs are met by residents, that will reduce their spending on other things. High subsidies will increase taxation or reduce public expenditure on housing elsewhere or on other services. All these processes will have deflationary effects on the local or the wider economy. In the longer run, better quality housing will, in a market economy, attract richer (or younger) and displace poorer (or older) people, and both processes will make an impact on other neighbourhoods. This will not happen significantly under the housing association programme which is designed to benefit existing residents and to give them control over access to vacant houses which may become available later.

The third scenario is even more complicated. Improvement of backcourts, the cleaning of stonework, the pointing of window frames – all widespread in the housing associations' projects – make an impact on the environment. So may the mobilisation of energy brought about by the residents' participation in these projects. People's perceptions of the neighbourhood may then change and that may attract richer or younger residents – as in the previous scenario – or if prices increase private investors may be attracted to buy, improve or build other houses; and these effects may in time spread to nearby areas or even to the whole city. This is not merely fanciful: the successful 'Glasgow's Miles Better' campaign subsequently launched on a nationwide scale by the city did not rest only on the rehabilitation of the east end, but it could not have been convincingly mounted until a great deal of that job had been done.

Conclusion

We cannot trace and measure all the effects outlined above but it is clear that in broad terms rehabilitation in Glasgow and its, east end has been effective, if expensive. Decrepit housing and the neighbourhoods in which it stands have been greatly improved without turning out the people who live there. However, the people responsible for this work know well that it could have been better done. The comments which follow are designed to offer some help to those who will be tackling such problems in future.

1 A better framework for planning is needed – one which will

relate and evaluate the impact of public intervention in various sectors of the local economy and provide the information required to monitor these processes.

2 Within the housing sector, policy for public and private housing is separately planned and financed, although the development of the District Council's corporate Housing Plan has undoubtedly helped to bring these things more coherently together since 1980. Policies and procedures still do not recognise the complex mixture of tenures found in small areas within the east end. Inner areas in Britain now need a revitalisation strategy embracing all tenures.

3 The powers provided by rehabilitation legislation for dealing with housing have often disregarded the need for action on other matters such as abandoned private factory buildings, the shortage – or surplus – of schools, and so on. The SDA has done a great deal to improve vacant land and cleared sites in the east end, but again a more purposeful programme for dealing with every kind of land use is required.

4 Little has been done to change the size mix of dwellings, or the demographic and social mix of the households living in them. In this respect, the new private investment considered in the next chapter may be of major importance.

5 The energy and collaboration evoked by public participation in these projects should be brought to bear on planning for other services too – possibly through local management committees of some sort. As the housing associations come to focus upon management issues, their committee structure may already need rethinking and reorganisation. Such a re-examination could provide the basis on which to build a wider range of planning and management activities concerned with other aspects of the economy.

6 Revitalisation policies must recognise the need to concentrate resources for housing and environmental improvement in chosen areas. Pepper-potting of grants for internal improvements to housing will have little impact beyond the houses themselves. If public expenditure on improving run-down British neighbourhoods is to remain very restricted it would probably be more effective if channelled away from individual improvement grants to housing association activity, at least at this stage of revitalisation.

7 Rehabilitation strategy has to be dynamic. Investment changes attitudes as well as houses. In the British context, government should take a long view. Intensive initial subsidised rehabilitation may generate longer run private funding. That has happened in Glasgow's east end as the next chapter will show. Time and inflation will reduce the real exchequer costs of current rehabilitation investment and public money may attract a private response.

7 NEW OWNER-OCCUPIED HOUSING

Duncan Maclennan, Moira Munro and Douglas Lamont

Owner occupation in GEAR

Private housing in the GEAR area has long been of exceptionally low price and low quality. There was once a large, privately rented sector and, in the 1970s, this was still the major location for low-quality furnished lets in the city (Dawson *et al.*, 1982). The owner-occupied sector, which has always been more extensive than most people expect in central city areas, housed almost a fifth of residents in the GEAR area in 1977 and in 1982.

Most of the existing stock is tenement housing, with an average price of around 30 per cent of mean tenement prices in the city. During the 1970s a low proportion (less than 20 per cent) of these sales was funded by building societies. Tenement flats in the east end were generally purchased by lower income, first-time buyers who could not get a building society mortgage, or by home-owners moving around within the low income market. A distinctive cheaper segment within Glasgow's owner-occupied market has been identified in previous research and a significant proportion of that sub-market lies in the east end. The area was not regarded as being inaccessible or unsuitable relative to workplace locations (Munro, 1986; Dawson *et al.*, 1982). A study of the Glasgow housing market made in 1977 showed that first-time buyers in all income groups avoided the east end primarily because they perceived it as containing housing and environments below the standards they desired and were able to find elsewhere (see page 121). This lack of confidence did not, however, lead to vacancies in or abandonment of private housing. Demand was, if anything, lower for poor quality public sector housing on peripheral estates and it is there that the bulk of housing abandonment in the city has occurred.

Changes in the price of owner-occupied housing in GEAR throughout the 1970s were similar to those of the rest of the

135

owner occupied stock in the city. However, the growth in the proportional scale and real value of owner-occupied housing in the GEAR area in the 1970s probably did little if anything to regenerate the area. Purchasers had low incomes and frequently had been unable to secure suitable alternatives in the council sector. Because of the pattern of financing and reliance on 'rental-purchase' arrangements, they received few subsidy benefits through tax relief on mortgage interest or through option mortgages. Since tax relief is an important source of assistance to home-owners, this is a severe loss to individual residents in the east end.

Throughout Glasgow, a great deal has been done in recent years to revitalise older housing. The last two chapters have described many of these initiatives. Although rehabilitation may, in the long term, stimulate growth in owner-occupation in inner city areas, in the GEAR area in the 1970s these policies had little impact on the owner-occupied sector. There was, relative to the rest of the city, a low uptake of improvement grants. Housing association activity reduced the numbers of owner-occupied houses: for all the housing associations in Glasgow, owner-occupation fell from 30 per cent to less than 10 per cent (Maclennan and Brailey, 1985).

There was a substantial long-run increase in demand for home-ownership, but the reputation of the east end deprived the area of its share in the growth of middle and higher income owner-occupation which occurred elsewhere in Glasgow and the surrounding region. These patterns were reinforced by the local authorities' planning policies for owner occupied housing which generally sent developers to the metropolitan fringe for sites. However, since 1979, changes in planning policy towards owner occupation, the slowdown in demand for the more expensive houses and the building societies' need to search for new outlets for housing finance all combined to change investors' attitudes. Construction of new housing for sale within inner city areas became a major concern of housing and urban policy in most British cities. Such schemes have been attractive to central government as they combine objectives of urban and housing policy by steering private finance to inner areas, diversifying socio-economic structures and generally expanding home-ownership.

So far, no systematic and detailed evaluation has been

made of the ways in which new housing built for sale in the central city may strengthen the local economic base. The development of these houses has been seen only as a contribution to the welfare of their buyers or as the fulfilment of broad political objectives. But housing policy can have a more pervasive, long-term effect on an area, both by creating new demands for labour, short term and long term, and by changing the character and status of neighbourhoods within the city. If more conventional economic policies such as factory building have a limited effect, then housing policy may play a useful supporting role – even possibly a leading role – in diversifying and strengthening the local economy. We explore that possibility in this chapter and lay some of the foundations on which a more thorough study of this policy could be built.

New housing – the potential benefits

Rehabilitation programmes in the east end have generally rehoused people as tenants. New building and extensive rehabilitation for sale can diversify the range of owner-occupied housing available. Since these houses are sold in an open market, available not only to existing residents, they may generate a series of benefits to the local area which depend not only on who constructs the houses but on who purchases them. These benefits include the jobs and incomes arising from new construction itself, the investor and consumer confidence arising from the creation of sizeable groups of new houses which may bring more people or new kinds of people to the area. Construction activity may use local labour, which in turn may use local services. It will also remove some of the negative effects of vacant or derelict land. The creation of sizeable 'blocks' of new housing may reduce the risks which building societies and other investors see in these neighbourhoods. And if people prefer to live amongst others with similar incomes and social characteristics, a concentration of investment may also reduce the risks which house-buyers feel themselves to be taking and improve prospects for resale when they come to move on. Existing residents who might otherwise have to leave the area to seek better housing will find broader and better choices available to them in the east end. Multiplier effects flowing from the introduction of higher income groups into the area may include a raising of the demand for local retail, educational and other services, together with the attraction of new businesses catering for them.

This kind of policy may also have damaging effects for some people. It may disrupt a settled community by bringing unwelcome newcomers into the area. And if the new housing attracts demands from other tenures and locations, success in the GEAR area may produce new problems elsewhere. A reduction in the price appreciation rate of housing in the more fashionable western inner area of the city would do no great harm, but a growth in the numbers of empty and hard-to-let flats in the less popular peripheral housing schemes might have more destructive effects.

In June 1982 we surveyed home-owners in new houses and in reconstructed dwellings in the GEAR area. They live in fairly small groups widely scattered throughout the east end. Similar schemes now being developed outside of the area were not examined (but see Fielder, 1985). We tried to interview 183 people at five sites constituting a 100 per cent sample of the households then living in the newly built schemes. Of these, 110 interviews were successfully completed. Those omitted were mainly people we could not contact at home after repeated calls (23 per cent of the initial sample) and people who refused to answer the questionnaire (14 per cent).

The houses Some 15 per cent of the completed sample of dwellings were tenement flats rehabilitated for sale and 85 per cent were new houses or (more often) flats completed during the last two years. The types of dwellings and their price ranges are shown in Table 7.1. Several important points emerge from this table. First, the mix of house types made available was significantly different from existing owner-occupied dwellings in the GEAR area; 37 per cent of the new dwellings were semi-detached or terraced. Second, the price of this housing was approximately four times as high as the mean price of older owner-occupied housing in the area. The price range of new houses was closer to the Scottish average for new house prices than to that of the existing GEAR stock. Clearly the housing built and rehabilitated represents a significant shift in the type, quality and price range of east end housing. Indeed, the new dwellings (70 per cent of which were purchased by first-time buyers) had markedly different characteristics from houses purchased by first-time buyers in Glasgow as a whole in 1977. Only 10 per cent of Glasgow first-time buyers had gardens, compared with 49 per cent in the GEAR area schemes. Eight per cent had central heating, as against 35 per cent in GEAR. Table 7.2 shows this extension of choice of house type for people moving as 'continuing households' to the new houses. Almost 70 per cent of those living in semi-detached or terraced dwellings had moved from some form of flatted accommodation, for example.

The households The sample was evenly split between new and continuing households, but most of them – almost 70 per

Table 7.1: Purchase price by new house type

Price	Semi-detached		Terraced	Flats	Rehabilitated Tenements	Total All Types
Price	Number	%				
Under £10,000	0	(0.0)	0 (0.0)	0 (0.0)	1 (5.6)	1 (0.9)
£10,000-£14,000	0	(0.0)	2 (11.1)	13 (26.5)	17 (94.4)	32 (29.6)
£15,000-£19,000	14	(60.9)	5 (27.8)	30 (61.2)	0 (0.0)	49 (45.4)
£20,000-£24,000	5	(21.7)	11 (61.1)	6 (12.2)	0 (0.0)	22 (20.4)
£25,000 and over	4	(17.4)	0 (0.0)	0 (0.0)	0 (0.0)	4 (3.7)
Total[1] (per cent of all those interviewed)	23	(20.9)	18 (16.4)	51 (46.4)	18 (16.4)	110 (100)

1 Including two flats for which price information was refused.

Table 7.2: Previous house type by new house type

Previous house type	New House Type					
	Semi-detached or Terraced		Tenement or Flats		All House Types	
	Number	%	Number	%	Number	%
Semi-detached	2	(6.5)	1	(4.0)	3	(5.6)
Terraced	7	(22.6)	3	(12.0)	10	(18.5)
Tenements	17	(54.8)	12	(48.0)	29	(51.9)
Maisonettes	1	(3.2)	1	(4.0)	2	(3.7)
Flats in high rise	2	(6.5)	6	(24.0)	8	(13.0)
Four-in-a-block[1]	2	(6.5)	2	(8.0)	4	(7.4)
Total continuing Households	31	(100.0)	25	(100.0)	56	(100.0)

1 Four-in-a-block houses are four flats in a building that looks like a semi-detached house, but has entrances at the side to lead to the upstairs flats.

cent – were first-time buyers. Purchasers of new private housing in the GEAR area have an age structure somewhat different from the rest of the population (Table 7.3). There was a similar proportion of children of school age in the new dwellings, but a markedly higher proportion of adults in the 15-45 ranges. Correspondingly there was a lower share of old people. These are mostly new households and young families.

Building for sale has also diversified the social composition of the area (Table 7.4). Fifty-five per cent of purchasers were non-manual workers. The great majority of people were working; about 75 per cent of all adults were in full-time employment. The new housing, at least in the short term, diversified age and family structure, increased the rate of

Table 7.3: Age distribution

Age groups[1]	New Private Housing Survey		Main 'GEAR' Survey
	Number	%	%
0-4	18	7.0	4.4
5-15	28	10.9	14.5
16-29	119	46.5	20.2
30-44	63	24.6	14.6
45-59	22	8.6	22.7
60 and over	6	2.3	23.7
Total (excluding age unstated)	234	100.0	100.0

1 Comparable age groupings used in the Main GEAR Survey were 0-4, 5-15, 16- 30, 31-45, 45-59/64, and over retirement age respectively.

Table 7.4: Socio-economic composition

Socio-economic Groups	New Private Housing Survey		1981 Census
	Number	%	%
Professional	5	2.7	5.4
Employer/Manager	9	4.9	
Intermediate and Junior Non-Manual	88	47.6	9.1
Skilled Manual	45	24.3	24.4
Semi-skilled	27	14.6	16.7
Unskilled	5	2.7	11.2
Armed Forces and Inadequately Described	6	3.2	32.1
Total Economically Active	185	100.0	

economic activity and raised average incomes – not because it brings in a lot of rich people (car ownership rates are unusually low for owner-occupiers) but because husbands and wives are usually both at work and they have few or no dependants to care for.

Comparison of gross household incomes shows that new house-buyers had markedly higher incomes and superior employment status compared with other GEAR residents (Table 7.5). It seems that a minimum household income of around £5,000 a year was necessary for those buying a rehabilitated house. For the new houses and flats, probably around £7,500 was needed. This would suggest that less than 10 per cent of existing GEAR residents could purchase such a dwelling and further sales of new dwellings (if prices, subsidy and mortgage arrangements are to remain broadly constant) will depend upon the capacity of the area to import housing demand from the rest of the city.

Table 7.5: Gross household income

	New Private Housing Survey		Main GEAR Survey
	Number	%	%
Less than £2,500	0	0.0	29.4
£2,500-£4,999	3	2.7	38.5
£5,000-£7,499	14	12.7	10.2
£7,500-£10,000	51	46.3	9.2
More than £10,000	21	19.1	n/a
Refused	17	15.5	5.6
Don't know/not answered	4	3.6	7.1
Total Respondents	110	100.0	100.0

Where did the buyers come from? The origins of the purchasers of new and rehabilitated dwellings are shown in Tables 7.6 and 7.7. Of continuing households 30 per cent came from within the GEAR area. Some 15 per cent of members of new households also originated in this area. This would imply that around 20 per cent of new opportunities were taken up by households who might otherwise have left the area. Roughly 85 per cent of purchasers overall appear to have originated elsewhere in the city and comparison of the socio-economic status of these incomers with first-time buyers in the GEAR area in 1977 shows a marked improvement in the capacity of the area to attract moderate income home-buyers. The distribution of purchasers by previous tenure is also revealing. Some 43 per cent of continuing households had moved from other owner-occupied houses and more than a third of all purchasers came from local authority dwellings. Half of the first-time buyers came from parental homes. This suggests three main 'streams' of demand: households trading up within the owner-occupied sector, households moving from public housing, and newly formed households previously living with their parents. All come mainly from Glasgow.

Finding housing in the east end Previous studies in Glasgow (Munro and Lamont, 1985) have shown that buying a house

Table 7.6: Previous address of new and continuing households

Location	Continuing Households		Adult Members of New Households	
	Number	%	Number	%
Within GEAR area	17	30.4	13	13.7
Elsewhere in Glasgow district	32	57.1	66	69.5
Outside Glasgow	7	12.5	16	16.8
Totals (excluding address unstated)	56	100.0	95	100.0

Table 7.7: Previous tenure of newly formed and continuing households

	Continuing Households		Adult Members of Newly Formed Households	
	Number	%	Number	%
Rented from local authority	23	41.1	26	26.0
Housing association	1	1.8	0	0.0
Other rented, furnished	5	8.9	4	4.0
Other rented, unfurnished	1	1.8	0	0.0
Owned occupied	24	42.9	5	5.0
Rental purchase	1	1.8	0	0.0
Other	0	0.0	9	9.0
Lived with parents	–	–	49	49.0
Don't know	1	1.8	7	7.0
Total	56	100.0	100	100.0

often calls for an expensive and time-consuming search. Our survey shows that searching for new housing in the GEAR area was relatively simple. The bulk of purchasers (78 per cent) encountered no significant problems and their search for finance (in contrast to observations on the search for finance for older cheaper housing) was straightforward for 90 per cent of households. Nearly all borrowed money from building societies, in marked contrast to those previously buying older, cheaper housing in the GEAR area.

Households were asked where they had searched for housing elsewhere in the city (Table 7.8). Almost 45 per cent said that the east end was the only place they had looked and since, at most, only one-third had originated in the east end this implies that at least 12 per cent were particularly attracted from other places to the developments in the GEAR area. The pattern of search elsewhere suggests that new house provision in the GEAR area will have, at least marginally, reduced demand for higher value tenements in the west end and for other types of housing in residental suburbs outside Glasgow.

Table 7.8: Areas of housing search outside of the east end

Location	Number	%
West end[1]	18	16.4
South side[2]	10	9.1
Croftfoot, King's Park, Rutherglen and Cambuslang	9	8.2
Elsewhere in Glasgow District	7	6.4
Outside Glasgow	17	15.5
No other areas considered	49	44.5
Total Respondents	110	100.0

1 Including Jordanhill, Partick, Hillhead, Dowanhill, Kelvinside and Woodlands
2 Including Shawlands, Strathbungo, Battlefield and Govanhill

Reasons for selecting the GEAR area

Explanations of the ways in which people choose a place to live are particularly complex. A house provides not only shelter and investment potential, but also a location giving access to workplaces and other 'activity sites' and a neighbourhood context.

The houses built for sale in the east end are distinguished

by their newness. Nearly 60 per cent of the households interviewed, however, did not particularly wish to buy a new house rather than an old one. The majority of new house purchasers were attracted by the level of housing services provided rather than their vintage. In the course of time, as other new houses are built elsewhere in Glasgow, the east end may have to compete more keenly with other locations. We tried to find out whether there were any other factors influencing households to seek a GEAR location. Here we do not examine the factors triggering households into moving in general or into owner occupation in particular but instead emphasise why GEAR was chosen.

We asked for the 'main reasons' influencing the choice of new houses in the GEAR area and the answers are shown in Table 7.9. Almost 25 per cent cited a main reason related to house type, price and financing arrangements, conditions which could be replicated throughout the city. Almost one-third of households had friends or family in the area or had previously lived there. This is an important localising feature within GEAR and should be examined further. The key question (which cannot be answered with existing data) is whether the set of 'returning' households identified here exhausts the possibility of attracting previous residents back to the east end or whether substantial latent demand remains for these or perhaps for larger houses in this area.

Some 20 per cent of households stressed the good accessibility of this area to their work and other activities. Past patterns of housing development in the city have virtually compelled owners of terraced and semi-detached houses (especially if new) to make long journeys to work and have implied suburban living with car ownership. In the present sample of households only half were car owners and three-quarters used public transport to travel to work. These proportions are respectively very low and very high for a sample of owner occupiers, especially in new housing. If they can find or create suitable sites for building houses for sale, urban renewal agencies and developers working in inner cities should stress the transport savings of living in such areas.

These advantages could be considerable for long-distance commuters working in the city centre – particularly if several members of the household have to travel to work each day.

Our survey shows that 25 per cent of these people work in the GEAR area, 37 per cent in the city centre and a further 4 per cent in adjoining areas. The remaining third work further afield.

Table 7.9: Reasons for choosing the east end

Main reason

	Number	%
Family, friends live in area	18	16.4
Brought up in, used to live or always lived in east end	17	15.5
Close to work	16	14.5
Attraction of price, purchase arrangements and value for money	14	12.7
Suitable houses available	13	11.8
Centrality, accessibility in general	8	7.3
Liked neighbourhood or location of houses	6	5.5
Other reasons	8	7.3
Don't know or not answered	10	9.1
Total respondents	110	100.0

Perceptions of the GEAR area

The closeness of the east end to the city centre attracted many house-buyers but this feature of the area had been recognised as being a positive one by many in our 1977 sample of house-buyers who did not move to the GEAR area (Dawson et al., 1982). The 1977 sample rejected GEAR for a range of environmental and social reasons. The most important reasons for rejection, in rank order, were: the need to improve the quality and range of private housing (76 per cent); vandalism (74 per cent); violence and crime (73 per cent); and the need to clear derelict land (73 per cent).

The provision of new housing has itself done something to improve the quality and range of private housing in the east end. It is also interesting to consider the rank order of area problems perceived to exist by new house-purchasers in 1982, to assess whether policy has reduced the disadvantages identified in 1977. Area problems perceived by the 1982 sample of new house-purchasers are shown in Table 7.10. The high 'visibility' of poorly maintained roads and pavements

145

may be largely attributable to the recently completed nature of
the new housing sites. They may be put right soon, but signs
of past decay (drab and decayed appearance, waste ground,
empty and derelict houses) still concern a lot of people. So do
crime and vandalism. The new house-buyers stress the poor
surrounding physical environment more than existing residents do, but they seem to worry less about vandalism and
crime. It is also noteworthy that new purchasers are less
concerned about 'lack of interest in the area' by public
authorities. Nevertheless, a great deal of environmental
improvement is still required in the GEAR area and a high
proportion, one-third, of new house-buyers regarded the
appearance of the area as being 'fairly' or 'very unattractive'.

Table 7.10: Perception of GEAR area problems

Problems positively identified	New Private Housing Survey		Main GEAR Survey
	Number	% of all respondents	%
Pavements and roads in poor state of repair	59	53.6	60.8
Not enough things for teenagers to do	49	44.5	59.8
Drab and decayed appearance	42	38.2	26.1
Vandalism and hooliganism	40	36.4	50.6
Waste ground	37	33.6	24.2
Empty or derelict houses	35	31.8	26.6
Too much violence and crime	30	27.3	34.1
Rubbish in the streets and backcourts	29	26.4	35.5
Local people not caring about area	29	26.4	23.0
An area with a bad reputation	27	24.5	26.3
People who make trouble	23	20.9	20.5
Lack of interest in the area by local authorities	23	20.9	42.7
Not enough trees or green areas	8	7.3	11.0

Short- and long-term reactions

When households make choices which they regret, they can
either move again or, since movement costs are substantial in

the short-term, they can remain and express discontent or perhaps try to change things. Satisfaction with their present houses and with public transport among these house-buyers suggested that they were pretty well contented. However, compared with east end residents as a whole, fewer said they were 'very satisfied' with their local area in general (Table 7.11), and a significant proportion of households (41 per cent) were 'dissatisfied' with 'area appearance'.

Table 7.11: Satisfaction with local area

	New Private Housing Survey		Main GEAR Survey
	Number	%	%
Very satisfied	22	20.0	31.7
Fairly satisfied	66	60.0	49.3
Not very satisfied	16	14.5	11.4
Not at all satisfied	2	1.6	7.2
Don't know or not answered	4	3.6	0.5
Total respondents	110	100.0	100.0

These problems have not, so far, prompted an abnormally high proportion of people wishing to move. Their intended length of stay (Table 7.12) is not short in comparison with that found on other new build sites in Glasgow (Fielder, 1985) and although a quarter of the households interviewed were seriously thinking of moving house again, the reasons prompting such a move were rarely related to the qualities of the environment. Firmer conclusions about the success of these sites must await a longer period of residence.

The most important reason given for leaving the present house and the GEAR area is related to changes in family size and stages of the life cycle. Larger houses, or houses with gardens, are being sought.

This raises an important planning question. Could these life cycle demands be met within the GEAR area or will these people inevitably move out to other areas? There are at present very few houses of larger size and equivalent quality to their present homes available to buy in the east end. That could be put right, but at this stage in their lives these families may be even more concerned with schools, health services, recreation

147

Table 7.12: Intended length of stay in present house

	Number	%
Less than 5 years	19	23.8
5-10 years	13	16.2
10-20 years	1	1.2
20 years or more	6	7.5
Indefinitely	13	16.2
Don't know	28	35.0
Total not seriously thinking of moving	80	100.0

and the social composition of their neighbourhoods than with their housing. A whole package of resources may be required to retain them in the east end. It is at least arguable that this option should be available for those who want to stay in the east end. The whole topic calls urgently for research because their decisions will help to shape the future of this area. Any area specialising in starter homes for first-time buyers may enjoy buoyant conditions for a short while, perhaps with a rapid turnover of people, but a surfeit of small houses might develop in the future, depending on demographic changes. The first purchasers of new houses in GEAR received a 'once and for all' subsidy because their homes may have been built on land sold to the developers by public authorities for very low prices. The houses themselves, therefore, are likely to re-sell for somewhat higher prices and the subsequent buyers may not feel they have done so well.

Potential multiplier effects
There is considerable evidence that the 'back to the city' movement of prosperous households in the USA generally creates 'enclaves' of childless couples and some small families who do not use local amenities and services (Leven et al., 1976). Such enclaves make little contribution to local economic and social resources. Residents in new private housing in the GEAR area clearly do not correspond in origins or family status with American 'gentrifiers' and Table 7.13 shows that they do use local facilities and services. Indeed, they use them more than other residents in the GEAR area. Visiting a local pub is their most frequent pastime. However, roughly half the new residents do take their main food shopping outside the GEAR area (Table 7.14). That is probably because many of

them work in the centre. The data available do not allow us to pursue this theme in more detail. We must stress, however, that a fuller evaluation of the contributions which new residents make to the areas in which they live is an essential component of a well-planned redevelopment programme.

Table 7.13: Use of local recreational facilities

Leisure activities	New private housing survey				Main GEAR survey
	Not used/ participated	Gone to outside east end	Gone to elsewhere in east end	Gone to local area within east end	
Pictures	69.1	30.0	0.9	0.0	1.0
Bingo	89.1	1.8	1.8	7.3	12.3
Social Club	75.5	12.7	3.6	8.2	21.7
Pub	27.3	26.4	0.9	45.5	32.3
Theatre	76.4	20.9	0.9	1.8	0.9
Disco/Dance	62.7	26.4	3.6	7.3	9.4
Swimming Pool	58.2	8.2	4.5	29.1	3.5
Indoor Sports	67.3	11.8	4.5	16.4	3.9
Outdoor Sports	67.3	16.4	5.5	10.9	4.8
Watching Football	69.1	10.9	10.0	10.0	6.7
Church	62.7	5.5	3.6	28.2	34.8
Library	51.8	10.0	5.5	32.7	25.3

Table 7.14: Shopping patterns

Areas used for main food shopping	New Private Housing Survey	Main GEAR Survey	
	Number	%	%
Within Gear			
Bridgeton/Dalmarnock	10	9.1	9.0
Shettleston/Tollcross	27	24.5	34.7
Other GEAR locations	0	0.0	23.8
Outside GEAR			
City centre	30	27.3	5.5
Duke Street	16	14.5	10.4
Rutherglen/Cambuslang	8	7.2	5.7
Other area (location unspecified)	18	16.3	10.1
Don't know/not answered	1	0.9	0.8
Total respondents	110	100.0	100.0

Conclusion

We could see for ourselves that, with the exception of one small and rather badly chosen site, the houses built for sale in the east end were popular and successful. The older houses rehabilitated for sale were somewhat cheaper and also attracted a long queue of potential purchasers. Typically the purchasers were young, childless couples where both partners were working, many in non-manual occupations. Many of them had either moved or returned to the east end and so had an attachment to the area, but equally many purchasers were simply attracted to the price, quality and accessibility of the new developments. These developments have brought opportunities for buying small but reasonably good new houses to neighbourhoods which were previously unattractive to both building societies and the potential purchasers.

While it must be remembered that these developments are currently only on a small scale, the potential benefits of such new housing schemes are wide-ranging. They have allowed diversification of the age and social structures of the existing population and have brought into the area people with relatively high incomes. The houses widen choice by providing a combination of house type, location and tenure not previously available. The image of the area is improved by the physical improvements that arise when unattractive vacant land is replaced by attractive residential environments, and also by the less tangible benefits that result from signs of rising social status and investor confidence. The individuals who come into the area also bring potential benefits for the local economy. We showed that they make quite extensive use of many local facilities and must thus boost the demand for local retail and service businesses. A more detailed examination is needed, however, before any quantitative estimate could be made of local multiplier effects.

Some slight reservations should be expressed about the future of the schemes. Houses built since our study was made are selling well, but as this is chiefly small, first-time-buyer property, it is inevitable that many of the initial buyers will wish to move to larger houses either as their income increases or as they start a family. The continued demand for these houses will then depend on demographic features. There is good reason to expect that there will be growing numbers of small households in Glasgow. But more small houses are being built elsewhere in the city. The east end will always have the advantage of its accessible location which may continue to support the demand for these houses even if other similar new ones are built elsewhere in the city. But it will have difficulty in providing a physical environment that matches Glasgow's best.

What have been the costs of the new schemes? The main cost to the community has been the provision of land by the District Council at a low cost to private developers. The most valid cost to consider is the 'opportunity cost', that is the value of the next best use to which the land could have been put. In the case of east end land we can perhaps think of three main alternative uses. First, the land might have been sold on the open market to firms or private developers. In this area, investor confidence and the demand for industrial sites were so low that the price on the open market was likely to be very low, if indeed any buyer could be found without some further incentives. Second, the land could have been used to build factory units for sale or rent to local businesses. The benefits from such a strategy might include increased employment, although not necessarily of local residents – as we show in Chapter 4. Third, the District Council could have retained the land for future development of local authority houses. (We have said in Chapter 5 that this is unlikely.) Which of these alternatives is the 'next best' or indeed whether any of them is actually more beneficial to the GEAR area and the objectives set out for it would need careful comparison of the benefits from each with the benefits from the new housing schemes.

The development of new housing schemes has met some of the population and social mix aims of the GEAR project and the potential benefit from these schemes is very great. The new residents can play an important part in revitalising the area and the local economy. More importantly the role of a revitalised housing sector in giving a lead to the local economy and in increasing confidence in the area and its future should not be underestimated.

8 SOME ENVIRONMENTAL CONSIDERATIONS

Shiela T. McDonald

It is scarcely necessary to repeat that much of the east end of Glasgow in 1976 provided a distressing and distressed environment. The state of the area was such that in the GEAR Household Survey of 1977-8 'appearance of the area' came second only to 'crime and vandalism' as a problem identified by people living in the area. The background to the existence of the vast urban deserts in Glasgow's inner areas which contributed to this poor environment has been outlined in Chapters 1 and 3, and by other commentators (Checkland, 1981; Smith and Wannop, 1985). The waste areas were the visible evidence of failure to keep the various parts of programmes in phase: decentralisation of population from the congested and outworn areas was meant to be accompanied by redevelopment, but was not. Population declined more rapidly than anyone expected: the outflow of people to new towns, suburbs and further afield was massive. Industrial change meant that unwieldy factories were vacated and left to decay. The time lag between clearance and redevelopment may now be thought to have had some longer-term advantages in that the era of high-rise development had passed before renewal in the east end began in earnest, but this would have brought small comfort to those living in the area in 1976.

The Scottish Development Agency was set up under a Labour administration in 1975 to further economic development, generate and safeguard employment, promote industrial efficiency and improve the environment. Its remit gave it scope for linking economic and physical planning, an approach which is part of the Scottish tradition in regional planning and development. The Agency took over the functions of the Derelict Land Unit in the Scottish Office and many acres of spoil heaps and disused industrial sites have been reclaimed in the ten years of its existence. Smaller-scale environmental improvements have also been undertaken by the Agency. Increasingly, in both the manufacturing and service sectors of the economy, people at work find themselves in attractive surroundings, making environmental action all the more necessary in areas where the Agency hopes to stimulate revival.

The east end of Glasgow is of particular interest because it is one part of one city in which environmental improvement and 'greening' has been a prominent feature of a massive urban renewal effort with central government funding injected into the area through the intervention of the Scottish Development Agency. The scale of this funding might well arouse the interest of other authorities: between 1975 and 1985 some £12.5 million was spent on environmental improvement in GEAR alone. This compares with £156 millon spent throughout Scotland in the same period.[1] Additional components of greening in GEAR are leisure and recreation projects amounting to around £7.5 million, funded by the local authorities and the Scottish Development Agency, and the Cambuslang Investment Park created through the assembly and reclamation of many hectares of land. These varied elements contribute significantly to the overall impression of greening in GEAR.

The greening of cities with the help of programmes of environmental improvement has become a significant part of urban renewal in the UK and many other parts of Europe in the past few years. One manifestation of the trend is the acceptance in the UK of the notion of the Garden Festival as a means of reclaiming derelict land, improving the urban image, drawing in visitors, providing sites for industry and housing, and creating new public open space (Chetwynd, 1984). The extent to which this and other policies have been developed and implemented is readily apparent from evidence provided in a review of green policy prepared by the Association of Metropolitan Authorities (AMA Green Group, 1985). The review demonstrates that schemes to link green areas, provide footpaths and cycleways, create recreational spaces, remove eyesores, establish nature reserves, and carry out tree-planting burgeoned through the involvement of different groups and agencies able to draw on a variety of sources for funding. In the metropolitan authorities of Britain's biggest cities environmental projects became a major focus of attention. Specialist teams were built up to initiate and organise the work. This was less marked in the Scottish regional authorities because of the existence of the Scottish Development Agency.

No coherent national policy existed in the UK in relation to greening. Disparate schemes were gradually drawn together, aided by thinking at strategic level in the local authorities. At local level action was taking place with a measure of community involvement. For the metropolitan authorities there was considerable worry over lack of finance and the difficulties of developing and implementing wide-ranging programmes in a climate of uncertainty stemming from the likelihood that these strategic authorities would be abolished without any guarantee that their programmes would be safeguarded and carried on. The AMA review stresses the need for allocation of adequate resources and suggests that central government must recognise the importance of green issues by the allocation of resources to back a statement of central support for local initiatives. The refinement of policies put forward to implement ideas on nature conservation is apparent also in the Greater London Council's work prior to abolition (GLC, 1985b).

Clearly whatever can be learnt on this theme from the GEAR project *should* be learnt. The intensity of the action experienced in this area is unlikely to be repeated for a long time. In looking at the outcome so far, and at expected future outcomes, this chapter focuses on social outcomes and does not attempt a detailed cost-benefit appraisal. It takes the view that some of the main benefits of the programme cannot be measured in money values. Even the Department of the Environment in its guidance on appraisal (DoE, 1983) acknowledges that environmental improvement may have wider benefits which cannot be quantified immediately, such as the attraction of economic development, and the retention of employment. It warns against the concentration of resources on the basis of 'worst first' rather than in areas where the chances of attracting private investment are greatest, but does not concern itself with the extent to which the labelling of an area of poor environment can adversely affect the image of a much larger area and demoralise its inhabitants with devastating social and economic consequences.

In the GEAR area there has been a deliberate effort to coordinate the workings of different agencies and authorities with the guidance of a governing committee chaired by a

Scottish Office Minister. The participants have been led by the Scottish Development Agency and include Strathclyde Regional Council, Glasgow District Council, the Housing Corporation, the Scottish Special Housing Association, the Manpower Services Commission and the Greater Glasgow Health Board. Between them they have been responsible for over £202 million of expenditure in the area. Each organisation has retained its statutory responsibilities and this has meant that programmes have had to be drawn together in a spirit of co-operation which has not always been easy to engender. Much that was done at the outset to generate momentum could be said to have taken the easiest options on this account. It must, however, be remembered that ideas about greening and nature conservation have developed so fast during the last ten years that it would not be very fruitful to dwell largely on the early stages of the GEAR project with all the benefits of hindsight.

What then has been accomplished in the east end of Glasgow?

GEAR and the improvement programme

By 1982, when a review of the project took place, the physical environment had changed dramatically. Some of the worst features had been removed and the impact of others had been reduced. New houses and new workshops, modernisation and rehabilitation projects for housing and shops, new roads and traffic management had all contributed to the change. A major thrust of the Scottish Development Agency's effort had been towards environmental improvement, reflecting not only local concern but also the responsibilities of the Agency itself. Derelict and vacant land already in public ownership had been transformed into green areas through temporary or more permanent forms of landscape treatment. Cleaning featured as well as greening. Smoke control measures had made a remarkable change in the atmosphere, and backcourts had been upgraded. Buildings had been cleaned, an often costly exercise with scaffolding required for the tall, four-storey, sandstone tenements which are typical of older housing in Glasgow. The expenditure was strongly directed towards one of the major objectives of the GEAR project which was to improve and maintain the environment. The immediate results were highly visible and provided early evidence which helped to convince people that GEAR was indeed to be a programme of action.

Responses to improvements within the area

The initial response of people living in the area to these improvements was favourable. Compared with early evidence of concern about waste ground and the lack of trees and green areas, the findings of the social survey we made in 1982 suggested that work carried out under the GEAR programmes had reduced the grimness of the waste land in a significant way.

Levels of satisfaction varied throughout the area. The lowest levels were found to be in sectors of poor environmental quality where there were traffic problems or large numbers of children. Visits undertaken in 1982 showed that public use of 'green' sites was variable and that some sites were more popular than others. Some of the early sites were temporary, cosmetic improvements which improved the look of ground bought perhaps in advance of road improvements. Some had had a previous use in the sense of providing short cuts for pedestrians. Where this was not recognised by providing paths the 'improvement' was simply ignored and the site continued to be walked over. Some had been found acceptable as pleasant places for the elderly. (One respondent put it nicely: 'I like the wee project they have done over there – the old folk can have a wee seat on the bench'.)

Other sites were well used, with factory workers playing on a kickabout pitch at lunchtime, mothers sitting watching toddlers, and youngsters playing ball on the grass. These were happy sites which added greatly to the social amenity of the locality. A few sites showed evidence of dumping of rubbish, broken saplings, glass on kickabout pitches, graffiti, damaged fences and play equipment, and litter, especially among the shrubs. Some little-used sites were close to sites proposed for future housing. Others did not have the close relationship to housing which would best satisfy the principles of defensible space.

The visible evidence on the ground, and the responses in the social survey, made it abundantly clear that aspects of the environment which were the concern of two or more public services, such as the litter in the shrubs or the broken pavements left by statutory undertakers, caused a great many problems. Finding solutions to such problems severely tested the ability of participants to collaborate effectively.

Thus the cleansing department of the District Council made an application for urban aid funds to enable it to set up an amenity cleansing squad in the areas suffering most from litter. This allowed extra and more flexible resources to be deployed, literally to pick up the pieces left by existing work practices. Such squads are seen to be important because of the support they give to caring residents who may become disaffected in areas where there are shared entrances, backcourts and front gardens, and a minority of residents who through unwillingness or inability to accept a share of responsibility create a mess.

Responses from outside the area

Already by 1982 people outside the area were responding to the greening and cleaning. The private sector had begun to recognise the existence of GEAR and the opportunities provided by inner city sites where the short-term temporary improvements had included site clearance and preparation. The private house-builders acted swiftly once they could be assured of continuing supportive developments on surrounding sites and sales have justified their decisions to build. People passing through the area were aware that it was being cleaned up because many sites fronting the main traffic routes were among those tidied up in the first years, and GEAR signs were prominently displayed.

The revenue implications

One of the most difficult aspects of landscape improvement – that is, maintenance of the sites to a sufficiently high standard to counter any initial vandalism and to sustain the high profile image which was an essential part of the scheme – was tackled decisively from the start. The first year of the work on establishing a new landscape was covered by the initial contract, and a further three years by separate contracts funded by the Agency and supervised by landscape consultants. This innovative procedure was intended to ensure that the good impression created by improvements would not be lost and that the eventual handover to the local authorities would be readily accomplished. This latter aspect has not yet been tested because the Agency has continued to maintain sites in the GEAR area. Nevertheless, one of the points which stood out in our consideration of these environmental improvements was that the cost of maintaining the improved sites would in time fall principally on the District Council. The annual cost to the Agency of maintenance in GEAR was £400,000 in 1982-3, so this was not a minor matter.

Maintenance of the existing improved environment will continue to incur costs whatever arrangements for handover may be developed. There is, however, some evidence in parts of GEAR of local interest in maintaining gardens and communal areas as in the case of Fairbridge Tenants' Co-operative, or the initiative by tenants at Barrowfield in relation to front gardens. This interest should be fostered and encouragement given to tenants' associations and to community councils wishing to take over and organise maintenance of the sites as they become established. This need not always be on an unpaid basis. Work of this kind could provide opportunities for drawing on the organisational skills of people in the area. Local interest in maintaining gardens and communal areas deserves every encouragement but can never cater for more than a limited part of the maintenance requirements.

The monitoring of sites through maintenance contracts and other means is needed to identify sites where full use is not being made of facilities and to discover the reasons behind lack of use. Sometimes the employment of personnel to join in activities and help people to learn to make use of facilities is required; at other times removal of the supposed 'improvement' and its replacement by something that is more welcome may be the only sensible answer.

A related point was that there could be a continuing supply of vacant land which, if treated in similar ways, would also have to be maintained at high cost. Alternative uses of sites and ways of treating land to reduce maintenance costs or to generate income might help. The potentially most useful alternatives here seem to be the encouragement of more natural areas requiring a different and less manicured regime, the creation of 'community greens' of rather larger size and the gradual elimination of small sites which are costly to maintain. The ideas put forward here have been for the most part employed elsewhere in the UK and represent the next steps forward from the stages of development reached in 1982. Some, as will be seen later, have been taken up: others have not.

Natural areas. The opportunity for young children to learn from contacts with living things in the natural world can play a significant part in their development. It is easy to forget how limited are the opportunities available to many children in the east end, where even the temporarily vacant land which is often their only play space is barren and dangerous. The lack of natural, wild areas makes the retention of two such places particularly important. One is a unique area within a tight loop of the River Clyde which is difficult to reach. Some school teaching in biology and nature study has been carried out there and its retention as a field laboratory seems especially important. The other is a site at Auchenshuggle leased on a short-term basis by the British Trust for Conservation Volunteers. This site has the only area of mature woodland in the east end (as opposed to mature trees within public parks) and is therefore of considerable value. The creation of more natural habitats of this kind would be particularly valuable for low income families who find it difficult to get to the more distant country and regional parks.

Community Greens. At the small-scale local level, open space in the form of an area of rough grass which can be used in a variety of ways by whole families can be very welcome. Some areas provided by the Agency have begun to develop in this way, and each could in time acquire an individual identity by being used in different ways by the local community. The concept of a community green is useful because it can allow for changes in patterns of activity stemming from changes in attitudes to work and leisure.

Allotments. The development of more allotments may well be justified. The GEAR area has few allotments. Our social survey found only four households with an allotment but ninety-six households expressing an interest in working one. However, initial help is required if ground which is rough and badly drained is to be brought into use by residents with no strong tradition of gardening. The problems and expense of breaking new ground which is weed-infested and badly drained should not be underestimated if new allotments are provided.

Urban Farm. Glasgow already has an urban farm at Greater Possil on a six-acre site alongside allotments and any interest from residents in the east end could usefully be encouraged. A suitable site would have the character of a smallholding, preferably with a house occupied by a project worker.

Cycling tracks. Bikes of all kinds have long fascinated youngsters and traffic conditions make independent routes very necessary in built-up areas, especially when the pedal cyclist becomes a BMX rider or motor cyclist. Our field surveys showed that the banks of the River Clyde were being eroded in places by young motor cyclists in the absence of a designated 'scramble' area. This is the kind of use which generates opposition and so the problem is avoided rather than faced up to. The GEAR area is a place where action may be justified and feasible, even if what is offered is training on a disused factory site rather than Swindon's extensive track (Ball, Taylor and Blezard, 1985).

Driving course and maintenance workshop. Equally controversial for different reasons would be the use of ground for a driving course and maintenance workshop. One way of widening job opportunities in inner city areas is by providing driving tuition. The low car ownership rates and the high cost of tuition suggest that driving is a skill which many capable people in the GEAR area will continue to lack unless positive steps are taken to help them learn. A scheme of this kind would have to involve the driving schools, the police and government funding agencies, but – once developed – the resources might be available to residents in other parts of the region.

None of these uses would of itself generate much revenue, but each could be of social benefit, and collectively they could reduce the maintenance costs of substantial areas of land. In this way such schemes could help to ensure that the credibility of environmental improvement is not impaired through lack of upkeep. Widening the appeal of the programme to encompass the interests of more people in the area is a worthwhile objective.

Another point to be made in relation to the GEAR environment was that in the longer term the success of the improvement programme must depend on the extent to which local people become involved and come to regard the improved sites as community assets. Unless there is some interest by residents, 'improving and maintaining the environment' can be an impossibly large commitment for any organisation. Landscape and townscape treatment of the main traffic routes have enhanced the image presented to the world outside by the GEAR area. Improvements to the external environment also have a contribution to make in fostering a social environment robust enough to bear comparison with times past.

Wider benefits from improvements
In an area with high percentages of elderly and frail people, low incomes and unemployment, people can very easily become isolated and withdrawn, afraid to go out and not able to go far afield when they do go out. Pride in place was seen as a factor in retaining and restoring morale for those already in the area, and in generating interest amongst possible newcomers to the area. Environmental improvements had then a part to play in furthering the GEAR objectives of fostering the commitment and confidence of residents, and overcoming their social disadvantages. On the townscape side, thinking on these lines drew attention to the importance of reinforcing the traditional focal points of the east end, such as Parkhead, Bridgeton and Shettleston where many changes have occurred as thousands of people living nearby have moved away. In earlier days Glasgow's traditional townscape in tenement areas gave prominence to nodes of activity by accentuating the corner properties with roofscapes of turrets, cupolas and clocks. Nowadays the buildings sometimes remain although changes in traffic movement, population densities and usage may mean they no longer have the same importance in marking nodes of activity. This has been the case in the east end but the cleaning of the buildings and planting on the approaches to these focal areas have been a part of the townscape strategy emerging from local plans and from the GEAR project team. Form and function, symbol and substance have to be integrated if the townscape improvements are to have lasting value. It is here that townscape policies must be related to a broader spatial strategy which recognises the need

for maximum accessibility and improved service delivery to focal points, and the psychological value of familiar places where the reassurance of human contact and known faces can be expected. If these problems are ineptly handled, a mismatch may occur between the visual messages of the townscape and the social reality. A stage without actors may be created.

Environmental work has provided a vehicle for social and community development. People in the area have taken part in a rich variety of schemes with help from the Agency, from other authorities participating in the GEAR project, and from conservation bodies and community workers, some of whom have been funded by MSC and urban aid. Community councils have provided the main point of contact. Where residents' groups exist they have been drawn in, as have tenants' associations and housing associations. The process has not always been simple or straightforward. It has to be considered as a learning process for all who take part whether lay or professional. At times it may have seemed to be a public relations exercise, at others the desire to listen and to respond to residents' wishes may have led to 'overdevelopment' of sites.

For the people living in the GEAR area meetings are often frustrating and sometimes uninformative. It is all too easy for discussion to be deflected and for people to realise afterwards that they have been unable to communicate with public officials or to reach productive decisions. Community workers in the area have helped local people to take part in meetings, but they are aware that if success is measured in terms of wider participation rather than the commitment of a few activists community development is a very slow process.

Involvement in the environment
Two examples may serve to illustrate the complexities of generating wider involvement in environmental matters. In one case school children took part in the planning, design and planting of a playground located within a street block and overlooked by many dwellings. The playground once built was taken over by older children and had then to be altered. This experience showed that such a space is only defensible if all those overlooking it are of like mind. In the GEAR area,

as in other places, that can be difficult to achieve where there are more than a few dwellings in the neighbourhood.

However, the general findings from our survey do suggest that the planting and green areas are subject to less vandalism than the structures on the same sites. This is encouraging in view of the work carried out in schools in the GEAR area by the British Trust for Conservation Volunteers which has created gardens in school grounds where previously there was only barren asphalt. Members of the Trust's team have run trips by minibus to country parks and have given children the opportunity of planting trees. They have also worked in the only area of mature woodland in the east end and defended it against a private housebuilder, as well as supporting the retention of the semi-natural area in the Cuningar loop on the River Clyde referred to earlier. This area is now included in the second review of Strathclyde's Structure Plan as an area of interest for nature conservation (SRC, 1985).

Another example of consultation with a tenants' association which influenced the form of an open space was one which led to the development of allotments and a semi-formal garden enclosed by cast-iron railings. Strong local activists achieved a result of considerable quality with a sitting area and trees. Supported by a gardening club at a local neighbourhood centre this scheme reflects the aspirations of one group, but needs to be complemented by an open, less restricted area if the needs of different age groups are to be fully met and especially those of teenagers. It is a very different type of space from that created in Hackney by residents working with Free Form Arts Trust (Wates, 1985) which has no direct counterpart in GEAR, although GEAR has had community artists working from the Dolphin Arts Centre.

What the scheme does illustrate is the emergence of a supportive network through the concentration of different activities taking place concurrently with different sources of financial backing. It is this that offers great promise for the future of the east end since, whatever limitations current schemes may have, the ability of people in the area to take part in discussion leading to decision-making has been greatly enhanced by the intensity of activity in the GEAR project and this must be one of its longer-term benefits – hard to measure though it may be. Consultations on the future of a disused railway line recently brought out clearly the differences between early ideas by professionals for the use of the route and those of local people who are keen to eliminate the threat of what could be an alternative route for football supporters leaving the Celtic ground.

Alongside projects associated with the residential developments, businesses have been encouraged to improve the look of their premises, and local police have offered advice on security and design. An Enterprise Trust has been set up to help stallholders to rejuvenate the Barras market in the inner part of the area, and historic buildings and examples of industrial and commercial products of the past have been conserved.

Pointers to the future
The GEAR project was a test bed for ideas and policies which might be adopted elsewhere. It has informed thinking on other SDA projects in Scotland. Subsequent projects have drawn back from the range of activity tried in the GEAR project and operated with more restricted objectives and more measurable targets (Gulliver, 1984). This could mean that some of the long-term benefits of the more imaginative features of the GEAR scheme and its more open-ended features may be lacking in the Agency's later schemes. The impact of concentration in one specific area is likely to be less marked in that the supportive networks built up through the presence of many personnel, often funded by urban aid, are less likely to develop. Experience in the east end shows that it is not enough to put in capital without also putting in revenue, and that the support of local people is a vital element of any programme of environmental improvement.

The notion of a separate working-class culture which has no truck with the refinements of middle-class greening can never be far from the minds of those exploring the GEAR project. There is indeed robust evidence of differing appreciation of things that can be seen in the sharp reactions of different groups to the pigeon lofts which colonise the various open spaces. Nevertheless there is substantial support from within the area for improvements overall. Most people do prefer green areas to shale and rubble strewn with rubbish.

The GEAR programme demonstrates a difference in style

from much work carried out by local authorities in England. The difference lies in part in the fact that the local authorities in England built up staffs to carry out much of the work themselves. The staffs in the new Scottish authorities which emerged from the reorganisation of local government in the early 1970s did not develop in precisely the same way. The presence of the SDA with its role in land renewal has meant that while programmes are agreed with local authorities the Agency personnel act in a managerial capacity and put much of the work out to consultants. This has led to a growth in the numbers of landscape consultancies and is in line with the present central government's approach in that the ebb and flow of work is accommodated in the private sector while staffing levels in the public sector are restricted. There may be pointers here to what will happen now that England's metropolitan counties have been abolished.

The approach to environmental improvement in the GEAR area falls a long way short of the full development of a philosophy based on ideas of greening to reduce pollution, and provide closer contact with nature and the changing seasons. But it is a considerable advance on the outlook which allowed deterioration to reach the appalling levels to be seen in the east end in the early 1970s. In presenting a more human face the project raises again historic questions of whether area rejuvenation is for the benefit only of those who live within the area or whether it is also for the benefit of a larger population. The project is dealing with the most extensive area of dereliction in Glasgow, and without it there could have been no *Glasgow's Miles Better* campaign. The state of the east end would have made such sentiments derisory. A city can be labelled every bit as destructively as a difficult-to-let housing estate, and Glasgow was so labelled. Shedding that stigma is a slow and costly process in which the GEAR project plays an important part. It has certainly contributed to the confidence with which Glasgow has embraced ideas of central area rejuvenation, tourism and even the Garden Festival of 1988, and it will have effects which last well beyond the lifetime of the individual projects which have enlivened these once drab and dreary acres.

[1] Hansard, 1985.

9 ACCESS TO THE HEALTH SERVICES

Isobel M. L. Robertson

Our studies of the GEAR project dealt with many aspects of the health and welfare services. In this chapter we focus on a particular issue which should concern health service planners in an area of this kind.

When the National Health Service was set up over thirty years ago it was committed to offering equal care for all members of the population. Recent studies cited in the Black Report (Townsend and Davidson, 1982) have shown that standards of health still depend heavily on social class – more heavily than ever in certain age and sex groups. For example, post neo-natal death rates, one of the more sensitive indicators of class inequalities in health, show a general decline in all classes but the difference between upper and lower classes has not narrowed (Walters, 1980). While it is still difficult to prove exactly how poverty and the class structure are related to ill-health there is less doubt that the situation could be improved by a comprehensive anti-poverty strategy.

This chapter focuses on two questions. How easy is it for people in the east end to get to a doctor, a chemist and other branches of the health services? Is public policy making it easier or harder for them to reach these services? We begin by posing them in a more revealing way. Then we look at the kinds of people who live in the east end and their health record, making comparisons with two other areas. Next we compare the accessibility of general practitioners, hospitals and chemists in these three areas. Finally we look at the impact now being made on these patterns by the new health centres which are being built in the east end and draw some conclusions for the future.

Equal access to health care is difficult to achieve for a variety of reasons. The needs of individuals and their ability to use the National Health Service vary. Young children, pregnant women, the elderly and the disabled generally have a greater need for care than other people, and often they find it harder to get to the places where care is available. Mothers of young children, for example, may have a very demanding day which includes ferrying children to and from school, shopping and housekeeping and perhaps a part-time job which together allows little time for visits to clinics, particularly if these have to be made by public transport. The cost, the time and trouble of a bus journey have to be weighed against the probable benefits of medical advice. Attendance at pre-natal or child clinics is much easier for car owners. The elderly, in contrast, may have more time but less mobility because of disability or the lack of a car.

Perceptions of the value of the health service also vary. It has been shown (Phillips, 1979) that middle-class people are more likely to overcome the obstacles of time and distance because they give greater priority to matters of health – and perhaps because they get more out of the health services. They also make more telephone contacts (Weiss and Greenlick, 1970). Lower socio-economic groups, on the other hand, are generally less inclined to consult doctors, and are much less concerned with preventive medicine (Townsend, 1974). The anti-smoking campaign, for example, has found most support among the middle classes. Levels of education influence the demand for and the ability to use medical services to maximum effect, and the speed with which people learn from recent research about smoking and other dangers to health.

The location and variety and quality of medical facilities also help to determine access to the general practitioners through whom other branches of the health service have to be approached. Thus the uneven distribution of their surgeries across the map may reinforce patterns of social disadvantage – and not only in Britain. Similar patterns have been demonstrated in New Zealand (Barnett and Newton, 1977), Australia (Freestone, 1975) and in the USA (Sparer and Okeda, 1974). In 1971, Tudor Hart (1971) described what he termed the 'inverse care law' by which he implied that in areas of most sickness doctors shouldered heavier case loads, had less hospital support, less effective traditions of consultation and more obsolete premises. Physical access to a surgery is closely related to the frequency of use (Hopkins *et al.*, 1968). Studies of inner city areas where surgeries may be shabby, overcrowded and poorly equipped show that many patients prefer to seek treatment at hospital out-patient departments or to resort to patent medicines purchased at pharmacies (see, for example, Thornhill Neighbourhood Project, 1978).

We investigated the provision of health services in the GEAR area and made comparisons with two other communities of comparable size, also in the Glasgow area – a peripheral, working-class estate of local authority housing (Drumchapel) and a prosperous owner-occupied suburb (Bearsden). We measured the accessibility of services in terms of time, distance and the choice available, contrasting different methods of transport. Potential visits to surgeries, hospitals, clinics, health centres and pharmacies were computed using a time-space model called PESASP (Robertson, 1984). Various indicators of health in the three communities were also compared.

Socio-economic characteristics of the three communities
As Table 9.1 shows, both GEAR and Drumchapel have lost population over the last decade but the much more rapid decline in the GEAR area, where population halved, has brought it into line with Drumchapel in terms of numbers. Although Bearsden has grown in the last ten years it is still smaller than the other two communities. In age structure the GEAR area differs by having fewer children of pre-school age and fewer young adults. But its retired population, at 22.2 per cent, far exceeds that of Drumchapel and Bearsden. Thus the east end, because it once supported a much larger population, poses problems of accessibility which are in some ways easier and in some ways harder than those faced by the two newer, smaller, suburban areas. It has acquired over the years facilities to serve the much larger population it once had. But its remaining people are scattered over a much larger area.

The two working-class areas clearly have more urgent needs. Unemployed and temporarily sick people are almost as numerous in the GEAR area as in Drumchapel, and both are far in excess of those in Bearsden. There are great disparities in the proportions of socio-economic groups. The GEAR area has only 5.4 per cent in professions and management while Bearsden has 46.5 per cent. Unskilled workers, often a vulnerable group, amount to 11.2 per cent in the GEAR area and even more in Drumchapel but scarcely reach 1 per cent in

Bearsden. Educational qualifications are insignificant in both GEAR and Drumchapel, while Bearsden has one of the highest concentrations of graduates in the whole of Britain. It has also an exceptional car ownership rate of 84.6 per cent, giving great mobility to those who actually have the use of those cars. The GEAR area and Drumchapel have only 20.4 per cent (our

Table 9.1: Comparative analysis of socio-economic characteristics of GEAR, Drumchapel and Bearsden

	Inner city GEAR	Peripheral council estate DRUMCHAPEL	Owner-occupied suburb BEARSDEN
Population and area			
Total population 1981	40,852	31,379	26,387
Total population 1971	81,900	38,029	25,017
Area	14 km²	3.5 km²	11.7 km²
Age structure (percentage of total population)	%	%	%
Children 0-4 years	4.6	9.1	6.6
Young adults 25-34	10.1	13.9	13.3
Retired (60/65 and older)	22.2	8.7	13.9
Socio-economic class as % of all households			
1 Professional and managerial workers	5.4	2.6	46.5
2 Non-manual workers	9.1	17.6	28.9
3 Skilled workers	24.4	29.3	11.1
4 Semi-skilled workers	16.7	30.3	3.5
5 Unskilled workers	11.2	13.5	0.9
* Others	32.1	6.7	9.1
* Mainly retired persons with no previous occupation stated			
Social characteristics Unemployed and temporarily sick as % of economically active	26.2	30.4	4.1
Single parent families as % of all households	0.6	3.1	0.2
Large families (4+ children) as % of all households	2.1	5.3	1.6
Possessors of degrees, professional and vocational qualifications as % of adults over 21	3.4	0.8	33.3
Housing Housing tenure as % of all tenures			
Owner occupiers	19.8	2.4	88.9
Council tenants	67.9	94.3	8.0
Travel Mode of travel to work as % of all travel to work			
Bus	35.3	36.4	10.3
British Rail	4.8	6.8	9.7
Car	20.9	10.6	64.8
On foot	21.0	8.8	5.8
Car ownership (% of all households)	20.4	17.2	84.6

Data derived from Small Area Statistics of the Census of Population, 1981 own survey, made the following year, showed an even lower proportion of car owners – 14 per cent) and 17.2 per cent of car-owning households respectively. As a result, travel to work by car (and probably to social and other facilities) is easily the commonest form of transport in Bearsden. In the east end and Drumchapel people go by bus or – particularly in the GEAR area – they walk (21.0 per cent).

Health and sickness

Adequate measures of the health of an area are not easy to obtain. One index is provided by hospital admission rates but these have some disadvantages. For example, one individual may have several admissions in the course of a year. Further, doctors vary in their propensity to recommend hospitalisation. Hospital admission rates have been compiled for the GEAR area for 1980-2, with the help of postcodes attached to the address of all patients.

Table 9.2 shows the rates of admission to hospital for different age and sex groups for the three areas compared. The overall average rate per head of population is 19.6 per cent in GEAR, considerably higher than the 11.1 per cent in Drumchapel and 6.6 per cent in Bearsden. One of the reasons for the difference between GEAR and Bearsden is that doctors often advise hospitalisation when home conditions are inadequate or patients have no close relative living nearby. Another difference between the two communities may be their varying use of private medical facilities. GEAR has a lot of old people who are likely to boost the hospitalisation rate, but when different age groups are inspected it is obvious that GEAR leads the field in most of them – and particularly among men over 45. It has an average of 57.2 per cent of males aged 75 and over in hospital at some time during a year in comparison with 47.7 per cent in Drumchapel and 27.8 in Bearsden. The contrast between both working-class areas and the more middle-class Bearsden is marked in every age and sex group.

In other indicators of morbidity (Table 9.3) GEAR again compares unfavourably with Bearsden and in some cases with Drumchapel. For example, in new cases of TB during 1981 GEAR had fifteen while there were only two in Drumchapel and six in Bearsden. Hospital admission in the first year of life tends to be more common in Drumchapel than in GEAR but that may be a reflection of the larger families found there. In Bearsden over 80 per cent of babies are fully immunised against diphtheria, tetanus and poliomyelitis one year after birth. The proportion in the east end varies from 50-80 per cent in different parts of the area. The incidence of low birth rate, often associated with the mother's smoking habits, is higher both in the GEAR area and in Drumchapel than in Bearsden. Underweight babies have a poorer chance of a healthy childhood than those of normal weight. More of the elderly in the east end and in Drumchapel are on the health visitors' books. This is not necessarily a reflection of ill-health but may be related to the absence of support from friends and relatives.

Children are examined medically when they enter school and again when they leave. Frequently found defects are inflammatory conditions of the ear and eye, speech and language disorders and dental caries – all of them things which the average family can normally put right very quickly with a bit of professional help. Some caution is necessary in the interpretation of this data because doctors vary in their propensity to report defects. There is no standardisation. Table 9.4, however, shows that the average number of defects per 1,000 children examined in GEAR is considerably above the Glasgow mean, and these defects are higher absolutely and by comparison with other areas when the youngsters leave school than when they started. By 1983 the situation in Glasgow had considerably improved. No data were available for GEAR.

Mortality in the GEAR area from all causes in the years 1980-2 is summarised in Table 9.5. In this table, large values of Chi^2 generally mean that the difference between the GEAR experience and the figures which would be expected in a typical Greater Glasgow population of these ages and sexes is large and unlikely to have arisen by chance. The high Chi^2 values together with the small standard errors signify a population which has much worse health experience than that to be found in the Greater Glasgow Health Board area as a whole. The GEAR area had, in fact, the highest Chi^2 values of any Area for Priority Treatment identified by the local authorities in Glasgow.

Table 9.2: Rates of admission to hospital*, 1980-2, by age and sex

	Age group in years. (Percentage of each group)																	
Community	0-4		5-9		10-14		15-24		25-44		45-64		65-74		75+		Mean
	M %	F %	M %	F %	M %	F %	M %	F %	M %	F %	M %	F %	M %	F %	M %	F %	%
GEAR	23.6	14.5	13.2	9.4	7.4	5.6	10.6	10.9	14.8	15.6	27.7	16.9	45.5	25.9	57.2	34.6	19.6
Drumchapel	19.8	16.3	12.0	8.5	9.8	6.9	10.3	12.7	13.9	14.9	21.4	14.8	25.2	18.1	47.7	42.1	11.1
Bearsden	8.2	6.4	7.0	5.3	5.4	4.1	5.0	6.3	4.4	7.5	8.9	9.2	21.6	16.4	27.8	25.8	6.6

* Hospital admission for all specialities except geriatric appraisal, geriatric long-term and young chronic sick.

Data supplied by Greater Glasgow Health Board Information Services Unit.

These percentages represent the average annual number of cases of hospitalisation in the period 1980-2 over the total males or females in each age group in 1981.

Table 9.3: Some indicators of morbidity in postcode sectors within GEAR, Drumchapel and Bearsden

	GEAR	Drumchapel	Bearsden
Hospital admissions in the first year of life per 100 births	24.2-29.0%	29.9%*	12.8%*
1980 births fully immunised against diphtheria, tetanus and and poliomyelitis by November 1982	50-80%	60-69%	80+%[†]
New cases of TB during 1981	ø15	2	6
Elderly (65 years and over) on health visitors' books, 1981	4.7-35.7%	7.7-35.7%	0.8-10.6%
Incidence of low birth weight as % of live births 1980-1981	0-20%	7.1-20%	0-4.7%

ø 4 are in institutions (hostels and lodging houses).

* aggregated postcode sectors, one each for Drumchapel and Bearsden.

[†] 80+% in all postcode sectors.

Data supplied by Greater Glasgow Health Board Information Services Unit

Table 9.4: Average number of defects per 1,000 children examined at school

Area	1978		1983			
			Entrants		Leavers	
	Entrants	Leavers	Boys	Girls	Boys	Girls
GEAR	71.9	83.6				
Eastern District Health Board	75.5	55.5				
Greater Glasgow Health Board	64.4	55.1	39.6	36.8	33.0	27.7

Source: Information Service of Greater Glasgow Health Board

Table 9.5: All causes of mortality: GEAR area, 1980-2

Population Cohort	SMR	SE	*Chi^2
Aged 0-64, male and female	131	5	+47.7
Aged 0-64, male only	132	7	+31.8
Aged 0-64, female only	128	8	+15.9
All ages, male and female	119	2	+71.82

SMR Standardised mortality ratio
SE Standard error of SMR
* Comparison with Greater Glasgow Health Board

Source: Information Service of Greater Glasgow Health Board

The news is not all bad. The GEAR area shows declining perinatal and infant death rates since 1974 (see Table 9.6). Both series of figures rose, absolutely and in comparison with Greater Glasgow figures, between 1975 and 1977, but then fell again and were significantly lower in 1980 than in other parts of the city. These data are encouraging but must be treated with caution because of the relatively few births in any one year within the GEAR area. The ratio of births to deaths in GEAR was 54:100 for the years 1980/1; in Drumchapel it was 171:100 and in Bearsden 169:100.

Accessibility of primary health provision

When we began our research in 1982, the GEAR area had some thirty-one doctors' surgeries. Four were operated by one doctor on his own, but most were group practices with between two and nine partners. Most of these surgeries were well located in relation to public transport. They were, however, in some cases, dilapidated in appearance. The ratio of patients to doctors must have been one of the lowest in the country (see Table 9.7) but it must not be forgotten that these figures show the numbers of patients living in each area, not the numbers on individual doctor's lists. Because many of the families displaced from GEAR to the peripheral estate of Easterhouse retained their former doctor the numbers on east end lists may be higher than these figures suggest. In a study of Swansea, Phillips (1980) has pointed out that a desire to maintain a link with a doctor known to the family for a long time appears to be stronger than the wish to minimise the distance to general practitioners' surgeries.

The space-time model PESASP used in this exercise is a sensitive and practical instrument for measuring accessibility. Not only does it examine space and time simultaneously but it can handle a sequence of activities rather than one at a time. For example, the accessibility of a doctor's surgery can be measured simply by the time or distance from home to surgery, but for many individuals the trip in reality will be HOME → BUS STOP →. SURGERY → PHARMACY → BUS STOP → HOME. Distance to bus stop, time-table of buses, opening times of surgery and pharmacy and the individual's own daily pattern of activities must all be taken into account.

Figure 9.1 shows the travel time to and from the nearest

Table 9.6: Perinatal and infant death rates, 1974-80 (deaths per 100 live births)

| | Perinatal Death Rate | | | | | | | Infant Death Rate | | | | | | |
	1974	1975	1976	1977	1978	1979	1980	1974	1975	1976	1977	1978	1979	1980
GEAR	2.4	2.6	2.5	3.5	2.5	1.7	0.7	2.2	3.1	2.7	2.7	2.2	0.9	0.4
Eastern District	2.6	2.9	2.5	2.4	2.1	1.6	1.8	2.2	2.6	2.6	2.3	1.7	1.7	1.0
Greater Glasgow Health Board	2.3	2.3	2.0	2.0	1.6	1.3	1.4	2.0	1.9	1.7	1.8	1.4	1.3	1.3

Source: Greater Glasgow Health Board (Information Services Unit)

Table 9.7: Numbers of doctors, patients and pharmacies, 1982

	No. of doctors	Resident population per doctor	No. of surgeries	No. of pharmacies
GEAR	61	669	*31	20
Drumchapel	16	1961	6	3
Bearsden	12	2198	3	3
Greater Glasgow	–	#1872	–	–

* As of 1982. Six practices have since moved into the Bridgeton Health Centre where the total number of doctors is 20. Two practices moved into Townhead Health Centre where there are 19 doctors and two to Baillieston Health Centre where there is a total of 12 doctors. Overall provision is little changed but locations are different.

Patients per doctor, Department of Health and Social Services. Scottish Health Statistics, 1980.

surgery on foot or, if necessary, by bus. In most respects GEAR is better off than the other two communities. Every individual in the GEAR area could reach and return from a surgery in less than thirty minutes. The situation is similar in Drumchapel where surgeries are reasonably well located but much fewer in number. There the doctor-patient ratio is lower, in line with Glasgow as a whole (Table 9.7) but the area is smaller and its residents more concentrated. An 'ideal' distance to a surgery has been estimated at a maximum of 15 minutes on foot (Hillman, 1973). In the GEAR area and Drumchapel, with the surgeries as located in 1982, most inhabitants were within this limit. In Bearsden, however, only 20 per cent of the population live within a convenient distance on foot from the three surgeries. As car ownership is high many patients will use this form of travel, but mothers at home may not have the use of the family car during surgery hours, and many of the elderly have given up driving. A journey by bus to a surgery from some parts of Bearsden can take a return trip of between 45 minutes and an hour or more. The ratio of patients to doctors is higher than in the GEAR area or Drumchapel but this is probably an overestimate because some residents may go to doctors in neighbouring Milngavie or in the city of Glasgow who have been excluded from this computer model.

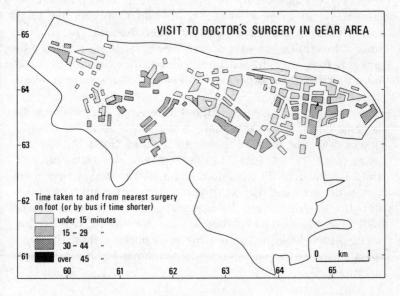

Figure 9.1 Travel times to doctors' surgeries

Our PESASP model also enables us to measure the amount of choice that people have. The ability to choose is an important ingredient in the quality of life. Many accessibility models assume that the potential customer will use the nearest facility. But even if he is content to do so, it may not be open when he needs it. Since most of our activities occur as sequences fitted into the daily routine of sleeping, eating, shopping and working and since most individuals have to dovetail their timetable of activities with the opening times and locations of service points, the question of choice is more complex than at first appears. An activity sequence involving a visit to a doctor and then to a chemist was simulated for the three communities. In GEAR with thirty-one surgeries and twenty chemists the maximum choice was 620 (31 × 20) provided that all are open at the same time. On foot within a total of 30 minutes travelling time some 6 per cent (i.e. 37) of the potential choices were available from certain locations. The situation in Drumchapel is similar, but use of public transport increases the choice in a few neighbourhoods by a factor of 2. Bearsden presents greater contrasts. Some individuals have a choice of five out of the nine offered by three surgeries and three pharmacies, in under 30 minutes total travel time on foot or by bus. In other Bearsden neighbourhoods the choice is very restricted, even for those prepared to travel a long way. In all three communities the use of a car permits virtually 100 per cent choice within the same journey time.

If a visit to a pharmacy without a previous trip to a surgery is considered, most indviduals in the GEAR area could reach one or more chemists on foot in 15 minutes. Some indeed had an exhaustive choice, although others, for example, in Dalmarnock, had no conveient chemist – for reasons we note in Chapters 11 and 15. As dispensing facilities are part of the new health centres now being set up, the number of chemists will probably decline. If they are the first line of defence for many individuals, gaps in their distribution which become even larger than present ones must have some impact on health.

Health centres
Since 1982 three health centres have opened within the GEAR area and one on its margins. These are purpose-built complexes housing the offices of general practitioners, nursing and ancillary staff, child clinics, chiropodists, dentists, physiotherapists and other services rarely available in the average surgery. Most doctors have moved from their surgeries

into these centres. Journeys from home to and from the new health centres are shown in Figure 9.2. The result of the change in provision is that the pattern of accessibility is now much worse – comparable with that in Bearsden (see Figure 9.1). For at least 70 per cent of the population the time necessary to reach a GP has increased. For some, particularly in Tollcross and Shettleston, an inconvenient and costly bus journey is necessary. The GEAR area houses a lot of those in poorly paid jobs, large numbers of elderly and unemployed people, and very few car owners. Health centres are better equipped than the old surgeries. They may provide other services not previously so easily available to patients, such as a physiotherapist, and they certainly provide a more pleasant and fulfilling environment for medical and nursing staff. However, research, quoted earlier in this chapter, by Hopkins *et al.* (1968) and Weiss and Greenlick (1970) has shown that distance can have an inhibiting effect on the frequency of use of surgeries and other facilities, particularly among poorer people and people without cars.

Given the socio-economic character of the east end, it must be questioned whether health centres are the best way of providing primary health care. In talks with residents' groups and others involved in the GEAR project it was clear that the Health Board is widely felt to be aloof from local people and unwilling to join with other services in corporate planning. That need not be the case. An interesting exception to this attitude was found in relation to the establishment of a Day Hospital for psychiatric patients at Bridgeton. Two consultant psychiatrists arranged meetings with the local Community Councils to discuss problems at an early stage in the development, and residents joined in a support group to help on the project. They told us that they accepted the hospital as something which belonged to the community and served it.

If health centres are deemed to be the best form of provision of primary health care, greater efforts must be made to locate them in the most accessible sites and to improve transport services for patients. It is acknowledged (McCreadie and Macgregor, 1979) that 'the health centre cannot be convenient to all' as it requires a large catchment population to 'justify the economic provision of a broad range of diagnostic, treatment and rehabilitation services'. Although 40-50,000 patients were

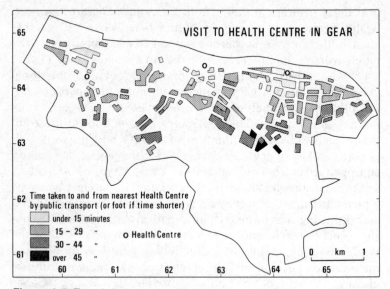

Figure 9.2 Travel times to health centres

at one time considered to be the ideal catchment size
(McCreadie, 1974) most Scottish centres now cater for 10-
30,000 persons. In this respect the GEAR health centres are
typical. They are, however, in far from optimal locations.

In order to test how far these health centres are from the
most accessible locations in the east end a data base of
population was set up for the whole Eastern Glasgow Health
District of which GEAR is a part. Using an accessibility
maximising technique, the TORNQVIST algorithm (Robertson,
1977), we found the optimum sites for the six centres now
operating in that area (Figure 9.3). We also computed the
catchment areas for the actual locations. Comparison of the
two maps in Figure 9.3 shows that only one centre (in
Easterhouse, outside the GEAR area itself) has been located
within one kilometre of the optimum site. The distributional
pattern of the other five centres is far from optimal.
Townhead, in the extreme north-west part of the Eastern area,
as well as having a peculiarly elongated catchment shape,
has proved to be difficult to reach because of the disposition
of bus routes. The shape of a population catchment determines its degree of accessibility to those who live within its

boundaries. The more compact the area, the greater the ease with which a facility can be reached by potential customers. It is obvious that very few of the actual catchments, if any, have the regularity and neatness of the optimum areas.

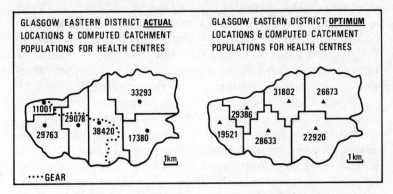

Figure 9.3 Optimum and actual health centre locations

It is appreciated that it is not always possible to obtain a suitable building site at the optimum location. The Health Service complains that sites 'can usually be obtained only after protracted, difficult and frequently frustrating negotiations' (McCreadie and Macgregor, 1979). Local resident groups, however, are not convinced that the Health Board put sufficient emphasis on accessibility. Factors such as nearness to existing hospitals (Townhead is a case in point) may be regarded as more important. Townhead's proximity to the Royal Infirmary gives it the unhappy appearance of being part of that intimidating Victorian edifice. Bridgeton Health Centre, on the other hand, built right next door to a long-established pub which local residents managed to save from demolition, may seem incongruous but is more likely to be regarded as an integral part of the community.

The journey to hospital
Most people make journeys to hospital from time to time to seek help from out-patient and casualty departments, or to visit friends and relatives who are patients there. The GEAR area is better served than either Drumchapel or Bearsden for this purpose. The nearest large hospital to the east end is the Royal Infirmary. A journey there and back by public transport

takes from 30 to 90 minutes for most households in the GEAR area (Figure 9.4). As can be seen on the maps, this compares well with both Drumchapel and Bearsden. From some parts of Bearsden total travel time to a hospital by public transport is over two hours. A return journey to the nearest children's hospital (Yorkhill) is generally over one hour, and nearly two hours from some districts. The situation is similar in Drumchapel where over half the estate live at least 1 hour 30 minutes from Yorkhill. In Bearsden public transport travel times are generally greater than in Drumchapel. For over 70 per cent of the area two hours are necessary for a return journey by bus. Adjacent to Yorkhill are maternity facilities used by Bearsden residents. Mothers in the GEAR area, however, can use the Royal Maternity Hospital which is within 30 to 90 minutes total travel time. The advantages of the east end apply mainly to people without cars. For car drivers these differences are not so important. Thus it will be mainly in Drumchapel, where car ownership rates are low, that people have to make really long journeys to hospitals.

Summary

The relationships between poverty, unskilled work, unemployment, poor education and ill-health outlined in the Black Report seem to hold in the GEAR area. Present policy for primary health care will not change those patterns. Our recommendations included a plea for more health education workers in the east end, and we understand some action is being taken about that. But the replacement of small, well-located surgeries with large, badly-sited health centres means that most east end people now have to travel further in order to visit a general practitioner. Some local chemists may have difficulty in keeping going. It is possible that pleasant and well-equipped medical facilities may in time attract more doctors and nurses to work in this inner city area, but thought will have to be given to improving the mobility of non-car owners – particularly elderly people and mothers with young children – all heavy users of the health services. Consideration should also be given to the use of health centres for other purposes which will help the community: for example, as solvent abuse clinics, and as centres for working with alcoholics – both badly needed in the east end. They could

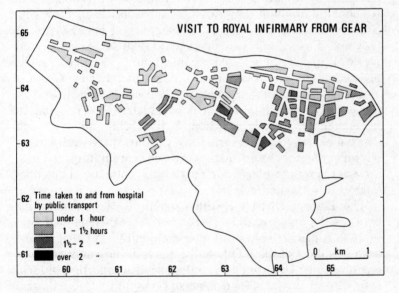

Figure 9.4 Travel times to hospitals

also be open in the evening for self-help groups and for advice and counselling sessions of various kinds.

In a wealthy urban country like Britain, where lethal epidemics have been eliminated and housing standards are generally good, health depends to an increasing extent on life-style, on whether people smoke, how heavily they drink, how much exercise they take, whether they live and work in harsh or protected environments, or whether they can work at all. Health education is particularly important in an area such as Glasgow's east end with its high mortality and morbidity levels. Despite widespread interest in prevention of ill-health only a very small proportion of resources has so far been channelled in this direction. One health education worker serves the whole of the Eastern Glasgow Health District.

While alcoholism is a recognised problem in the east end of Glasgow there are no day-care facilities. Provision of an Alcohol Information and Advice Centre has been discussed actively for several years, but it has not yet been set up. A Solvent Abuse Clinic was opened in 1980 in Bridgeton and was run initially by voluntary contribution. Since 1983 it has been formally approved and funded by Greater Glasgow Health Board. In 1984 it handled 138 cases (114 male and 24 female). The development of a psychiatric day hospital in Bridgeton, as already mentioned, has been the first such experiment in Glasgow and has proved successful largely because of its close links with the community. It can, however, provide places for only thirty patients, about one-quarter of estimated needs.

The Eastern District Health Council is the main bridge between the public and the Health Service. Since its inception in 1975 it has actively dealt with complaints and suggestions from members of the public and from voluntary and statutory organisations. Unfortunately, only a small proportion of local residents are aware of its existence. Community Councils also play a role in influencing decisions on local health care, for example on the provision of the Day Hospital for mental illness at Bridgeton.

Problems of ill-health in the inner city call for a corporate response. One aim of the GEAR project was to involve local government and central agencies, and to help both forge closer links with the local community. In the course of our research the health services were frequently criticised for their failure to consult and involve the public. At a time when improvements in public health depend increasingly upon public education, that is particularly sad. Healthier living will call for a broadly based strategy for jobs and incomes, education, housing, transport and the physical environment. The health services should be prepared to play a fuller part in formulating that strategy in collaboration with the public and with their colleagues in other public services.

10 LEISURE AND RECREATION

Alan Middleton and David Donnison

Introduction

It has become an accepted part of academic thinking and popular wisdom that we are becoming more and more of a 'leisure society' and that people need to be educated for the use of their new leisure time (Shaw, 1984, p. 8; Chairmen's Policy Group, 1982, p. 31; Parker, 1971, p. 16; Parker, 1976, p. 93; Simpson, 1973, pp. 278-88; Roberts, 1970, pp. 116-19). Engendered by the post-war growth in car ownership and the rapid expansion of participation in sport and active recreation (Chairman's Policy Group, *op. cit.*, pp. 30 and 44), this optimistic view of ever-expanding leisure time is rooted in a pre-OPEC era of full employment. Much of this literature offers a prospect of a 'leisure society', linked to increasingly high-tech work, permitting shorter working hours which would enable everyone to share this new-found freedom. The key problem will be how to provide for this new pattern of living an education which helps people with their 'leisure management' (Shaw, 1984, p. 8).

Recent changes in the economy have destroyed much of this optimism. The rapid rise in unemployment and the growing numbers of older pensioners are making a substantial impact on the demand for leisure activities. For those in work, increasingly to be found outside the conurbations, demand for recreation is likely to continue to increase. But for some 4 million unemployed, 9 million retired people and 1 million one-parent families there are few opportunities of joining the 'leisure society'. The fact that many of these people have a great deal of time on their hands makes their exclusion harder still.

In the most poverty-stricken areas, where these people are heavily concentrated, leisure facilities are often scarce or obsolete. Libraries, swimming pools, theatres and cinemas – often built in the nineteenth or early twentieth century – are decaying. New capital expenditure is needed to upgrade or replace these things and to construct new ones. This would not be so important if the people who remained in these areas had access to facilities elsewhere. In the UK as a whole the majority of households now own a car, and this has greatly improved access to recreation in the suburbs and the countryside. But in the inner cities things are very different. The urban poor are unable to travel far for their recreation.

In this chapter we shall turn our attention to some of these issues and consider how those responsible for leisure policies in the east end of Glasgow have addressed them. First, however, we must consider how the changes which have been taking place in society affect the relationship between work, leisure and non-work.

Leisure and the assumption of full employment

Stereotyped ideas about recreation go far to define for governments how people are expected to use their leisure time, and how public resources should be deployed in this field. The rural and middle-class bias in central government's spending on leisure can be seen in Table 10.1. With the exception of expenditure on sports (which will have minimal impact on deprived groups) and the IBA (which may contribute to passivity rather than activity), government funds are oriented towards the countryside, the arts and tourism. This expenditure is consistent with the view that there are 'worth while' ways of spending leisure time and that other pursuits need no encouragement from the state. The strength of the bias also influences education for leisure, in that this attempts to instil ideas about what is 'worth while' (Parker, 1976, p. 93). It is proper that education should be concerned to improve the quality of people's experience but that should not lead merely to an emphasis on predominantly middle-class activities.

How should policy-makers respond to this dilemma? Young and Willmott have argued that leisure throughout society will become more varied and more active, as the activities of the higher income groups filter down to the poorer sections of society. If they were right, the state may be justified in supporting recreations which all will ultimately enjoy. Television viewing and other passive activities, Young and Willmott said, are likely to decrease while participation in everything else, particularly in sports, is likely to increase –

Alan Middleton and David Donnison

Table 10.1: Government expenditure on leisure and related* services in the United Kingdom in 1980-1

	£ million	
Home-based and social activity		
Independent Broadcasting Authority	38	
Sub-total		*38*
Sports		
Sports Council	19	
Scottish Sports Council	3	
Sports Council for Wales	3	
Sports Council for Northern Ireland	1	
Department of Education (Northern Ireland)	6	
Sub-total		*32*
Day trips and outings		
Countryside Commission (England and Wales)	7	(a)
Countryside Commission for Scotland	3	
Government grant to National Park Authorities	8	
Historic Buildings and Ancient Monuments	28	
Royal Palaces and Royal Parks	15	
British Waterways Board (cruising waterways)	12	
Forestry Commission (recreational budget)	5	
Nature Conservancy Council	9	
National Heritage Memorial Fund	5	
Department of Agriculture (Northern Ireland)	0.5	
Department of Environment for Northern Ireland (Conservation Branch) and Ulster Countryside Commission	1	
Sub-total		*93.5*
Entertainment and the arts		
Arts Council of Great Britain	72	
Museum Purchase Funds	1	
Area Museum Councils	4	
Arts Council of Northern Ireland	2	
Department of Education (Northern Ireland)	4	
Sub-total		*83*
Tourism		
British Tourist Authority	14	(b)
English Tourist Board	14	
Northern Ireland Tourist Board	2	
Scottish Tourist Board	6	
Wales Tourist Board	4	
Department of Economic Development (Northern Ireland)	3	
Sub-total		*43*
TOTAL		289.5

* For some agencies, such as the Countryside Commission, Nature Conservancy as will the search for culture in museums and adult education. According to these authors, plans for the environment will need to allow for the growth of many different types of activity. Golf, tennis, badminton and squash are likely to become much more popular, along with sailing, water skiing, swimming and other water sports. The demand for camping, caravanning, walking and driving in the country will also grow. With the spread of car ownership, others will follow the middle classes into more dispersed recreational networks (Young and Willmott, 1973, pp. 236-7).

For many people in the inner city this view of the future must now appear utopian, not only because it takes full employment and increased earnings for granted but also because it assumes a particular relationship between work and leisure which no longer holds. As changes in the nature of work take place, the concept of leisure is continually being redefined. In Marx's day, when all respite from work could be categorised as the 'reproduction of the labour force', the average working week was about 75 hours and there was no leisure as the working class know it today (Dumazedier, 1967, p. 5). In a society dominated by the work ethic, the value of recreation is considered to be that it makes people more fit for work (Anderson, 1961, p. 42; Mead, 1957, p. 13). According to the protestant work ethic, idleness is sinful, and in the late nineteenth century leisure which was not positively 're-creative' was identified as idleness (Dumazedier, 1967, p. 8).

From the early 1900s to the 1960s leisure was identified as 'time which was free from work' (Dumazedier, 1967, p. 12; Anderson, 1961, p. 33). It was 'time not paid for, one's own time' (Soule, 1957, p. 16), or the time we are free from the 'duties which a paid job or other obligatory occupation imposes upon us' (Lundberg *et al.*, 1943, p. 2). Leisure was still largely conceived of in relation to work (Domenach, 1959, p. 1103). Even today, for most people, work and leisure are

---

Council or British Waterways Board it is not possible to separate expenditure on leisure services from that on other functions such as landscape enhancement, nature conservation, drainage or water supply.

(a) Excludes Grants to National Parks
(b) For overseas promotion.

Source: Chairmen's Policy Group, p. 31

binary concepts which can only be understood in relation to each other. Work and leisure tend to be treated as mutually exclusive, with work being characterised by payment, obligation and non-pleasure, while leisure is distinguished by non-payment, freedom and pleasure (Young and Willmott, 1973, p. 207).

From the mid-1960s onwards, however, the relationship of leisure to obligations outside work was also explored. For Dumazedier, 'leisure is activity to which the individual may freely devote himself outside the needs and obligations of his occupation, his family and his society, for his relaxation, diversion and personal development' (Dumazedier *et al*, 1961, para 54.5). In this definition, leisure time is distinguished from the time devoted to the obligations not only of work, but also of the family and society (see also Dumazedier, 1967, pp. 16-17; Young and Willmott, 1973, p. 207). 'It is first and foremost liberation and pleasure' (Dumazedier, 1967, p. 14). Its three main functions are relaxation, which gives recovery from fatigue; diversion or entertainment which spell delivery from boredom; and personal development which serves to liberate the individual from the daily automatism of thought and action, and involves the free exercise of creative capacity. Dumazedier presents a list of activities which he says are undisputably contrasted with leisure – a person's job, supplementary work or occasional odd jobs, domestic tasks, care of the person (meals, bathing, sleeping), family rituals and social and religious obligations, and necessary study (Dumazedier, 1967, p. 13). He stresses that it is wrong to contrast leisure only with one's job.

For these theorists, however, the state of being both without work and without leisure is not given serious consideration. In describing this condition, sociologists have rarely developed concepts which take us further than the nineteenth-century idea of 'idle time', with its connotations of laziness. In times of full employment people move in and out of unemployment fairly quickly and the moral condemnation directed at 'idleness' is focused on those who stay unemployed. But in times of recession huge numbers of people have time which is free from work and, as Beveridge pointed out, this 'free time' is not leisure. (Beveridge, 1944, p. 20). More recently it has become common sense to refer to unemployment as a form of 'enforced free time' (Chairmen's Policy Group, *op. cit.*, p. 3) or 'forced leisure' (*ibid.*, p. 23). However, these concepts are confusingly self-contradictory and do not fit well with the notion of freedom incorporated in the concept of leisure proposed by Dumazedier and Young and Willmott. The time of the unemployed may be free from work, but it may not be free in any other sense. Unemployment, as we shall see, reduces recreational activity.

Patricia Apps draws a helpful distinction between work defined as 'production for trade' which involves social interaction and exchange, and leisure defined as 'production for own consumption'. Work may include exchanges of services within the household which are not 'monetised': although a housewife's services may have no money price on them, they may, in effect, be supplied in return for a 'wage' provided by her husband. Conversely, in industries sufficiently well protected from competition, where workers control entry to their occupations, a good deal of activity may be 'production for own consumption' – business lunches, overseas conferences and the like which partly constitute leisure, encouraged by the fact that this type of consumption is not taxed as highly as it would be if the expenditure they entail were distributed in wages. People in such occupations – predominantly the more highly qualified males – are thus likely to get more recreation both inside and outside what are usually described as working hours (Apps, 1981, Ch. 4).

This contrasts vividly with the situation of the unemployed, the elderly and the disabled. The working class in Glasgow have retained the term 'idle time' and distinguish this from 'leisure time'. This concept of 'idle time' does not, however, have an association with laziness. If work is about payment, obligation and non-pleasure and leisure is about non-payment, freedom and pleasure, then 'idle time' is about non-payment, non-freedom and non-pleasure – neither 'production for trade' nor 'production for own consumption'. As unemployment rises, as the numbers of the elderly grow, and as the population and those in work become redistributed in space, the people affected by the restriction, boredom and anguish of 'idle time' are increasing and becoming concentrated in our older industrial cities.

Parker, acknowledging that analyses of leisure activities

191

assume that all adults are in full-time paid work, said in 1971 that this was true for 70 per cent of cases (Parker, 1971, p. 29). That was probably an overestimate even for the early 1970s, but it bears no relation to the situation in the inner cities in the 1980s. In our survey in the GEAR area of Glasgow in 1982, only 32 per cent of the adult population were in full-time work. Twenty-three per cent were wholly retired, 11 per cent were seeking work and 7 per cent were sick or disabled. In addition to this total of 41 per cent who were neither in paid employment nor full-time study, a further 5 per cent of adults were full-time housewives who would have liked a job if they could have got one. That is, 46 per cent of adults were looking for work, retired, sick or disabled – more than those in full-time and part-time work put together (Table 10.2).

Table 10.2: Activity status of GEAR adults in 1982

	Number	%
Full-time work	535	31.5
Part-time work	121	7.1
Seeking work[1]	193	11.4
Temp. sick or disabled	23	1.4
Wholly retired	392	23.1
Perm. sick or disabled	89	5.2
Full-time student	30	1.8
Non-employed housewife[2]	282	16.6
Other/non response	35	2.1
TOTAL	1700	100.0

Notes: 1 Represents a rate of unemployment of 22%.
   2 Eighty-seven housewives (5.1% of all adults) indicated that they would like a job if they could get one.
Source: GEAR Survey, 1982

In some parts of British cities the present rate of unemployment will be much higher than that of the GEAR area in 1982 (which was around 22 per cent). In pockets of Glasgow male unemployment can be as high as 60 per cent. Parker points out that the unemployed and the retired, whom he classifies as being in the same position as the unemployed, may occupy themselves with 'trivial tasks and time-filling routines' and that lack of money restricts the range of activities in which they can engage. In 1971, Parker could optimistically propose that 'with increases in the incomes of the unemployed through such measures as wage-related unemployment benefits, people out of work may be able to purchase a "standard of leisure" comparable to that of those in work' (Parker, 1971, p. 31). Once again we must doubt that this was ever the case, but by 1982 these short-term, wage-related benefits had been abolished and long-term unemployment and unwilling early retirement had become familiar features of working-class life. For many working class people the 'worthwhile' middle-class and rural pursuits which continue to be subsidised by the government are out of reach, and we can no longer comfort ourselves with the hope that rising wages and social security benefits will one day bring them within reach.

Those responsible for leisure services are aware of some of these changes. Indeed the Chairmen's Policy Group, consisting of the chairmen, directors and other senior representatives of statutory agencies and local authority associations which have roles to play in the field of recreation, have pointed out that the number of retired people, particularly those over 75, will increase over the next decade, and that there has been a steady increase in single-parent families and those who are living alone. They acknowledge that these groups have fewer opportunities for enjoying themselves (Chairmen's Policy Group, *op. cit.*, p. 10). Thus policy-makers are aware of the large numbers who are short of income and other resources, affected by ill-health and other disabilities – including the 'low-paid, many of the growing millions of pensioners, the disabled and the handicapped and those who are unemployed' (*ibid.*, p. 4). But their authorities have had to cope with a series of particularly heavy cuts in grants from central government.

These cuts have some democratic justification, for leisure is not what people want most from life; good health, a satisfactory job, a reasonable level of income and a happy family life usually take precedence over leisure in surveys of people's desires. In times of recession, jobs and incomes become even more important. Another major problem is that the providers of recreational facilities have little experience of dealing with 'idle time' and its restrictions. This has not been part of their professional training and experience. As the leisure needs of the growing urban poor become clearer, it also becomes more apparent that community education and social work agencies, voluntary organisations and community groups all have substantial roles to play.

The GEAR project in Glasgow offered an opportunity for closer collaboration between all these services by bringing together the Scottish Development Agency, the Regional Council and the District Council – the main providers of leisure and related facilities in the city. The Agency's environmental improvement programme could develop in co-operation with the District Council's Parks and Recreation Department and each of these could be co-ordinated with the Regional Council's concern for community education and care of the elderly. Let us now consider what happened.

Leisure provision in the GEAR area

At first, plans for leisure and recreation in the GEAR area were given a high priority and were expressed in terms of compensation for the other problems of the area (SDA, 1978a, p. 22). Participation was said to be limited by apathy, low incomes, limited local leadership and a fear of anti-social behaviour. Its potential role was that it could harness the energies of young people and ease the burden on the elderly, the disabled and the unemployed. The project set out to co-ordinate the organisations providing and operating leisure facilities in both the public and private sectors, to improve the quality of existing facilities, to carry out new developments, to encourage participation, and to convert vacant land and buildings for recreational use. As the population of the area declined, many commercial facilities had become unprofitable and had been forced to close and there were serious deficiencies in provision for indoor sports, swimming, public meetings, 'open space' and other facilities for young people. Officials wanted to respond to local needs but knew little about what was wanted. A preliminary survey of facilities led to an ambitious list of proposals. But progress was slow and the emphasis of policy changed as time went by.

By 1980, the status of leisure and recreation in the GEAR programme had been reduced from being one of the main aims of the project to being incorporated under the heading of 'improving the quality of life' as only one aspect of the project's six-point plan to meet this objective. Priority under the heading of leisure and recreation was given to providing the young with opportunities for enjoying their free time. The SDA had already spent around £800,000 on all-weather play and kickabout areas on what were previously gap sites and the Regional Council had provided floodlighting for a number of school football pitches. The SDA, the Region and the District had also allocated a further £4 million for major indoor and outdoor leisure and sports facilities.

The preponderance of kickabouts in the programme reflected the large number of previously vacant sites which could be easily converted. A programme of providing play areas also fitted neatly into the SDA's environmental remit, and raised fewer awkward questions about responsibility for management than did proposals for sports centres. The cost of maintaining the new play areas, however, was not negligible because they suffered minor vandalism, such as being strewn with broken glass and having play equipment broken. Their upkeep is quite expensive and their use is confined to good weather. They are also sexist in that they are mainly designed for and used by boys. Girls in the area complained that they had nothing to do while the boys could at least play football. The mix of public investment in leisure opportunities remained much the same in plans for succeeding years. It included, the following year, the appointment by the District Council of a specialist worker to oversee the development of leisure and recreation and to carry out a promotional campaign to publicise what was available in the area (SDA, 1980b, pp. 17-21). Plans for 1983 included the promotion of the use of leisure facilities in the countryside, additional informal meeting places throughout the area and growing use of educational buildings and play areas for community use. However, with the exception of proposals for the library service, which had been under consideration since the beginning of the project, the programme was still mainly concerned with sports facilities.

Leisure and recreation were being confused with sport. Nationally, participation in sport has grown rapidly over the last thirty years – in both the numbers involved and in the diversity of sports (Chairmen's Policy Group, *op. cit.*, p. 5). However, it is also recognised that substantial groups do not take part. Very few people in the GEAR area participate in active sport and no-one familiar with the class composition of the area and the age distribution of its residents would expect them to. Nevertheless, the sports facilities were 'needed'

195

under any criteria of comparison with facilities in more affluent parts of Glasgow and it was proper to do something to correct this imbalance. But if the aim was to help as high a proportion of the GEAR area's residents as possible, improvement of libraries or even bingo facilities would clearly help more people than the provision of new sports facilities. The provision of free television licences for elderly and housebound people might have met even more urgent needs.

As we shall see, libraries are most used by the retired, housewives and the part-time employed – who are also likely to be women. The unemployed are also more likely to use them than those in full-time employment. Because of pressure on spending, however, Glasgow District Council cut its expenditure on the library service. Plans for the establishment of a mobile library service to meet the needs of the elderly, the housebound and pre-school children, and for the library modernisation at Bridgeton and Tollcross were shelved. The failure to provide extended library services hit the poorest people hardest for they are least likely to participate in other leisure activities.

The new concern with promoting the use of leisure facilities in the countryside was also consistent with certain features of the area. We have already noted the importance of the car as a means of getting into the country. Glasgow, however, has the lowest rate of car ownership of all British cities and the situation in GEAR is particularly bad. Table 11.1 (page 209) shows the predicament of GEAR residents. Only 14 per cent of households in the area own a car, compared to 60 per cent in Great Britain as a whole.

Young and Willmott found that within occupational classes, the richer and the better educated did not have a much wider total range of activities than others, but car-owners did. Working-class car-owners were like people with cars in other classes in that they played more sports, ate more meals outside the home, and so on. In a regression analysis, age was found to be the most important variable determining the range of activities that people became involved in, but Young and Willmott found that this was followed closely by car ownership (Young and Willmott, 1973, p. 225). Those who were both poor and without a car suffered from a doubly severe deprivation with respect to leisure. The difference that car ownership in the GEAR area made to participation can be seen in Table 10.3. Those without the use of a car are much less likely than others to go to the cinema, theatre, disco or dancing. They are also much less likely to use swimming pools and to participate in other indoor and outdoor sports. As leisure policy changed, it tended to ignore these facts about the people in the area.

Table 10.3: Activities gone to in the last three months by car ownership and sex

	Total	Use of car	No use of car	Male	Female	Housewife
Respondents	862	154	706	352	498	86
	%	%	%	%	%	%
Pictures	11	16	9	11	10	5
Bingo	17	18	17	17	17	20
Social club	32	32	31	30	32	21
Pub	42	49	41	48	37	26
Theatre/panto	13	19	11	13	13	12
Disco/dance	20	30	18	22	19	9
Swimming pool	8	16	6	8	7	6
Indoor sport	7	12	6	7	6	5
Outdoor sport	8	16	7	9	8	7
Football match	13	14	13	15	12	7
Library	30	33	29	29	30	33

Source: GEAR Household Survey, 1982

The spread of car ownership and the decline of public transport have opened up a big gulf between the opportunities of different groups. Those without cars become increasingly isolated from the benefits of a 'leisure society'. If public transport cannot be kept going with sufficient reliability, more and more recreations will be out of reach of the poor and carless. The old, housewives whose husbands have first claim on a car if the family has one, and the young whose inability to find work makes car ownership impossible, will also suffer.

By the time of the production of the GEAR Project Report in 1983, the objective of 'improving the quality of life' had been adapted to 'overcoming the social disadvantages experienced by the residents' (SDA, 1983a, p. 16). These aims were mainly concerned with welfare rights, unemployment, and educational, health, transport and shopping provision; but the programme for leisure and recreation was retained. Quite clearly – and perhaps understandably, given the other problems of the area – the importance of leisure and recreation in the project had been diminishing over time and its role was also being perceived differently. By the end of 1983, outdoor sport and recreation facilities were being seen as 'an extension of the environmental improvement programme' (SDA, 1983b, p. 3) and these facilities were placed last on a list of social development policies.

We have outlined the changing recreational aims of the GEAR project. What was actually achieved? Between 1977 and 1983, the project provided thirty kickabout and local play areas, and five major new recreational facilities; four school football pitches were floodlit; the Shettleston public halls were modernised at great expense; an old wash-house was converted to a mini sports centre; tennis courts and pensioners' facilities at Glasgow Green and Tollcross Park were upgraded; the Glasgow Green Sport Medicine Centre was opened; the People's Palace – an attractive popular museum devoted to the history of Glasgow – was renovated; and the Whitevale Baths were converted to a Centre for the Unemployed. A total of £7,143,000 was spent on forty-four projects and a further £307,000 was to be spent on another five in 1983-4. This represented around £177 per head of population in the area and for the coming years a great deal more was in the pipeline.

But there had been disappointments too. In addition to the failure to enlarge the library service, there had been little success in extending the use of educational facilities for local adults, and little progress had been made in encouraging the development of commercial leisure activities (SDA, 1983a, p. 22). The failure to extend the use of school leisure facilities to the community is particularly disappointing. The Chairmen's Policy Group had proposed that education authorities need to break down the barriers between schools and the community, and to adopt new approaches in adult education (Chairmen's Policy Group, *op. cit.*, p. 6). Universities and technical colleges, wholly absent from the east end, also have responsibilities towards such areas which are generally disregarded.

The GEAR programme was intended to encourage the private sector to establish such things as cinemas, discos and roller-skating rinks in the east end. But there is little profit to be made in areas with large concentrations of the unemployed and the elderly, so it is not surprising that commercial operators have been reluctant to invest. East enders therefore have to rely mainly on voluntary and public provision for recreation outside their homes. The declining importance of leisure provision within the GEAR project is expressed in the fact that from 1983 onwards there was no-one on the GEAR management committee who was specifically concerned with leisure and recreation.

Thus far we have looked at the provision of facilities from the top downwards. It is time to consider what was achieved from the standpoint of the people living there. To do that we single out particular groups most likely to be deprived of opportunities and report their experience, drawing out evidence mainly from our own household survey, and comparing it with national patterns.

Recreational activity in the GEAR area

Social class. Participation in most leisure activities is related to socio-economic group. The upper middle classes are also more likely to report some link between work and leisure. Having occupations which are more likely to develop their capacities in satisfying ways, they are more likely to use recreation as an extension of their work or as an opportunity for using skills acquired in their work. The lawyer, journalist or town planner who goes to parties partly to make contacts and pick up news of professional interest, the chemist who makes his own wine, and the electronic engineer who builds radio-controlled model boats illustrate these patterns. The investment their recreations make in the development of their own skills, self-confidence and contacts then enhances their opportunities for professional success. Skilled manual workers also have opportunities for using their skills in recreative ways, but the less skilled, whose work is more likely to be alienating, more often seek from recreation a complete change from their daily grind. The working class are more likely to go to a pub, play darts and spend more hours watching television.

Skilled manual workers' participation in activities in the east end was around the average for all persons there, except that they tended to use the library less than others. Consistent with what would be expected, non-manual workers were more likely to use indoor and outdoor sports facilities and, perhaps surprisingly, less likely to use swimming pools. The semi-skilled workers were more likely to go to a social club or a football match and, again perhaps surprisingly, play an outdoor sport or attend a theatre. This may be related to the fact that the interviews were carried out just after the end of the pantomime season in Glasgow, but the city's excellent and relatively cheap theatres and its municipal golf courses may also help to create these patterns. The unskilled manual workers were least likely to participate in everything other than bingo.

The unemployed. Those in full-time employment were more likely than the unemployed to participate in all activities except going to a pub or a library. There were in our survey only four reported incidents of unemployed respondents taking part in a sports activity in the previous three months and those in employment were five times as likely to take part in these. Since the numbers of unemployed people who participated in anything other than going to the pub or library were very small, comparisons with the employed have to be made cautiously. However, the figures suggest that the employed were around four times as likely to go dancing, three times as likely to go to the theatre and twice as likely to go to a social club or bingo. The unemployed were just as likely as those in work to go to a cinema or a football match, but pubs and libraries were their main places of recreation outside the home (Table 10.4). For people who have difficulty in paying fuel bills, pubs and libraries offer a cheap way of keeping warm. The number of activities participated in by a person declined as unemployment lengthened. Those who were unemployed for up to six months mentioned, on average, 2.72 types of activity they had taken part in during the previous three months. Those who were unemployed for longer than this mentioned only 1.92.

Age and gender. The elderly, particularly those over 75, are less likely to go out than younger people. They increasingly need home-based recreation. When they do go out, retired people in the GEAR area are more likely than the unemployed to participate in all activities except going to the pub, the cinema or, by small margins, a swimming pool or a football match

Table 10.4: Activities gone to in the last three months by employment status

	Total	Full-time employment	Seeking work	Retired
Respondents	862	188	51	224
	%	%	%	%
Pictures	11	11	12	4
Bingo	17	22	12	12
Social club	32	36	20	28
Pub	42	39	47	32
Theatre/panto	13	18	6	12
Disco/dance	20	27	6	12
Swimming pool	8	9	4	3
Indoor sport	7	11	2	4
Outdoor sport	8	13	2	4
Football match	13	12	14	11
Library	30	21	25	31

Source: GEAR Household Survey, 1982

(Table 10.4). They were most likely to have visited a library, a pub or a social club.

Other studies have shown that women in all classes have less leisure than men, but middle-class women participate in more recreation than those in the working class. Women knit and sew more than they do anything else except watch television (Young and Willmott, *op. cit.*, p. 217). That is, women's leisure is to a large extent an extension of their domestic work. In the east end of Glasgow, however, women were as likely as men to participate in leisure activities outside the home. A similar percentage took part in all activities with the exception of going to the pub or attending a football match (Table 10.3). However, those people who classified themselves as full-time housewives and who were not retired, sick or disabled were less likely to participate in everything except playing bingo or going to the library.

Levels of education. National studies show that people with higher levels of education are more likely to participate in a wide variety of leisure activities. Although the GEAR area contains few highly qualified people, this pattern still holds good. Those with no educational qualifications were less likely to take part in activities outside the home than those with qualifications, but they were equally likely to play bingo.

It has been found, however, that if education is isolated from other related variables such as class, income and age, the impact of education is not particularly important. As we have noted above, within occupational classes the better educated do not have a wider range of leisure activities than other people (Young and Willmott, *op. cit.*, p. 224).

Membership of organisations. Thirty-nine per cent of respondents in our household survey were members of voluntary organisations. Of these, 24 per cent were members of organisations in their neighbourhood within the east end. The old centres of the villages around which the east end grew up during the nineteenth century were still the focal points for these clubs. The most popular types are social clubs, but only 18 per cent of the people interviewed were members of one. Eight per cent belong to adult church organisations and 7 per cent to sports clubs (Table 10.5). Clubs for the unemployed were not attracting significant numbers of members. Experience elsewhere suggests they are rarely an effective way of bringing unemployed people together (McArthur, 1985).

Table 10.5: Membership of organisations

	number of mentions	% of 862
Social club	156	18.1
Adult church organisations	71	8.2
Sports clubs	61	7.1
Elderly club	53	6.1
Residents'/tenants' associations	33	3.5
Youth clubs	11	1.3
Unemployed clubs	3	0.3
Other groups	44	5.1

Source: GEAR Household Survey, 1982

The handicapped. We were not able to make a special study of the needs of the disabled and the physically and mentally handicapped, but they should not be forgotten. To enable them to take part in leisure activity will often call for the adaptation of old buildings to permit easy access, the provision of special equipment or transport, help by paid staff or volunteers, exclusive use of facilities at certain times and so on. That will call in turn for closer collaboration between leisure providers and the health and social work services, partly because leisure activity can make an important contribution to physical and mental health, and hence has implications for savings in health and welfare costs. In the GEAR area, the leisure needs of the disabled and handicapped are partially met by health service staff who encourage activity which is both therapeutic and recreational.

Implications for housing and planning

The Chairmen's Policy Group argue that for those with restricted opportunities for recreation – mothers of young children, single parents and their families, the divorced, separated and widowed, the elderly, the housebound, and those on low incomes – provision should focus on activities in or near the home, and help to overcome the problems of mobility, by providing subsidised holidays, for example, or concessionary bus fares (Chairmen's Policy Group, *op. cit.*, p. 10).

Many people live in homes which are too cramped for the home-based recreations which have increased in recent years. Nearly half of leisure spending is on home-based leisure and one-third on social activities which involve contact with other people (Chairmen's Policy Group, *op. cit.*, p. 5). Home-based leisure includes watching television (which consumes most time), listening to music, reading, games and hobbies, needlework and knitting, caring for pets, decorating, do-it-yourself, vehicle maintenance and gardening. Housing standards should in future take account of the growth and diversity of home-based leisure activities, and particularly of the need for warmth, privacy and noise insulation in the home, and adequate indoor and outdoor space (Chairmen's Policy Group, *op. cit.*, p. 13). Although in Chapter 7 we welcomed the building of new houses and flats for sale in the east end, some of these are very small, with little or no private, outdoor space. Flats modernised by housing associations are generally more solidly built, but these, too, usually lack gardens. Much of this housing will become intolerable once the young working couples who now have so much of the owner-occupied property start new families and spend much more of their time in and around their homes. Larger houses with better insulation and gardens of reasonable size will then be needed to enable home-owning families who want to stay in the east end to do so.

House-owners in the east end of Glasgow are about twice as likely as renters to participate in indoor or outdoor sports or go to a library, a theatre or a swimming pool. They are three times as likely to go to the cinema and more likely to go to bingo or a social club. Those who hope to buy a house in the future follow leisure patterns similar to those of people who have already bought their homes.

Steps taken to enable people whose mobility is for any reason restricted to get about more easily may for them be more useful than direct investment in recreational resources. These possibilities will be discussed in the next chapter. They include cheap fares on public transport, more frequent and reliable services, and the improvement of street lighting and paving. In Chapter 8 we discussed the need for widely scattered, small public spaces where old people can sit and talk, and the attempts made in the GEAR area to provide little parks and sitting out places of this sort. We suggested that other uses for public open space should also be planned – always in close consultation with the communities to be served.

Many people are inhibited by anxiety about their own safety from moving freely about the streets. One of our researchers secured an elaborately detailed map, drawn up by school chidren in the east end, of the territories of different groups or gangs. These youngsters were well aware of the boundaries between one territory and the next, and knew in which parts of the town they could safely wander. Old people, too, were often anxious about going out in the dark. Providers of opportunities for recreation should consult their potential customers, transport authorities and the police before deciding where to put swimming pools, branch libraries and other resources.

Conclusion

The Chairmen's Policy Group argued that unemployed people suffer from a sense of guilt and a loss of self-confidence which derive from the dominant work ethic of our society, and that is why they do not avail themselves of opportunities for leisure (Chairmen's Policy Group, op. cit., p. 9). Having defined the problem as a failure to adopt an ethic better suited to the post-industrial world, they call for public debate about the ethical basis for a leisure society. While it may be true that such a debate is needed, we still have to recognise four things. First, culture – which includes the work ethic – has a material basis in society and is not likely to change if that material basis remains fundamentally unchanged. Second, the first priority must therefore be to provide jobs and other opportunities for economic activity – do-it-yourself, cultivating an allotment, and so on. Third, that calls for money and a reasonable standard of living for people in the inner cities. Recreation costs money. Growing vegetables on an allotment is no cheaper than buying them in a greengrocer's shop – particularly if transport costs to and from the allotment are high. Painting your front room may cost – in paint – a meal or two for the whole family. Not surprisingly, therefore, recreation is not high amongst people's priorities. Higher incomes come first. High unemployment is likely to be with us for some time, and the numbers of very old people will continue to increase. This implies, fourth, that we must continue to look to services outside the traditional leisure providers to help meet the leisure needs of the urban poor. Transport, housing, planning, education, employment and other services have important parts to play. ·

These points lead to a central dilemma. People concerned with sport, public parks, libraries, the arts and similar fields, from which those responsible for leisure and recreation services have been recruited, naturally aspire to provide facilities which attract a lot of customers and generate high attainment: an Olympic swimming pool which produces Olympic champions, for example; or a theatre in which local groups mount productions that win prizes at the Edinburgh Festival Fringe. We should take these aspirations seriously in an area which has long been in so many ways starved of excellence. Thus the maintenance and development of the Celtic football ground – one of the east end's few undeniable centres of excellence – ought to be encouraged.

But the priorities suggested by the kind of humane egalitarianism which underlies so many of the best innovations in social policy would focus attention not on star performers and the applause of thousands but on the needs of housewives, pensioners, lone parents, the disabled and the unemployed – the people who now get least recreation. Their needs must be partly met through the work of other services concerned with transport, street lighting, education, housing and so on: they will certainly call for close collaboration between leisure providers and those responsible for these services.

Faced with this dilemma between conflicting objectives, most practical politicians will seek a bit of both, and they are probably right to do so. But the pursuit of prestigious excellence and high rates of participation, so badly needed in a deprived inner city area, should always contribute something to the opportunities actually secured by its most deprived residents. If, when facilities are provided and events are staged, the pensioners, the unemployed and the rest do not come, steps should be taken to find out why and to break down the barriers which exclude them or to provide other opportunities which they value more highly.

11 TRANSPORT AND COMMUNICATIONS

D. Miller Allan

More than twenty years ago, the Buchanan Report *Traffic in Towns* (Ministry of Transport, 1963) confirmed that an era of motorway construction had finally arrived in Britain. Projects had been considered since the 1930s following the examples of other countries, and the London-Birmingham motorway was already in use; but this report was one of the first comprehensive statements of the requirements for the planning of transport facilities in towns and cities. Unfortunately, there followed an excess of enthusiasm among Ministers, city councillors and their advisers and many lavish road schemes appeared in the next few years. In due course the public backlash was equally excessive and often just as misguided, with little attention being given to the genuine needs and constraints which had been identified previously by researchers and transport planners. All this is well illustrated in the GEAR area where expensive transport investments are ill-suited to the needs of residents, who are likely to make little use of them.

The travel habits of people who live in the GEAR area are quite different from the national norms. In particular, they do a lot more walking and a lot less driving. Although attitudes towards public transport provision have improved since Barbara Castle's Transport Act of 1968, we have a long way to go before the true needs of such an area are properly recognised. That will not be achieved until guidelines from central government are formulated in the most general way possible, so as to maintain the widest scope for local initiatives. The present methods of allocating major local authority expenditure are not responsive enough to local needs. Capital spending on particular forms of transport is planned to meet Scottish and regional needs and there is no shortage of these in Strathclyde which is by far the largest region in Scotland. Thus a reduction in the GEAR area's road programme would be unlikely to release funds to improve other means of communication there, or indeed for other local purposes. Extra expenditure on roads elsewhere would probably be approved instead. This sort of inflexibility is difficult to avoid where different responsibilities have been divided among separate departments within the central and local authorities.

In this chapter we look first at roads and public transport in the GEAR area, then we consider the people who live there, and how they get about. Finally we draw some general conclusions about transport planning in such areas.

Transport in the GEAR area

The transport facilities of the GEAR area are not inferior to those in other sectors in the city. Bus services are as good as anywhere. The east end is crossed by two lines of the Trans-Clyde rail system and at the time of our study the reinstatement of a third line was a possibility which would have linked all of the main centres of activity with each other and with the city centre. There is also a comprehensive main road network and most of this is underused. Additional road capacity has been provided recently at several busy locations, and three extensive schemes are planned or under construction. One of these is related directly to a major new development within the area itself but the others have been promoted as part of the citywide network.

At least three factors prevent local people from making fuller use of these facilities. A high proportion of residents are elderly, and for many of them the use of public transport presents problems, particularly during the evening. The area also has a high proportion of unemployed teenagers. Despite the poverty of these people fares are as high as in any city in Britain. Meanwhile, car ownership is significantly lower than in most of the city and in the Region (see Table 11.1). So only a minority of residents benefit directly from the growing road system of the east end. Much of this investment is more useful to outsiders. So far as residents are concerned, expenditure on new road schemes can only be justified by the general environmental benefits it may bring. Whether there are any is hotly disputed but it is clear that they are unlikely to be significant. Larger revenue support for public transport, bringing lower fares and more frequent and varied services, would benefit east enders a great deal more.

Table 11.1: Car ownership in the GEAR area and elsewhere

Proportion of households where one or more cars are owned	
	%
GEAR area 1978	16
GEAR area 1982	14
City of Glasgow District 1981	29
Strathclyde Region 1978	39
Strathclyde Region 1981	45
Scotland 1981	51
Great Britain 1981	60
West Germany 1967	51
West Germany 1977	83

Source: GEAR Household Survey, 1978; Glasgow University Household Survey, 1982; Census 1981

Roads

Three strategic roads cross the area, fanning out in radial directions from the city centre. All have extensive residential and shop frontages in places, but a new radial motorway (the M8) just to the north has drawn off much of the through traffic, greatly improving the roadside environment. Even without the new schemes now in the pipeline, this sector of Glasgow's road network is already less heavily used than the roads elsewhere in the city (Table 11.2).

Table 11.2: Peak hour usage of Glasgow's road network

Peak hour traffic volumes as a proportion of sector capacity	
	%
North-East	87
East End	56
South Side	103
South-West	57
North-West	77

Source: Strathclyde Regional Council (1977), *Strategic Transport Planning Unit – Technical Note No 17*

The new Hamilton Road Route now being built is intended to provide direct access to the underdeveloped areas north and west of Cambuslang, as Figure 11.1 shows. The Regional Council expects that this new road will also produce environmental benefits just as the M8 has done. It was proposed in 1965 as a link between the northern end of the

Glasgow-Carlisle motorway (the M74) and the East Flank of
the Inner Ring Road at Glasgow Green. It was retained in the
Region's first Structure Plan and evidence at the Examination
in Public in 1979 suggested that the cost of construction (to
expressway standards) would not be excessive compared with
the alternative of upgrading the existing route along London
Road. At 1976 prices, the comparison was between £17.6
million and £10 million. It was argued that a completely new
route would improve things by diverting greater traffic
volumes from streets nearby but the case was not too
convincing and, in view of the figures in Table 11.2, this is not
surprising.

In reaching a decision, the Secretary of State was faced with
a related issue: whether to approve the completion of
Glasgow's Inner Ring Road by constructing the East and South
Flanks to which the Hamilton Road would be connected. The
existing sections of the Ring Road provide the only continuous high-grade route through the city centre but its traffic
capacity is limited because it was designed on the assumption
that the remainder of the Ring Road would be constructed
later. At Charing Cross – its most central point – there are only
two traffic lanes in each direction. The East Flank was to be
built along the High Street leading to the original centre of the
city at Glasgow Cross, a particularly sensitive location. The
Secretary of State decided to delete from the Structure Plan
the remainder of the Ring Road and the connecting link
through Glasgow Green to the Hamilton Road route.

This decision was perhaps not surprising but the consequences appear to have been disregarded. If there were doubts
about the Route's viability before, clearly they became more
substantial when the ring road to which it would link was
deleted from the system. Yet the truncated version (east of
Dalmarnock) is already being constructed. The shorter route
will not divert as much traffic from adjoining streets, and
indeed some will be busier with the traffic that will be
attracted through Dalmarnock and Bridgeton to the new road.

The threat of this road extension which has so long over-
shadowed the Dalmarnock area has had seriously damaging
effects. Commercial investors, even those who have obtained
planning consents (sometimes with some difficulty) have been
reluctant to risk commitments in the area while the road and

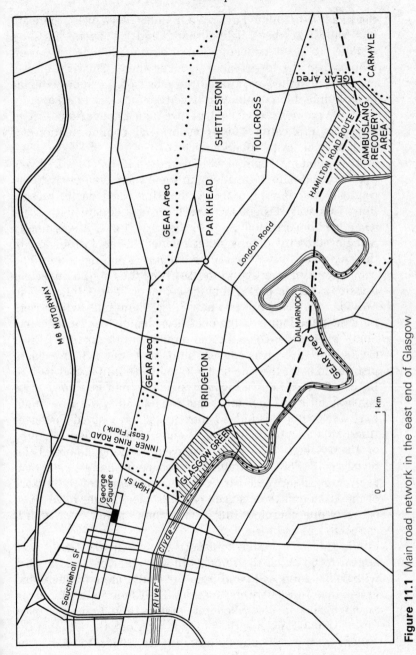

Figure 11.1 Main road network in the east end of Glasgow

the line it is to follow have been in doubt. As a result there are few shops in the neighbourhood and no chemist's shop despite the heavy concentration of old people who have been rehoused in the tower blocks erected there. This is a classic example of failure to foresee the effect of transport policies upon vulnerable people who have been brought to an area by other government services. Later we note a converse failure to note the implications for transport and communications of initiatives taken by other services.

This dilemma might never have arisen if the city's highway planners had paid more attention some years previously to the original reasons for proposing the Ring Road on its present line. This was designed in the form of a square with sides some 2 kilometres long, but in the early 1970s it was finally recognised by the planners that a wider line enclosing more of the city would have been more suitable. The line chosen had been approved long ago in the 1940s by the City Engineer, Sir Robert Bruce, as part of his master plan. It was intended to provide a link between two new railway terminals which were to replace the four existing ones near the city centre. The new South Station was to be located on the south bank of the River Clyde but this was never built and one of the main justifications for the line of the Ring Road disappeared with it. In the 1960s the city's highway planners had less need to be constrained by former ideas and a new and wider line might have been adopted; indeed they might have opted for fewer ring roads altogether instead of endorsing the plan for three of them which had been proposed so long before. Later revisions of their road traffic forecasts confirmed that this had been unnecessarily lavish. A greater awareness of the history of the issue and the changed circumstances might have given Glasgow one complete ring road by now, rather than the ill-connected parts of three.

Public transport Public transport services in the GEAR area appear to be much the same as in any other part of the city, with radial services to and from the centre more frequent and varied than those between suburbs. The Clyde Valley is served by an extensive electrified rail system, and two lines pass through the GEAR area. It is easy to overlook the fact that the system was good enough even in the 1960s to allow the transport planners of the day to concentrate most of their attention – and projected expenditure – on the development of a new road network. This was an advantage which was not shared to the same extent by other conurbations in Britain, except London. That explains and partly justifies the priority given to road building. Our travel survey showed that residents use buses six or seven times more frequently than trains. Fare levels are broadly comparable so the bus services must be far more useful. Compared with bus stops, railway stations are usually too far apart to compete for movement within the area, although a limited number of residents find them suitable for trips to the city centre and more distant places.

The reinstatement of the Parkhead Line would have connected several community focal points – Bridgeton, Parkhead, Tollcross and Carmyle – and it would have suited workers in the Cambuslang Recovery Area, as Figure 11.1 shows. A study by the Regional Council's Passenger Transport Executive, however, showed that this would require a substantial operating subsidy, and the proposal was subsequently dropped. In the light of rail closures elsewhere in the Region it is difficult to disagree with that decision, provided one accepts the conventional economic arguments. These may be questioned, however, in relation to an area of such low car ownership. Some believe that an opportunity to improve the east end's public transport has been lost. The subsidy would have been fairly insignificant compared with the projected capital expenditure on the Hamilton Road Route. The interest charges on this investment will certainly exceed by a substantial margin – perhaps as much as five or six times – the public transport subsidy which a renewed rail service would require.

Bus services are operated by the Passenger Transport Executive and by several independent companies within the Scottish Bus Group. The services receive much less direct subsidy than those of British Rail but it should not be forgotten that buses operate on a road system which is provided and maintained entirely from public funds. They are well used, and the operators claim to receive continual feedback from their customers via Community Council and other channels. Nevertheless, our travel survey revealed some criticisms of this service. Route licensing procedures have been simplified recently. The local legislation which has existed since 1930 to prevent complementary integration of the municipal and independent bus services in the city has also been revoked. These changes should enable services to be adapted to changing needs more easily and efficiently.

As in other parts of the city, conventional bus services have been supplemented in recent years by the use of community minibuses. These are provided by the Regional Council and their use and maintenance is supervised by local management committees. Running costs are partly covered by the charges which are made. Our observations suggest that they should be promoted more vigorously since they are not widely used and the Region's grants are not yet conferring their full potential benefits upon the east end.

Travel in the GEAR area

Our household survey included several questions relating to transport. Walking is by far the most common means of getting about within the area, as Tables 11.3 and 11.4 illustrate. The figures are so different from those observed in many other urban areas that the general conclusion is obvious. It is all too easy to categorise areas according to national stereotypes and this can lead to substantial errors. In our discussions with residents, two quite prosaic matters were frequently mentioned: the state of footway surfaces and of street lighting. For a population of walkers, many of them elderly, local government is failing to provide adequately the basic facilities of paving and lighting which were among the first tasks assigned to it as the cities of the first industrial revolution acquired their first public authorities.

Bus services were used by 69 per cent of respondents during the week of the Household Survey, mostly for shopping (33 per cent), social visits (19 per cent) and leisure or recreation trips (15 per cent). From a total of 862 respondents, 62 per cent found the services 'satisfactory', but 20 per cent were 'not very satisfied' and 10 per cent were 'not at all satisfied'. The most common complaints were of infrequent service (23 per cent), unreliability (11 per cent), high fares (5 per cent) and inconvenient routes (4 per cent). The general response was contradicted in Dalmarnock, however, where 51 per cent reported dissatisfaction, especially

Table 11.3: Work trips by GEAR residents and others

	Walk %	Bus %	Train %	Car %
GEAR residents:				
within GEAR area 1982	56	29	1	12
within GEAR area 1971	48	42	1	6
within conurbation 1982	33	40	5	19
Glasgow District 1981	16	42	9	29
Strathclyde Region 1981	18	28	6	43
Scotland 1981	20	24	3	45
Tyneside 1971	22	43	4	25
Greater Manchester 1971	21	36	3	30
West Midlands (Birmingham) 1971	20	35	1	34
Greater London 1971	17	23	24	26
Great Britain 1981	16	16	6	50

Source: GEAR Household Survey, 1982; Census, 1971, Census 1981

Table 11.4: Shopping trips by GEAR residents and others

	Walk %	Bus %	Train %	Car %
GEAR residents:				
within GEAR area 1982	73	14	0	4
within Glasgow 1982	63	25	0	10
National Travel Survey 1975-6	46	N/A	N/A	35

with infrequent services, but this was a considerable improvement over the 70 per cent who complained in a similar survey in 1978. The Concessionary Travel Scheme which is available mainly to the elderly is used by 86 per cent of those eligible to do so.

Residents were also asked if they rented a telephone. As an alternative to travel, this form of communication is particularly valuable in an area where many people find it difficult to get about, and where vandalism of public call boxes is more widespread than in the city as a whole. (Repair costs in the east end are some 10 per cent higher per unit than the city average.) In the GEAR area some 60 per cent of households rent a telephone compared with 72 per cent in the whole Glasgow telephone area: but the average figure conceals wide variations and in one area in the east end the proportion is only 32 per cent.

Conclusion

Every city is different and the lessons to be drawn from Glasgow's experience may not always be relevant to other places. Nevertheless, some general conclusions worth reflecting upon can be derived from our study.

The rebuilding and expansion of communications must play an important part in any programme for the renewal of decayed and semi-derelict urban areas. Their isolation from the rest of the world is a major part of the deprivations which many of their residents suffer. Yet in practice urban renewal programmes rarely give communications the central and integral role they deserve. Moreover, where those programmes do deal with communications, plans for roads, railways, buses and telephones are often formulated and implemented separately: money saved on roads cannot be switched to buses or telephones, for example.

Whatever plans are made should be based on thorough study of the needs of those who live in the area, through continuing consultation with their representatives. Communications will usually serve a much wider area of course, and the needs of other people throughout the surrounding region must be considered too. But if the residents of such an area, who already suffer severe deprivations of many kinds, do not gain a good deal from public expenditure and planning devoted to their communications, something is seriously amiss. That, in Glasgow's east end, means that the needs of pedestrians must be considered first of all; and next, those of bus passengers.

A sharp eye should be kept on the implications for communications of other new programmes affecting the area. In Chapter 9 we showed the serious loss of accessibility to health services which threatens to follow from the transfer of primary medical care to the three new health centres which are being set up in the east end. Perhaps these centres should operate something similar to the 'courtesy buses' which are run by every major hotel and car hire firms within reach of important transport terminals throughout the world. An extension of the ambulance service would be one possibility; community-based buses run by local neighbourhood groups may not be the best way of providing this transport unless steps are taken to improve their effectiveness. For frail or housebound people living on their own, a telephone may be even more valuable as a means of linking them with their relatives, the health and social security services and the shops. By meeting the basic rental charges for a telephone for such people, the community services might do a great deal at modest cost to improve their life chances and increase their peace of mind and the peace of mind of their relatives.

12 THE MANAGEMENT OF GEAR

Urlan Wannop and Roger Leclerc

Has GEAR been successfully managed?

To be fair to those who have managed GEAR, it has to be asked not just whether they were effective within the framework set for them but, also, whether that framework was as sound as they could have been given? We will return to these separate questions before going on to consider the transferability of the GEAR model.

A common criticism of GEAR, expressed by Booth *et al.* (1982), asserts that the project achieved little or nothing not already planned and in the programmes of the authorities and agencies working in the east end, or within their ability to achieve without the intervention of the SDA. We suggested in Chapter 3 that there was, in some respects, a hiatus in planning in the early years of the project for which the fact of GEAR was responsible. That is not enough to damn the project – it has to be considered whether delays led subsequently to better decisions and more productive action than would otherwise have occurred. Similarly, it is not enough to criticise GEAR because much of its investment was already in the pipeline before it began; it has to be considered whether this investment may have been more productive and flowed more smoothly as a result of the project.

To judge the fairness of criticisms of GEAR's management, two essential points must be recognised. First, the SDA was given a co-ordinating role of a kind unfamiliar to all the participants, and which satisfied few of the conventional precepts of effective administration. It was perhaps inevitable that criticism would focus on the Agency's team which had more responsibility than power and, initially, no capacity to demonstrate their presence quickly and convincingly. Unlike a development corporation for a new town to be built in green fields, the Agency was not allowed a period of grace of perhaps two years before making a visible impact on the landscape. Second, by comparison with the abrasive experience of the London Docklands Development Corporation in particular, there were fewer conflicts between the Agency and its partners than are reputed to have occurred in subsequent partnership initiatives in England. Some of GEAR's tensions arose only because the participants had difficulty in grasping the new role they had assigned to the Agency.

To satisfy public expectations, the GEAR project had to get moving quickly. It could not achieve this. The Director of Urban Renewal – a new post – joined the Agency four months after the project's launch in May 1976, but he had no staff to get things done until January 1977. Subsequently, the Agency team spent much time and effort in technical working parties, supported by the other participants to the project. Inevitably these working parties varied in competence, but some of them explored important administrative and policy issues which would not have been discussed but for the GEAR project. In general, the partners involved seem to have learnt a good deal about questions which would soon be posed by developments elsewhere. This can be seen in two notable cases: the housing working party led to initiatives in the east end in private housing and to a more liberal housing policy that would, at the time, have been regarded as politically premature for Glasgow as a whole. Second, the stimulus given to the District Council by a project for which the SDA was – rightly or wrongly – to earn most credit encouraged the launch of the Maryhill Corridor Project, a locally-grown initiative for which the District Council shared credit only with the Regional Council.

Nevertheless, despite these real achievements, the early progress of the GEAR project moved crab-wise, without any clear statement of over-riding priorities. The cumbersome system of working parties delayed the clarification of aims, and their eventual product – the 'Overall Proposals' considered by the Governing Committee in 1979 – came too late, was insufficiently clear sighted and failed to consider some fundamental questions about the use and demand for land. Similarly, the District Council's Local Plans provided no fundamental reconsideration of prospects for the east end within the City and conurbation. We show some of the results of that failure later in this book. Nor were these uncertainties about the cumulative outcome of the participants' individual programmes resolved by the GEAR Strategy and Programme produced in 1980 (Leclerc and Draffan, 1984), whose six basic social and economic objectives for the project had no firm dates attached to them, whose programme of action looked only a year ahead, and whose targets for three years ahead were apparently unmodified by any SDA review of relevant priorities amongst the participants' programmes.

In the managerial structure to which the participants were bound, the Governing Committee of principal politicians and officials, chaired by a Scottish Office Minister, helped to show the continuing high priority which participants gave to the project. A Consultative Group of senior officials drawn from levels just below that of the principal officials who, with politicians, represented participating agencies on the Governing Committee, became less effective as the project progressed. This Consultative Group was drawn from a level too close to that of the Governing Committee and too far from the day-by-day action. In 1980 it was succeeded by a Management Group, drawn more effectively and harmoniously from lower levels of these organisations.

By 1982, therefore, when we made our Review of GEAR management, it had gained sufficient support amongst the principal participants to ensure that it would go further. This reflected what people saw as its success. For Glasgow District Council the scheme was a tap for additional government investment which it wished to see flowing to Glasgow indefinitely. For leaders of the Regional Council, it gave to central government responsibility for an undoubtedly needy part of the region – although this priority was increasingly challenged by councillors who demonstrated that there were equally urgent needs elsewhere in Strathclyde. For the government, the scheme was a high-profile initiative which earned political credit, and also some co-operation from local authorities, becoming increasingly hostile about cuts in their rate support grant and expenditure ceilings. For the Housing Corporation, the project enabled Ministers to increase its budget, provided the Corporation could demonstrate it was focusing its efforts on the east end. The aggregate of capital expenditure by the partners to the project up to 1986, was estimated by the Agency as shown in Table 12.1.

There is no question but that GEAR brought more public and, perhaps, private investment to the east end than would

Table 12.1: Summary of GEAR project costs 1977-86
(£000's)

Authority	Total costs of projects established 1977-86		
	1977-85	1985-86 *	1977-86
Strathclyde Regional Council			
Infrastructure Transport	11,482	3,936	15,418
Education, Social Services, Community	7,212	5,304	12,516
Protection Services	4,262	–	4,262
TOTAL	22,956	9,240	32,196
Glasgow District Council			
New Housing	14,104	–	14,104
Modernisation, Rehabilitation**	49,742	12,328	62,070
Other	9,347	771	10,118
TOTAL	73,193	13,099	86,292
Scottish Development Agency			
Land Assembly – Site Preparation	10,395	608	11,003
Factory Building and Business Development	18,191	1,264	19,455
Environment, Recreation, Other Expenditure	29,139	3,966	33,105
TOTAL	57,725	5,838	63,563
Scottish Special Housing Association			
New Housing	20,348	2,328	22,676
Modernisation, Rehabilitation	17,718	1,031	18,749
Other	105	–	105
TOTAL	38,171	3,359	41,530
Housing Corporation			
Local H.A. New Housing	2,432	324	2,756
Local H.A. Rehabilitation	67,630	8,046	75,676
Other	75	295	370
TOTAL	70,137	8,665	78,802
Greater Glasgow Health Board	3,894	2,000	5,894
Manpower Services Commission	4,820	1,252	6,072
Other			
Dept. of Health and Social Security/PSA	1,060	–	1,060
Vol. Orgs. under Urban Programme	215	–	215
Total	£272,171	43,453	315,624

* 1985-6 financial information should be regarded as provisional
** includes £20,550,000 of additional expenditure incurred 1984-85

continued over

Table 12.1: Continued

Authority	Total costs of projects established 1977-86		
	1977-85	1985-86 *	1977-86
Private Sector Expenditure			
Private Housing			87,000
Industrial Plant and Machinery			48,000
Commercial Projects and Property Investment			49,000
Total			184,000

Private Sector Investment is based on projects completed, under construction or committed

Source: Scottish Development Agency

have occurred in the absence of the project. Nairn (1983) has made an item-by-item estimate that in the period 1977-82, capital investment attributable to the project, and not likely to have occurred in the area but for it, amounted to £12.3 million of a total of £15.6 million in SDA factory provision; £3.3 million of a total of £8.7 million in land assembly and site preparation by the SDA; £6.7 million of £9.5 million of the SDA's environmental programme; £5.9 million of recreational facilities provided by the SDA; £45.0 million of £222.5 million invested in roads, housing, health and other facilities by local authorities and public agencies other than the SDA; £2.6 million of the revenue expenditure in this area of £4.6 million in the Urban Programme; and upwards of £2.2 million on staff costs required exclusively for management of the project. Other revenue costs arising from special attention to the GEAR area's needs in education, social work and other initiatives not funded under the Urban Programme, have not been estimated. Nor have we included private sector investment in housing as described in Chapter 7.

These are impressive figures. But it is not clear whether this extra expenditure arose strictly from the Agency's initiatives in 'co-ordination' or from the separate efforts of the participants, at a time when trends in public expenditure might have deterred the participants from giving priority to the east end. Because the Agency's spending is not deducted directly from local authority expenditure in Scotland but falls within the allocations for regional aid in the United Kingdom, the local authorities can therefore perceive spending by central government agencies on the GEAR project as a helpful addition to their resources.

However, criticisms confined to the assertion that much of what has been done in the east end since 1977 was already programmed, or planned, miss the point of the project. Its main purpose in the government's mind was to speed up and improve the quality of local renewal programmes which, prior to 1976, had run behind schedule, been unsatisfactorily co-ordinated and eventually produced some very unattractive results. In these respects the project achieved a lot.

Unprecedently rapid improvements were made in physical conditions in the east end during the first five years of the project. They were undoubtedly due, in part, to the extra public investment attracted by the project. Naturally, because such investment takes a long time to get through the pipelines of the planning and building required, much of it was prepared in the years before the GEAR project began. Nairn also shows that whereas much of the extra investment came from the SDA, the local authorities and other participants provided most financing through their mainstream programmes. Accordingly, whereas the Agency would probably receive most of the credit from east enders, as our own household survey suggests, this does not do justice to the other participants. Even so, the project unquestionably brought new, higher standards of design in the environment, and in housing and industrial building. It greatly improved the landscape, as was shown in Chapter 8. And − equally importantly − it has led to a more effective attempt to consult and involve local people in planning new developments, after initial attempts which would be criticised by Nelson (1980) as being inadequately conceived and by Gillett (1983) as being unduly prolonged. It also produced some imaginatively innovative schemes such as the Templeton Business Centre and the Barra's improvement. Templeton's, a distinguished old carpet factory with flamboyant tile-facing on the edge of Glasgow Green which was closed and deserted, became a centre for launching and supporting new enterprises − offering workshops, offices, shared services and equipment, loans and grants, and professional advice. The 'Barras' (Barrows) is a market of small shops, second-hand stalls and street traders — Glasgow's Petticoat Lane — which has been renovated and improved. Close by, in what used to be a derelict area, small homes for owner-occupation are now in keen demand.

The SDA's open-minded thinking, its readier access to resources and its flexible powers must take a large share of the credit for all this. The effect of the same combination of ideas, powers and ready financing could be seen in the same period in other Agency projects, such as the work of the Clydebank Task Force. The SDA's contribution to the GEAR project may also have encouraged and enabled local authorities to bring a new impetus to improving the whole Clydeside Conurbation at this time.

The creation of a planning and co-ordinating team for the GEAR project was a stimulus within the Agency as well as to other participants in the project, bringing greater investment in the east end by mainstream directorates of the SDA. The GEAR team of planners carried a flag within the Agency for area-focused projects, contending with other staff who stressed the merits of the SDA's sectoral economic policies of a kind more familiar to industrial economists. This debate reflected the initial reluctance of the Agency's first Chief Executive to accept responsibility for co-ordinating the GEAR project, on the grounds that it would divert the Agency from its primary concern for the Scottish economy. Later, when the Agency took responsibility for sending Task Forces to Glengarnock and Clydebank, area projects (Gulliver, 1984) became more acceptable to Agency economists but were recast within the more rigorous mould of 'project agreements', with more clearly specified objectives, time horizons and contributions from all participants. Thus, the vaguer and more 'comprehensive' purposes which the government aimed for in GEAR were abandoned and the Agency's intervention confined to ostensibly economic objectives.

The tensions between the economic strategists of the Agency and the GEAR team of the Urban Renewal Directorate persisted until the Review of GEAR in 1982, commissioned by the Strategic Planning and Projects Directorate to bring the Agency's role in the east end within a framework similar to those devised for the various area projects managed by the Agency elsewhere in Scotland. Our report on the Future

Management of the GEAR Project (Wannop, 1982) was part of that Review. We suggested that the GEAR team's most significant roles were in fostering specific new initiatives and in the major Agency expenditure it arranged, more than as a co-ordinator of the work of other participants in the project. That depended more upon the cohesive political force of the Governing Committee. Some attempts at co-ordination had been unproductive and may even have delayed particular components of the participants' programmes. With one notably effective exception on housing, the efforts of the working parties, prior to the submission to the Governing Committee in 1979 of the Overall Proposals, appeared to have been no more than modestly useful in spreading an understanding of the GEAR scheme amongst executive and middle-management staff in participating authorities and agencies. The GEAR team also provided a centralised information service offering data on land, premises, employment opportunities and programmes, which neither the Regional nor District Councils organised so well for the east end or, indeed, for any comparable local area elsewhere in Strathclyde.

But the GEAR team were unable to co-ordinate local planning of the more conventional kind in the east end. Indeed, the project probably delayed action of this sort by District planners. We listed thirty-six unresolved issues in local planning, all of which were important for the improvement of physical conditions. We recommended that a Statement of Priorities should be prepared, establishing a programme for action by the participants over the remainder of the project. We saw the Statement as an overdue opportunity to consider priorities collectively, rather than as the sum of the programmes of individual participants. The SDA took on the task of preparing the Statement, but what was produced was closer in form to the project agreements then being compiled prior to the launch of the Agency's new area development projects, rather than to the sharper programme of action deriving from actual project experience appropriate to the concluding stages of a more advanced initiative.

We concluded, and the participants agreed, that the scheme in its present form should come to an end in 1987 – five years hence. By then, conditions in the east end would have improved to a point at which many other parts of Clydeside

225

would be in greater need of help, and the SDA, as the principal source of new initiatives, should turn its attention elsewhere, leaving the conventional administrative system to keep the renewal of the east end going. We suggested a transition from GEAR to an experimental form of area management, but left the arrangements for co-ordination between the two local authorities to emerge within the constraints of what would then be politically feasible. We reached our recommendation only after examining the most recent of the initiatives in urban regeneration launched in England since GEAR's inception. We were impressed with procedures for land brokerage already being pioneered by the Urban Development Corporations, which looked as if they might suit the GEAR area's needs for more flexibly and more quickly transferring land from dereliction or obsolete uses into uses benefiting the east end.

Following the Agency's Statement of Priorities in 1983, there was only slow progress towards arrangements to ensure the impetus of GEAR beyond 1987. Our report had recommended that leadership in co-ordinating the project should be transferred from the Agency to the local authorities in 1985, two years before the conclusion of the main project. We proposed that staff from the Regional and District Councils should be seconded into the GEAR team, anticipating the period beyond 1987 when the local authorities would be wholly responsible for managing the project's future.

But, by 1986, the GEAR team remained in place without local authority secondments to work alongside Agency staff, and a proposal by the Agency to establish a local economic Enterprise Trust to succeed GEAR was being debated with the Regional and District Councils. To the local authorities, an Enterprise Trust might have seemed too limited a contribution by the Agency to replace the scale of investment associated with the lifetime of the project. For their part, the local authorities had become more aware of the potential merits of a joint team with responsibility for continuing the impetus of GEAR after 1987. A new model for Glasgow was established in April 1986 in the Govan area, where a five-year initiative for economic and environmental recovery was launched on the lines of the Agency's earlier project agreements for other parts of Scotland. In Govan, however, the costs, staffing and leadership of the project team fell predominantly upon the local authorities, although the funding of the initiative incorporated a five-year capital commitment by the SDA together with support for training initiatives. The Govan model may have appeared attractive to the Regional and District Councils as a means of clearly representing the Agency's continuing commitment to renewal of inner Glasgow, and to the GEAR area in particular.

Returning to the two questions with which we opened this chapter, we incline to a favourable answer on both counts. GEAR's management was not instantly effective, but it adjusted to political circumstances and unprecedented working associations to reach a stable relationship amongst the participants. Other personalities might have more skilfully cultivated a strategic review of plans for the east end of Glasgow, or more winningly led the task of co-ordination but, within an unfamiliar framework, management was more often successful than not.

On the count of the effectiveness of the framework, we can see no other model which could have more completely and assuredly met the particular political and technical needs of the place and the time. We have little doubt but that fuller thought by government and fuller awareness in the SDA of the nature of the project could have helped shape a more immediately effective GEAR team, less hampered by the exaggerated ambitions surrounding its launch. Although the depth of prior analysis suggested by Booth and Moore (Lever and Moore, 1986, p. 90) as necessary for Agency projects is perhaps unachievably rational, given political imperatives, the brief evaluation of alternatives prior to selection of the east end, together with the accelerated launch of the project, brought difficulties for the GEAR team and the Agency which took time to dissolve.

Is the GEAR model transferable?
GEAR was the first of the series of major renewal projects launched in the United Kingdom from 1970 onwards. Its distinctiveness remains, because it is a model yet to be repeated either elsewhere in Scotland or in other parts of the United Kingdom, despite a succession of new initiatives in area renewal and management.

Since there was much satisfaction in the Scottish Office (Gillett, 1983) over the benefits of the partnership pioneered in the GEAR project, why was this comprehensive approach to urban renewal not repeated in other Scottish cities at least? In England, where there was no roving development agency at hand, the cumbersome process of designation for an Urban Development Corporation had to precede the kind of intervention which the SDA could very rapidly achieve in Scotland. In Scotland, the model could be quickly introduced wherever government wanted quick action; it enabled government to spend money on its priorities, not those of the local politicians; it appeared to achieve some innovations by local authorities which government had sought but had no other effective means of coercing. Why then, has there not been a second GEAR, in Aberdeen, Edinburgh, Dundee — or elsewhere in Glasgow?

The truth is that although nothing as intense as GEAR has subsequently been attempted over such a large area, and nowhere overtly including so generous a range of social objectives, the GEAR model of a multi-representative steering committee and an exclusive professional team has been adopted for projects throughout Central and Lowland Scotland. From the Garnock Valley project started in Ayrshire in 1979, up to the Govan-Kinning Park project begun in Glasgow in 1986, at least a dozen projects have been launched in which the SDA has been the catalyst for mutually supportive investment programmes by collaborating public and private agencies. Gulliver (1984) and Wannop (Barrett and Healey, 1985) describe the evolution of these. Some projects are preceded by Project Agreements setting out the action which the partners each intend, committing the spending that will ensue. The Agreements were initiated by the economists of the SDA to bring sharper purposes and a fixed life to projects which the more haphazard launch of GEAR had failed to define clearly. Particularly after the onset of the Conservative government of 1979, the Agency's projects were more completely centred on economic initiatives, including environmental improvement and supportive infrastructure. Social initiatives as part of a total approach to area renewal shrank to the margins. The idea of partnership which had underlain GEAR remained, but now bringing the private sector to the fore. Private participation was required not only by the ideology of the Thatcher government, but by the increasing influence of local urban and economic renewal experience from the United States.

Potentially the most significant of the partnership models to develop was Glasgow Action, the committee of local political, business and public figures gathered in 1985 at the Agency's instigation to restore the national status of the City Centre; with staffing confined to a Director without the supporting team enjoyed by GEAR, the seniority of the committee in private and public affairs nevertheless promised an even wider base of support. The GEAR model had been stripped to its essence in Glasgow Action, where brokerage and the power of financial patronage were combined in concentrated force. Similarly, the enterprise trusts proliferating in Scotland in the mid-1980s distilled some of the essence of the lessons of economic policy emerging from GEAR.

Lacking an equivalent to the SDA to forge enduring local collaboration, Inner City Partnerships and Programme initiatives in England and Wales have varied in their effectiveness, ranging from the Birmingham Partnership, commonly well regarded, to the Liverpool Partnership whose performance compelled the Department of the Environment to try a new tack, sending to the provinces a 'Task Force' of central government civil servants and businessmen. Although the disappointment expressed by some (Parkinson and Wilks, 1983) may do less than justice to these cases, it is clear that the Partnerships have not fulfilled the objectives of the Department of the Environment's White Paper (1977a) from which they emerged. Whatever GEAR's early difficulties, co-operation between the participants improved from awkwardness to at least collaborative tolerance, whereas the Partnerships in England appear frequently to have started badly and to have become worse (House of Commons, 1983).

There are many explanations for this difference. Scottish local government's longer experience of central government participation in local affairs may have made collaboration easier, or simply induced greater docility. The management structure of the Scottish Office in which all Departments answer to a single Secretary of State is integrated to a degree impossible in England, where the Department of the Environment cannot always gain corporate backing from other Ministries. Indeed, the DoE has been challenged not only from the Treasury but also from the Department of Industry. The Scottish experiment, now developed and widely followed in other parts of Scotland by the SDA in negotiated agreements with local authorities and the private sector, has been a more continuous organic growth, carried forward by Labour and Conservative governments alike, and bearing fewer of the marks of 'management by crisis'. It is our impression that public authorities in the GEAR scheme were more successful than their English counterparts in involving and consulting local people. That impression may be partly due to the fact that angry community groups in London probably find readier publicity than they would in Scotland. The London Docklands Development Corporation may not have abused its powers to a greater degree than the SDA did, but it certainly provoked fiercer dissent – perhaps because the Regional and the District Councils retained their planning powers and the GEAR area councillors accordingly retained their influence on behalf of their electorate. Moreover, in the community councils representing smaller areas within the District, Glasgow has a whole tier of publicly funded representative bodies, much used for consultative purposes, which is lacking in England.

The GEAR project, on the other hand, lacked some of the real managerial advantages possessed by Urban Development Corporations. The London Docklands are very similar to the GEAR area in total extent, total employment and total population, yet the Development Corporation has a stronger brokerage role in assembling sites for investment, if necessary by compulsory purchase, and improving their potential for development by an infrastructural and environmental improvement. All this was equally needed in the GEAR area, where the powers were diffused between the participants and lacked the single-minded impetus which can be mobilised within a Development Corporation. If this was a weakness of the GEAR project it should be remembered that it had, closer to hand, a battery of government agencies at the discretion of the Secretary of State in Edinburgh, each experienced in housing, environmental improvement or economic development. It may also be easier for established central and local agencies to act quickly in the early stages of a project and, later on, to withdraw from it than it is for a Development Corporation, set up for one purpose only and therefore 'starting from cold'.

Urban Development Corporations are supposed to have difficulties in working with the social, educational and other personal services provided by local authorities, but inextricably involved in renewal and development. The two agencies – the Scottish Development Agency and the Scottish Special Housing Association – which in the GEAR case combined many of the functions of a Development Corporation, might have had even greater difficulties of this sort. However, the quality of relations between agencies in local administration may be determined less by their numbers and powers than by the personal qualities and tolerance of the people concerned. Resort to the superior powers of Development Corporations may arouse greater friction than the patient, if protracted, negotiations implicit in Scottish practice.

Urban Development Corporations may eventually arise even in Scotland, in circumstances where the scale or quality of change sought is exceptional. The SDA's area projects have deliberately been confined to a limited, self-contained set of aims and areas. They may not prove adequate for Scotland's needs in every future case. Indeed, any policy for Clydeside's regeneration which depended primarily on GEAR and comparable area projects would fail. GEAR has demonstrated physical renewal to be the component of urban policy which can be pre-eminently successful within a local area frame. It has shown that the criteria for area definition differ for different elements of regeneration, whereby social and economic limitations central to comprehensive success will frequently be better related to client groups, labour market areas or the national economy, none of which can be as narrowly or precisely bounded as was the GEAR area.

PART III
Wider Perspectives

13 LESSONS FOR LOCAL ECONOMIC POLICY

Ivan Turok

The crisis facing Britain's inner cities and big peripheral housing estates arises from the collapse of the local economies which these communities depended upon. While those economies continue to decay, these neighbourhoods will fall still further behind the rest of Britain in the living standards they offer their people. Before we consider the lessons to be learnt from the GEAR project we must ask whether experience gained elsewhere in Britain offers hope that these economic problems can be resolved by action taken at the local level. Civic leaders in many cities are now trying to achieve that, with an urgency and a degree of political commitment that is often greater than that shown by national governments.

For the sake of simplicity we distinguish between two broadly different approaches to local economic development. The first and most common approach is pragmatic and *market oriented*. Local authorities attempt to cope as best they can in the circumstances, pursuing measures that conform with the advice of central government, adopting a residual kind of role that fits in with the activities of other public and private agencies to which they remain largely subordinate.

The second approach is newer, more experimental and less easy to define. It might be called *interventionist*. Local councils raise awkward questions about the merits of traditional policies and practices and attempt to make a more direct and profound impact on the situation. Such policies are based on a more explicit, coherent, longer-term strategy, and are frequently in conflict with market trends. We discuss each approach in turn.

The market oriented approach

Of the two, the market oriented approach is more low-key. Policies and programmes implicitly assume that growth and regeneration are necessarily progressive and that the benefits will trickle down to all groups in the population. They also assume that the economic role of the local authority has to be

235

a marginal one. There is a tendency to look elsewhere for economic solutions – both to the private sector and to other government agencies – and a reluctance to challenge established policies and practices. In some places this approach derives from a lack of strong political will. In others people believe that greater benefits are likely to be achieved by adopting a low-profile, consensual posture rather than a controversial or combative one. Specific projects and schemes are heavily influenced by the powers and resources conferred upon local authorities by central government or by organisations such as the EEC, which means that the council has little room for manoeuvre. In the inner cities local authorities may restrict themselves to using the powers and resources provided by the Inner Urban Areas Act and the Urban Programme. In the peripheral regions local action may be limited to supplementing the activities of what are perceived to be more powerful regional agencies.

Within this approach four main types of activity are carried out: physical, financial, promotional and training. *Physical* measures consist mainly of the provision of industrial sites and the building and letting of factory units. Local authorities tend to concentrate on small 'nursery' units and on the refurbishment of old buildings for small workshop space, leaving larger advance factories to be provided by regional development agencies or private developers. Other physical measures include the reclamation and servicing of vacant and derelict land, and general improvements in the quality of the physical environment. Such schemes are often encouraged by specific grants from central government. They may be implemented in a co-ordinated way by concentrating on particular run-down localities as in the 'industrial improvement areas' designated under the Inner Urban Areas Act, the object being to restore the confidence of private investors in the area.

Measures involving *financial assistance* usually take the form of loans and grants to companies and are an increasingly popular way of trying to promote economic development. Assistance is usually focused on small businesses and unconventional enterprises, the assumption being that larger firms are beyond the reach of local authorities and are in any case adequately served by regional aid and the financial institutions of the private sector. Local authority support is provided for a variety of purposes relating mainly to the acquisition and improvement of sites and premises, but for new firms small amounts of money may be available to help meet the costs of business consultancy, plant and machinery, employment and training, or other start-up expenses.

Promotion involves local authorities in advertising their localities, marketing particular sites and premises, producing registers of vacant property and directories of local companies, and providing advisory services for small firms. The intention is usually to attract inward investment or to facilitate the growth of new and established businesses. Non-local advertising may be delegated to regional agencies such as the SDA's Locate in Scotland and business advice may be organised through Enterprise Agencies which depend heavily on managers seconded from large private firms.

Finally, *skill training* provided by local authorities is usually limited to participation in nationally organised schemes, such as the Manpower Services Commission's Community Programme. Owing to the difficulty of the MSC in finding other sponsors, local authorities provide the bulk of such places in many areas. They may also support small schemes to train people for specific employers.

These simple descriptions obviously conceal considerable variety of experience and different levels of activity between areas. The appropriateness of particular measures will also depend to some extent on local circumstances. Bearing these qualifications in mind, we can summarise their main strengths and weaknesses. First, like many central government programmes, they tend to be based on small areas and *place-oriented* rather than directly aimed at local industries or at the disadvantaged people they are intended to benefit. Basic infrastructural projects improving the physical environment in run-down areas will lay the basis, it is hoped, for productive investment and retaining the local population, but they are not sufficient on their own to generate sustained economic growth or a lot more jobs. Indeed, where they do seem to have had some success, this may have been achieved simply at the expense of jobs and investment displaced from neighbouring areas.

Second, market oriented measures are frequently *property-led*, providing land and premises on a speculative basis or subsidising building improvements for specific firms. Such activities tend to be attractive to local authorities for pragmatic rather than strategic reasons. They have the necessary expertise, gained from their traditional land-use planning and estates activities, and any expenditure required is considered to represent an investment in fixed assets that should survive the possible demise of individual firms. On the positive side, new premises may bring about marginal qualitative improvements in the performance of their occupants, through permitting more efficient plant layouts and improved working conditions. But there is little evidence that physical measures have independently generated significant output or employment growth in assisted firms, or induced investment much beyond the levels that would have taken place in any case. To take the example of small factory units, the assumption behind their provision is that there exists a shortage of such property on the market and that this limits the growth of small firms. Judging from estates journals at the time, there was indeed something of a gap in the supply of these factories in urban areas during the 1970s and early 1980s (Richardson, 1985) but little evidence that such shortages seriously restricted the expansion or founding of small firms. The prospects of such firms depend far more on their ability to sell what they produce and to raise money when they need it (Lloyd and Dicken, 1982).

The third characteristic of market oriented activities is their tendency to be *competitive*. Many are designed to encourage firms to move into the area from elsewhere, through promotion, physical provision, financial incentives and by making the physical environment and social milieu attractive to outside investors. The hope is to attract the elusive large firms that would solve the local unemployment problem. These tactics have their origins in the 1960s and early 1970s when the conventional approach to spatial policy was to influence the distribution of industry through locational incentives. However, circumstances have changed and the distributional approach no longer works, particularly in the areas which most need help. During the depression of the last decade, investment has been lower and there has been less potentially mobile employment. The political climate has changed too, with restrictions on major public investment and cutbacks in regional assistance. Regional grants and development agencies such as the SDA's Locate in Scotland do not distinguish between localities and cannot be relied upon to direct inward investment to inner city areas or peripheral housing estates. Areas therefore compete against each other in a divisive and wasteful 'zero-sum-game' with no overall benefit. Worse still, individual authorities feel obliged to give incoming industries whatever they want, and exert little control over the level, security or quality of jobs created. Usually, far less consideration is given by authorities to the potentially more important task of retaining employment in existing firms, particularly in medium and larger sized establishments.

Finally, where less emphasis is devoted to attracting inward investment, considerable attention is given to encouraging new or established *small firms*. The reasons for this may be pragmatic, such as the failure of previous promotional campaigns to attract incoming industry, or they may reflect a view that small businesses fall more rationally within the province of local authorities, given the limited powers and resources they have. The present government promotes the notion that small firms are dynamic and contribute significantly to wealth creation, local economic development and job creation. Since the mid-1970s urban policy has also fostered the view that the inner cities are an appropriate 'seed bed' for new enterprises. In fact there is little evidence to support these claims and research suggests that the converse is frequently true. The small firms sector is a relatively backward area of the economy in which productivity, investment and competitiveness tend to be low (GLC, 1983; Storey, 1982). Consequently the quality of employment is frequently poor too, with wages relatively low, jobs less secure and working conditions worse than in larger enterprises. Beyond these simple generalisations it is worth pointing out that differences between industrial sectors are far more significant than differences between large and small firms *per se*. Most of the growth in jobs which took place in small firms during the last decade has been confined to a small number of service sectors. One of the dangers of encouraging the unemployed to start up in business is that they stand to lose whatever limited resources – houses and other assets – they own when their businesses fail, as many inevitably do.

239

Ivan Turok

We have listed some of the strengths and rather more of the limitations of market oriented approaches to local economic development. Many of the specific schemes and projects which come within this approach are worthwhile in themselves, but usually they only address some of the symptoms of the problem and do so on a small and piecemeal basis.

The interventionist approach

The alternative approach involves developing a more active policy of intervention which seeks to tackle some of the root causes of local economic decline by challenging market processes and traditional government policies in the interests of local communities. Much of the thinking which informs this perspective is derived from regional development agencies such as the SDA and from the experience of progressive authorities such as the Greater London Council (GLC), the West Midlands County Council (WMCC) and Sheffield City Council, which sought to develop alternative economic policies to the private sector solutions advocated by central government.

The interventionist approach incorporates measures altogether different in scale and character, employing greater resources and tackling problems on the basis of a more informed assessment of their origins. Recognising the limitations of the low-key and marginal programmes traditionally pursued, there is a willingness to act more strongly. Once again there is considerable diversity between the policies of different authorities, reflecting their different economic and political circumstances. Nevertheless, we can identify several major principles which, to a greater or lesser extent, inform the strategies of most of them.

First, there is a commitment to *defensive* actions intended to save jobs in plants threatened with closure and redundancy. Local councils have attempted to avert closures, salvage some of the jobs and strengthen the position of the remaining workers through extensive technical, financial and moral support, giving time for viable proposals to be put forward to keep plants open. The intention has been not simply to maintain older factories employing outdated production methods, but to work with management and the workforce to design improved products, identify new markets

240

and reorganise production in ways which improve productivity while at the same time giving workers more control over company decision-making. Defensive actions would have been particularly important during the slump in the early 1980s, though company failures have continued at a lower level. The emphasis within this approach has varied between authorities. The SDA, for instance, lays great stress upon commercial viability in its actions to support industry. Hence it is often criticised for its reluctance to help firms facing even temporary difficulties. When it does get involved, the advisory and other services are usually provided on a commercial basis and it is far less common nowadays for direct financial support to be involved. The GLC, in contrast, was more willing to intervene, to do so on not strictly commercial grounds, and to accord the interests of the workforce a high priority. In situations where company owners were keen to extricate themselves from the business, the GLC often supported the formation of workers' co-operatives. The policy of the WMCC lay somewhere in between – indicating a willingness to intervene but only where there were prospects of profitability, at least in the longer term.

The second strand of the interventionist approach is to go beyond one-off defensive actions to encourage more wide-ranging and longer-term *structural change* in the local economy. Key industrial sectors are highlighted for strategic intervention to promote restructuring through increased investment, modernisation, skill training and new product development. An overall, publicly organised strategy to promote reorganisation within each sector is considered necessary owing to the failure of external financial institutions and competitive market processes to do so in the interests of local people. In Scotland the SDA has indicated that high technology growth industries such as electronics, health care and advanced engineering are the priorities. It focuses attention on attracting inward investment in these sectors and provides some support to local firms, though only with mixed success so far. The GLC was considerably more ambitious, identifying and analysing in some detail twenty-three sectors in which intervention was required, ranging from those concerned with: (i) consumption (e.g. furniture, clothing, culture); (ii) caring and curing (e.g. domestic work and child care); (iii) engineering (e.g. motor vehicles and components, arms conversion); (iv) information and communications (e.g. computer software, printing, cable); (v) sweated trades and services (e.g. home working, cleaning, tourism); and (vi) infrastructure (e.g. public transport, energy, construction) (GLC, 1985a). These sectors clearly encompass a wide range of activities: old as well as new industries, manufacturing as well as service sectors, and both formal and domestic work. The scope and specific purpose of intervention in each was different but the broad intention was to challenge the principles on which these industries are currently organised – namely the reliance on market forces and the search for short-term profits which, during the last few decades, have worked against people in the major cities, where factories are older, operating costs are higher and labour is more organised. Instead an active strategy was pursued to seek long-term restructuring informed by wider economic and social goals such as providing satisfying work for marginalised groups, and producing goods and services in response to people's needs and in a socially responsible manner. Putting this strategy into practice was, not surprisingly, difficult, as we indicate later, but the approach to analysis and action was an interesting and important innovation in the field of local economic planning.

Third, in order to buttress the strategy of restructuring and ensure that it operated in the interests of the intended social strata, a different kind of economic planning was attempted – promoting *economic democracy*. Unlike the traditional top-down approach of indicative public policies backed by incentives, the new approach sought to increase popular participation by consulting and involving people more fully – particularly consumers, women, community groups and trade unionists. The principle of economic democracy is intended to increase the control of working people and communities over decisions which affect the local economy. Attempts have been made to put it into practice in a variety of ways. One of these has been called 'enterprise planning', which involves a combination of strategic investment policies, reciprocal planning agreements with employers and unions in companies receiving investment (covering jobs, wages, working conditions and so on), and subsequent 'hands on' monitoring of these enterprises to increase accountability to the wider community. 'Popular planning' is another objective, implying extensive community and workplace involvement in the formation of councils' own strategies. Social control over the economy has also been sought more directly through co-operative forms of economic organisation, community businesses, municipal enterprises and greater trade union representation on management boards. Finally, the position of workers disadvantaged in the labour market has been strengthened through targeted training initiatives and positive discrimination in local authorities' own recruitment policies – both designed to favour ethnic minorities, women and other disadvantaged groups. Local authorities have been more active in many of these fields than other agencies – the SDA, for instance, would consider the extension of public ownership and democratic control to be outside its remit, though others would argue that firms receiving public money should be more accountable to the Scottish people.

To put these broad aspirations into effect requires a much higher public sector profile. Whereas the traditional approach tends to cast public authorities in the role of attracting, assisting and enabling the private investor, this alternative requires the backing of sufficient resources for the local authority to be a major participant in investment decisions, and in a strategic rather than a servicing capacity. Local enterprise boards were set up by several authorities to perform this investment function, which they have done by buying shares in companies, providing long-term loans, strategic advice and technological support, as well as undertaking more traditional forms of property development in the context of the wider strategy. Funding is mainly from the rates although some success has been achieved in attracting investment funds from financial institutions as well. Local authority pension funds, for instance, represent enormous potential resources for investment in the long-term regeneration of local economies. Unlike conventional public investment agencies which are expected to adhere fairly strictly to criteria based on expected short-term rates of return, many enterprise boards were given a longer-term horizon and more wide-ranging guidelines. For legal reasons and in order to attract funds from external sources, commercial considerations have to be taken into account in making investments, but wider social objec-

243

tives can also be encouraged by offering specific grants and subsidies to top up the investment capital. These payments may be intended to help in creating some form of social ownership, to increase the numbers of black or women workers, to set up apprenticeships, to increase wages or to maintain jobs. This is a clear departure from the trend towards increased stringency in public investment, for it means supporting projects which do not show an immediate commercial return but which may be worthwhile in terms of wider social costs and benefits.

Not surprisingly, translating these ambitious plans into practice has presented many difficulties. Breaking with the orthodox approach to economic development and public investment provoked opposition from local authority administrators leading to bureaucratic obstruction. It was also hard to find enough committed staff with the necessary knowledge and expertise. Long-term investment in companies was hampered by numerous legal obstacles and by conservatism on the part of the pension funds and other financial institutions, and intervention was made more difficult by political hostility from various quarters. In addition, financial restrictions limited the ability to set up non-commercial ventures such as training projects and centres to develop socially useful products and alternative technologies.

Yet perhaps the most fundamental problem facing local employment policies is the limited economic power that local authorities can bring to bear on the wider economy. These alternative strategies have stretched the powers of local authorities to the limit but competitive market forces, the extensive control over production exerted by private companies, and the present harsh economic and political climate have all served to block progress. Local authorities have not had the time, resources or expertise to set up municipally owned enterprises on any scale, and their capacity to intervene in privately owned companies has been limited by several crucial factors. For instance, their desire to increase social control over private investment has generally deterred the stronger and strategically more important companies from approaching them for support. Consequently councils have been obliged to deal mainly with weaker firms and those that have previously been turned away by the established financial institutions. Many interventions have therefore been rescue packages, and a proportion of these firms have, not surprisingly, failed subsequently. A further, related difficulty has been to put into practice in successfully restructured companies the councils' wider social and redistributive objectives regarding job creation, working conditions, equal opportunities, worker participation, socially useful products, etc. in the face of pressure on the costs and efficiency of production arising from strong competition with more conventional producers. Difficult political choices have had to be made, with some of the social goals frequently being sacrificed in the attempt to achieve competitiveness and commercial viability. In firms where enterprise boards have held only a minority interest, they have frequently not even been in a position to make such choices, which raises the obvious question as to what, if anything, can be expected to be achieved in these circumstances.

Yet despite their limitations, there is evidence that interventionist policies have achieved tangible and worthwhile gains. After only a few years the enterprise boards set up by the metropolitan councils have secured or created several thousand jobs, and at a cost that compares favourably with the costs of unemployment and with the cost-effectiveness of traditional policy measures. On Merseyside over £1 million has been invested and 1,000 jobs maintained; in Lancashire investment of £4.5 million has supported over 3,000 jobs; and in West Yorkshire over 2,700 jobs have been secured with investment of £5.7 million (Miller, 1986). By mid-1985 the West Midlands Enterprise Board had invested £10 million in thirty companies and claimed to have assisted in saving or creating 4,000 jobs at a cost of £2,500 each (Dawkins, 1985). The Greater London Enterprise Board (GLEB) saved or created 2,300 jobs in the two years to the end of 1984 (GLEB, 1985). These were expected to rise to 3,500 within the following two years as firms carried out planned expansion. The cost per job of the 2,300 was £5,500 on the assumption that investments would realise only 50 per cent of their cost. The cost per job-year of the 3,500 existing and planned jobs was £3,300 on the same assumption. This compares favourably with the annual cost of £6,000 or more for each person kept on the dole, raising an important political point about the most effective use of public resources. Note, however, that as with all job creation estimates provided by public bodies, the local authority figures should be treated with some circumspection, and that in any case, the scale of job creation is far outweighed by the extent of unemployment and the pace of continuing job loss.

These simple numerical assessments of enterprise board experiments tell us nothing about wider, qualitative aspects of their achievements – in particular, whether any impact was made on what firms produce, how, by whom and for whom. Space does not permit a full evaluation here but there have been sufficient documented examples of successfully restructured companies, of enterprise planning and of new worker co-operatives to indicate that modest results have at least been achieved in these areas (GLC, 1985a; GLEB, 1985; WMEB, 1985). A variety of external economic, political, legal and financial constraints have prevented more significant inroads being made into the unemployment problem; but with greater powers, resources and time enterprise boards might have had more substantial effects. (Unfortunately the metropolitan authorities were abolished early in 1986 although their enterprise boards have survived in a weakened form.) More importantly, with the support of more sympathetic and expansionist national economic policies, their contribution to employment generation could have been considerably greater.

Conclusion

More significant than the material gains made by a few interventionist initiatives is the practical experience gained and the broader lessons that have been learnt about alternative policies. These active economic strategies were important explorations into the scope for quite new and innovative public policies to eradicate mass unemployment and move towards deeper changes in our economy and society. They have provided useful illustrations of what can be done with imagination and political will. Britain's depressed areas cannot rely on the slow adjustment of market mechanisms to make them attractive again to private investment. They need active local intervention to create the jobs and services required by local people.

Yet there are strict limits to what can be achieved by local action alone. Local and regional authorities currently have neither the legal powers nor the economic resources to counter the effects of wider economic processes and restrictive macro-economic policies. With more resources, however, a significant number of jobs might be created in public sector programmes providing the essential infrastructure and services (transport, telecommunications, energy, health, etc.) needed by industries and communities. With greater legal powers and more funds for investment public authorities might also make a bigger impact on the market economy – reorganising and promoting the expansion of specific industries, developing new products for manufacture, identifying new services to be provided and extending real training. Nevertheless there remain restrictions on what is possible at the local level, restrictions which require that constructive use is made of the various powers available to central government. Particularly important here are the powers to stimulate and expand demand in the economy through increased public spending. Without such an expansion many of the one-off actions taken to increase jobs in individual enterprises might simply displace jobs in others. There are also important actions that only national (and, indeed, international) authorities can take to challenge the power of large corporations and to introduce progressive reforms to the wider economic system of which they form a part.

Furthermore, neither local nor national interventions can be satisfactorily pursued independently. The spatial economy of Britain is too highly differentiated for regeneration to be left to broad national actions; and the economic forces lying beyond individual cities are too great for localities to be the sole focus of intervention. Coherent and integrated local, regional and national policies are therefore required; fired by the urgency and aspirations expressed in local communities, but able also to mobilise the economic power and resources available only at broader levels.

14 A STRATEGY FOR EDUCATION

Jean Forbes

1 Education and the problem of deprivation

The idea of putting extra resources into areas which were deemed to be 'deprived' was first articulated in an education document – the Plowden Report 1965. Later work by Halsey and others (1970) on the practical details of implementing such a policy set out clearly the way in which educational disadvantage is reinforced (and reinforces) other social disadvantages, the whole vicious circle turning from generation to generation. Disadvantages in education could not be treated alone and the positively discriminating policies directed to disadvantaged areas should consist of wider packages of social and economic measures.

Although the idea of positive discrimination crossed over into town planning and was subsumed during the 1970s into 'the area approach to deprivation', education policies have continued to travel somewhat apart from other policies in this activity. Extra efforts have indeed been directed into deprived areas' education, but the basic institutional and administrative structures which deliver those policies to the ground are unchanged, and effort has been channelled into a narrow range of curricula.

The whole system continues to gauge success by achievements in academic tests. Deprived people start handicapped in this race and the system continues to separate them out, advancing those few who can pass the tests, diverting the others to vaguer and apparently inferior futures. The system, too, continues to be very 'front end loaded' with major effort focusing on the school level and some effort continued to the formal sector of higher education. Adult education continues to be hopelessly under-resourced and neglected.

This is a bad thing for the population in general, when the weight of the age structure is changing away from the school age groups, and there is a clear need for recurring re-education even of the qualified throughout life. It is a greater disaster for deprived areas where the same characteristics occur but the people have, in addition, an inherited backlog of disadvantage to overcome.

The tenacity with which the problem of educational disadvantage persists suggests that educational (and indeed the other) policies directed to disadvantaged areas should be not just qualitatively different (e.g. more money, teachers, etc.) but different in kind as well. Educational disadvantage should be met with *both* more resources *and* custom-made institutional systems designed to fit the needs and characteristics of the areas concerned.

The following tabulation of the educational qualifications of residents in the east end of Glasgow demonstrates the urgent need for re-thinking educational policy for such areas.

Table 14.1: Qualifications reported in household survey by Glasgow University (1983)

	Total (%)		Men (%)		Women (%)	
School qualifications						
Lowers or O-grade	145	(9)	72	(9)	73	(8)
Highers or A-level	69	(4)	38	(5)	31	(3)
Leaving certificate	106	(6)	48	(6)	58	(6)
Sub total	321	(19)	158	(20)	162	(18)
Post school qualifications						
Trade apprenticeship	138	(8)	117	(15)	21	(2)
City & Guilds	44	(3)	41	(5)	3	(–)
ONC/HNC	9	(1)	8	(1)	1	(–)
Clerical or commercial	54	(3)	4	(–)	50	(5)
Other (not stated)	66	(4)	42	(5)	24	(3)
Sub total	311	(18)	212	(27)	99	(11)
No qualifications						
Nothing and 'don't know'	1192	(70)	505	(64)	687	(75)
Total questioned	1696	(100)	786	(100)	910	(100)

Note that some respondents will have more than one qualification, hence the sub totals add up to figures greater than the totals of the respondents.

There are two points to note in Table 14.1. First, 70 per cent of the respondents (64 per cent of men, 75 per cent of women) reported no qualifications of any kind. The second point to note is the severely disadvantaged state of women. Although they did about as well as men at school, subsequent training, traditionally biased towards 'men's work', gave men nearly

249

three times as many qualifications as women got. Only in traditional 'women's work', of clerical and commercial kinds, did women do better.

Table 14.2 shows how qualifications vary with age. The experience of each age group reflects the opportunities available at the time when they were at the age when most education and training take place.

Table 14.2: Qualifications by age

	Age Groups (% in brackets)				
Qualifications	16-20	21-30	31-45	45-ret.	ret.
School qualifications	78 (43)	92 (38)	38 (13)	72 (16)	40 (3)
Post school qualifications	15 (8)	70 (28)	75 (25)	95 (19)	55 (11)
No qualification	106 (59)	136 (57)	215 (71)	329 (70)	408 (82)
Total questioned	180 (100)	242 (100)	305 (100)	475 (100)	496 (100)

The apparent scarcity of post school qualifications among the 16-20 age group reflects the fact that many of them are still too young to have completed their training. Later they will probably share in the steady, if modest, improvement in qualifications which has built up over the years. Another question in our household survey showed that 97 per cent of respondents were not currently involved in courses of any kind – even courses of the leisure and recreation sort.

These patterns have important implications for educational policy in this area. So do the numbers to be expected in each age group. Figure 14.1 presents in diagrammatic form the projected trends of selected age groups. Assuming that various measures succeed in stabilising the population so that people now living in the east end stay there, it will be some considerable time before the current teenage bulge reinforces the numbers in the main working age groups. Following the present bulge is a very small age group now moving into and through primary and early secondary school. As that diminished cohort moves through secondary school the numbers of teenagers seeking work and of young people in their early

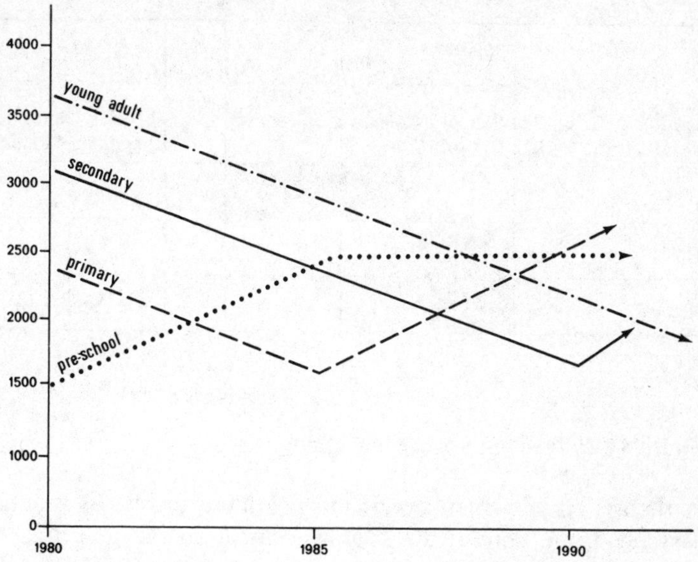

Figure 14.1 Diagrammatic projection of broad age bands assuming no in-migration and no out-migration

twenties will go down substantially. The primary school band may recover somewhat by 1985, the secondary by 1990, and the young post school group beyond that. If out-migration continues, that will make the downward slopes in the graph steeper; but in-migration, unless it is substantial and brings many school age children to the area, will do little to pull up the graphs until the 1990s and beyond.

A custom-built new system of education for such areas must first think out again the whole idea of educational need. For an area like the Glasgow east end what *kind* of curriculum, what *style* of learning, what *spatial pattern* of delivery on the ground and what structure of *management* is needed to break the vicious circle of educational disadvantage? First, we must see the population in GEAR as a whole, people of all ages having educational needs, not just the school age children. Then we should try to see the total, ideal, educational coverage whole before trying to design ways of bringing it to the people.

The present system apparently offers the following:

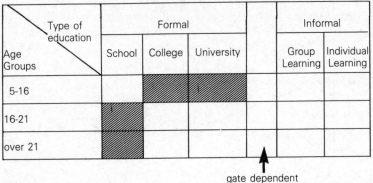

Age Groups \ Type of education	Formal				Informal	
	School	College	University		Group Learning	Individual Learning
5-16		▨	▨			
16-21	▨					
over 21	▨			↑		

gate dependent
on previous educational level

Figure 14.2: Types of educational opportunities

In theory all the open boxes are available to all. In practice passage from school to higher education is guarded by examination qualifications of various kinds, all devised by those who have, themselves, succeeded in the system.

Table 14.1 shows, in the formal sector, that very few deprived people progress beyond the minimum school leaving age since they lack the academic passports to do so. Also, as Weir (1983) states, some 'lack the confidence to return [to education] . . . They were depersonalised before, at school and do not want to risk that again' (p. 92). In practice also the use of the informal sector has long been known to be closely dependent on the student's previous attainment in the formal sector, thus effectively diminishing the deprived person's enthusiasm to use it or indeed capability to 'read' the system and grasp the opportunities that do exist. The experience of the Adult Education experiment in GEAR has fully demonstrated this with the relatively small uptake of the well-prepared and widely advertised courses available there.

New ways must be found to open the different *levels* of education to all citizens of whatever age, even if it means redefining the outlines of the institutional boxes.

If we are to turn our frequently disabling system into a system that enables everyone to get the most out of a world where all will have to look after and look out for themselves to a much greater extent than in the past, where learning and relearning will have to be a continuing part of life . . . then first, *capability* needs to be part of everyone's curriculum and *achievement* has to come in more than one guise. (Handy, 1984, p. 142, my italics)

2   Education and development

In theory there are three major purposes for which an individual pursues some educational activity:

1 for personal enjoyment;
2 for enhancing capability in relation to a group activity, which may be shared interest or work; and
3 for enhancing capability in matters which affect the local area and his neighbours in that locality.

The individual may undertake any of these learning pursuits either entirely alone on own initiative, or may join in collective learning such as a course tailored to the tasks of the group, or to the understanding of special problems of the locality. The mix is likely to vary through time as the individual ages and his needs change, but it will also vary as his capability increases.

In practice many people in areas like the east end have little hope of exercising this wide choice. They themselves have never been given the awareness of the riches education can provide, and the system is so structued that this range of offerings is seldom available anyway in such areas. Watts (1983) notes the 'dependency' which our present academic based system forces upon many such people. Although they 'fail' in the present system, they depend still upon it for education beyond school and they have no choice but to take what the system decides they need – usually this is labelled 'training'.

People's sense of themselves is crucially affected by the messages that are fed back to them about their places in their immediate community and the wider society. (Watts, 1983, p. 186)

Rising unemployment in Britain has led to the promulgation of an array of policies to increase 'training' opportunities for young school leavers and (to a much lesser extent) retraining for older workers made redundant by the closure of traditional industries.

In spite of this activity there is considerable confusion about what 'training' should consist of and how best it might be delivered. The process at present is still part of the dependency style of education for the non-academic. The work illustrations in current television advertisements for the Youth Training Scheme show:

(i) more young men than young women;
(ii) far more examples of manual jobs (like assembling a car engine) than managerial (low level) or design jobs; and
(iii) no examples of social development or local leadership jobs.

There is an in-built assumption that training is about operating somebody else's system.

Le Boterf (1983) points out the basic dilemma posed by too narrow a concept of training.

> Training designed to produce narrow specialities, or people equipped to do only one specific job has helped to create a cultural pattern of dependence that conflicts with the current need for the active and broad ranging involvement of human resources in the search for solutions. (p. 27)

Narrowly defined training is insufficient preparation for an uncertain future, and if this is all the 'education' deemed useful to give to disadvantaged people then it is likely merely to compound their disadvantage after initially raising false hopes. The skills needed are those which give flexibility and adaptability, and those depend on knowing how to think and how to steer one's own learning and re-learning in pursuit of opportunities as they arise. These will be both skills of doing and skills of thinking, each founded within a larger understanding of the purpose for which they are used.

Knowledge is power, and if we are genuinely to effect a sharing of this power within our society then 'not only knowledge but control over what counts as knowledge will have to be shared' (Schuller, 1979, p. 109). We have to seek some adaptation of the education system within deprived areas which will be developmental for both individual and community. It must foster in individuals the *capability* and the *confidence* to act both:

(i) *independently*, when confronting wider society and seeking a career path within it;
(ii) *inter-dependently* with others in interest groups or on behalf of the local community in development discussions.

'Community development' policies must be built on a carefully designed programme of community learning which will wind up the awareness, the capability and the confidence of the members of that community. The difference between areas like GEAR and more favoured areas is that in GEAR there is a vast backlog of educational failure to be overcome, before the point is reached at which the whole community begins to feel a sense of forward movement – its collective progress.

From the policy-maker's point of view, developmental education will fuel rising aspirations and the articulation of demands on all services. Demands will be initiated not just for quantity of services but for quality of both the product and the management thereof, providing a basis for participation. Participation is itself educative and its effect too will accumulate.

> The educator has a role to play not only in transmitting
> skills and knowledge as a pre-requisite for action, but also
> in assisting adults to derive the maximum educational
> value from the community learning . . . which occurs in the
> course of community action. (Brookfield, 1983, p. 106)

The locality itself is important in any locally organised educational policy. In GEAR and similar areas, people are relatively immobile, either through age, poverty or lack of confidence. The locality is the secure 'home'.

The educational policy must appear visibly at known local places, i.e. there must be a clear spatial logic to the design of the delivery of the service. This is a key service, and it requires to be located spatially in association with other supportive services and where people can get at them.

The locality itself is likely to be the strongest key to starting interesting lines of learning via locality based curricula –

whether related to the environment, local workplaces, local social activities and so on.

Educational policies seldom pay attention to this geo-graphic scale of planning. Without sensitivity to locality, as place and topic for study, an educational policy for a deprived area is likely to make little impact and its failure will diminish the chances of the rest of the community develop-ment policy package succeeding.

3 Problems in management

Looking at the visible outlets of educational activity in GEAR, it might seem that the provision is adequate.

There are at present four secondary and seventeen primary schools in the GEAR area. The secondary schools are two non-denominational mixed schools and two Roman Catholic schools – one for boys and one for girls. The school catchment areas over-run the GEAR boundary – this is especially so in the case of the two single-sex schools. Nevertheless, the schools form a visible educational presence. Nursery schools serve the pre-school population. Beyond the stage at which people go to school, provision is rather sparse. There is no College of Further Education within (or even close to) the area, although a specialist branch college of the city centre College of Building is located in the Bridgeton area. Commu-nity education services and an adult education experiment (the latter funded from temporary Urban Aid money) are separately organised from rooms within St Mungo's Secon-dary School. Alongside the more conventional educational system, the Dolphin Arts Centre in Bridgeton – also on temporary funding – has been innovative in reaching young people through art, drama and ceramic classes. A Resource Centre, located within St Mungo's school buildings, can provide archive material and equipment to support both school and post school educational projects.

It will be noted that most of the post school provision is located in school buildings. Given the marked alienation of this population from anything connoting school, this is a serious mistake. It may make economic sense to use redun-dant school space, but it does not make social sense in such an area.

The adequacy of this provision is a delusion. The elements

visible on the ground in GEAR are the only manifestation of
education which local people see. Viewed from their position,
the service seems to consist of scattered fragments, each
operating in isolation (see Figure 14.3a). It is left to the
consumer to try to construct some totality from these glimpses
of its parts, and to design his own best path through that
dimly perceived system. The education service is very
centrally organised and highly subdivided vertically. There
are five major subdivisions.

  (i) Pre-school
 (ii) Statutory schooling
(iii) Further Education (formal)
 (iv) Higher Education (formal and specialised)
  (v) Community Education and Adult Education.

Each of these has further subdivisions. Each element is
marked off from the others by its own line management
configuration, its own staff with their particular qualifications,
career structures and even particular trade unions. Each
element carries particular kinds of 'curriculum' with particular requirements for admission. Neither staff nor potential
students can transfer easily between channels, once launched
upon one. It is quite impossible for anyone to 'pack his own
qualification' by collecting 'credits' from different channels.

Finally, there is no sense anywhere in this school-biased
system that many people other than school teachers have
expertise and ranges of knowledge that make them important
in any locally based learning system. Education is largely in
the hands of a priestly caste of present or former school
teachers.

The managerial threads of the system are cross-linked only
at Regional Directorate level and even there the link cannot
include the specialist central institutions or the universities
which are funded by central government. Down at locality
level in the GEAR area there is no cross-linked delivery
system. Innovations and devoted work abound, but each rises
and falls within its own sector, unable to capitalise on the
mutual support which an integrated system would provide. It
is ironical that the simplest route through the educational
system is the one the 'academic' pupils will take to the
University and the professions. The most complicated and

Jean Forbes

half hidden pathways are set before the people least able to understand the map. We have an educational equivalent of the well-known Inverse Law of uptake of health service facilities (those who need the system most use it least).

4 Guidelines for designing an area-based system
The approach to designing a better system in the east end must confront the following issues:

(i) The structure of the population is showing diminishing cohorts in the statutory school age groups for some time to come; this suggests that greater attention should be given to post school provision, and that there will be spare resources for the purpose.

(ii) The present population has passed through the school system with minimum benefit. At the very least, policy must be directed massively to compensate for this, again focusing priority on post school provision.

(iii) There is substantial alienation from the very idea of school, so some means must be found to accord post school education an independence and status in its own right.

(iv) Any plan for education in this or a similar area, must make its ideals and its design clearly visible on the ground, in the shape of accessible and welcoming places where an estranged population might once again feel inclined to re-establish a working contact with the education system.

(v) The new system must be designed upwards from a reappraisal of student needs, not downwards from what the existing institutional structure finds it convenient to deliver.

(vi) It must be made clear from the beginning that the new system will operate on a partnership basis, with the local community and its representatives having a direct input to the continuous improvement of the curriculum.

(vii) The new system must overcome the current fragmentation of management in education, as perceived by local people.

(viii) It must be made evident to all that policy for developmental education is an integral part of any package of policies for the social and economic developments of an area such as GEAR. All aspects of this package must be seen to be designed and implemented *together* at locality scale. This is a challenge to the traditional professional paradigms of public administration. Political will called the GEAR scheme into existence in the name of promoting community renewal. Political will must follow through to provide the means of achieving that.

5 Outline specification for a new system in GEAR
Organisational structure, curriculum content and style of teaching and learning are tightly inter-related. The ideal shape of one presents opportunities and constraints for the other. An overall design for a new system will be the result of a trialogue between these three elements. Moving from the problem issues defined above, we can sketch some specifications for a GEAR education system, in which the three fit together.

(a) Organisation
- (i) spatial structure – select one or more places from which to organise and 'sell' the education service, locating these points physically adjacent to other community service outlets and to shops (in brief – high profile at busy places). Extend the service from these centres using other places and means as appropriate.
- (ii) Management – incorporate a community information system within the educational plan; constitute local elected representatives and those representing interest groups as the foundation for a local education committee the functions of which will be to steer the system locally and to negotiate on its behalf with city, regional and central government authorities.

(b) Kind of curriculum
- (i) Scope – the system must give access to the full range of education facilities, from nursery to university; the curriculum structure therefore must provide
  - – direct local access to all the formal and informal curricula which can be organised at this scale; and
  - – easy 'plug in' links to the curricula of the higher education facilities of the city and region.

It is imperative that the range of curricula should not

be chosen for the area by some distant officials, but developed in consultation between area-based officials and local opinion.

(c) Style of teaching and learning

(i) This should be based on a model of partnership

– between professional teachers and other professionals, especially those like architects, engineers, planners, social workers, health workers and police, who are actively working in and for the area;

– between all professionals and citizens

the community is a considerable reservoir of human and material resources, which we have seldom sought to involve in the creation of its own education. (Batten, 1980, p. 33)

All professionals engaged in this kind of learning enterprise will themselves learn even as they impart their technical expertise, and many citizens will find themselves teaching about the workings of community and the economic history of their own area, from knowledge carried in family memories of shared experiences. Such knowledge is as vital to the development of plans for area development as is technical expertise.

(ii) Use of information technology

– this gives any area system the technical capacity to create archives of local information or teaching materials, to support 'distance learning' (home-based learning in this context), to interconnect with educational establishments outwith the area and to exploit materials produced by the national media and the Open University. Technology provides the means to bring a vast range of knowledge right to the doorstep of the citizens of GEAR and other areas. Any failure to do so will be organisational not technical.

6 A model for a local educational system

(a) Organisational structure Figure 14.3 outlines the basic organisational proposal – the creation of a cross-link, called here the Local Learning Centre, the main purpose of which

Model 1 – Multiple vertical organizational channels

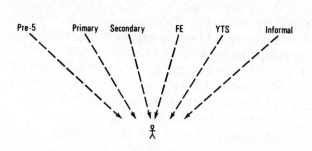

Figure 14.3a Existing organisational pattern of educational provision in a local area

Model 2 – Simplified structure with local co-ordination

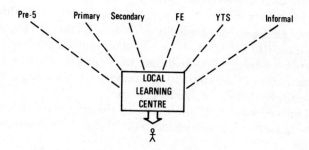

Figure 14.3b Locally based simplified system using coordination device of Local Learning Centre plus associated network

will be to gather together all the separate streams of educational effort currently travelling into GEAR in parallel, and to redesign the structure on a local network pattern and redeploy the skills accordingly to be visible to and attractive to local people.

To set this proposal into the actual geography of the Glasgow east end, it was necessary to examine patterns of accessibility and the present (rather scattered) distribution of other service outlets. It was evident that one major step in the renewal of this area would be a physical regrouping of needed services to exploit points of maximum local accessibility. This is important in the case of a relatively immobile population. One of the major proposals of Glasgow University's study of GEAR was that there should be a hierarchy of service points, one centrally located at Parkhead – the most accessible point for east enders – two additional centres linked to it (at Bridgeton and Shettleston), and three minor outlets – each a satellite to one of the three main centres. The whole geographic pattern should operate as a single delivery system for a unified service package. Our proposed model for the delivery of the community-based education service is given the same geographic pattern, in expectation that it would work in close geographic and functional co-operation with the other community services.

It is very important that the Learning Centre itself, being the key to the whole education network, should have a high profile location at the accessibility centre of GEAR – Parkhead. There it may be seen as the visible official commitment to treating all local post school education as an important thing (no longer to be hidden away in abandoned school buildings) – a place working for the community on a site where passers-by can 'drop in' en route to the shops or the bus stop, and find something to help or interest them.

The Learning Centre should be the organisational core of the education network and would have four interlocking tasks:

(i) It should co-ordinate the work of local schools, libraries, resource centres and arts centres in collaboration with its two sub-centres. In effect these three centres could act as neighbourhood '*campuses*' from which the education network could branch out.

(ii) It should provide the locus for the design of a totally *new curriculum package*, to which all people ought to have access on a 'life long' basis.

(iii) It should be an *expertise and research centre*. Employers currently link directly with the local schools to give pupils job experience. The Centre should encourage such contacts and back them up with special courses, information or advice and should provide the channel by which local firms collaborate in skill training programmes. It could also provide the missing contact with higher education establishments, inviting their help, and directing it to the places where it is needed. The universities in Glasgow are now much better disposed towards helping their parent city than they used to be. But so far as the east end goes they might as well be on another planet, so few are the operational links connecting them to it. Many have pointed out that some new kind of mechanism is required to support people at the very earliest stage of starting a business. The Scottish Business School tries to offer such help, but there is no framework which can put forward local need to it or bring its expertise to ground at this level.

(iv) It should develop a *Community Information Service* to provide clear, unified and accessible information for local people about what is going on in education.

Developing beyond that, it should also provide information on welfare rights, grants-in-aid, transport timetables, social events and so on – much of it in response to the needs of local community groups. Moving on in due time from this kind of administrative information, the Centre could become the site of a community data archive. The archive would take in information from research studies of the area made by both public service agencies and local schools (through their studies of the locality as part of a community orientated curriculum). It is extremely difficult at present even for professionals to assemble a range of research data for sub-areas within the city. The collecting agencies (the separate departments of local government) all work with different sets of area units. Data assembled within the area for administrative, educational or research purposes should be available to local people themselves – a fruitful interpretation of the ideal of 'freedom of information' and something which makes the idea of 'people's plans' a good deal more practicable than it is at present.

Figure 14.4 summarises the proposed organisational struc-

Jean Forbes

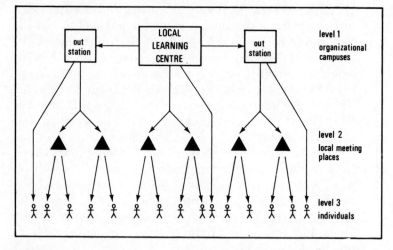

Figure 14.4 Organisational levels in the proposed locality education system

ture of the network system: the Learning Centre and its out-stations providing the nodes around which local clusters of educational activity are woven. Each node is both a potential site for incoming students (in those cases where curriculum items require to be specially housed at a central place) and a point from which learning is delivered out through the network to the cellular level (of ad hoc groups meeting at convenient places) and beyond to individuals. All work which would travel out would be fully backed up by the resources of staff and materials based within the campuses and be channelled through the organising centres into the network. Figure 14.5 shows the spatial pattern of the proposed system.

Several elements of the proposed campuses are already in place in GEAR and we can describe the gaps which clearly require to be filled. Secondary schools and public libraries exist close to the three chosen sites. However, there is only one resource centre (in St Mungo's school) and one arts centre (in Bridgeton). Two more of each are required. Resource centres are potentially very important as they provide learning materials, information, study space and reprographic facilities, all significant for many community activities. The Dolphin Arts Centre provides a vital point of contact between educationally impoverished people and a new world of self-

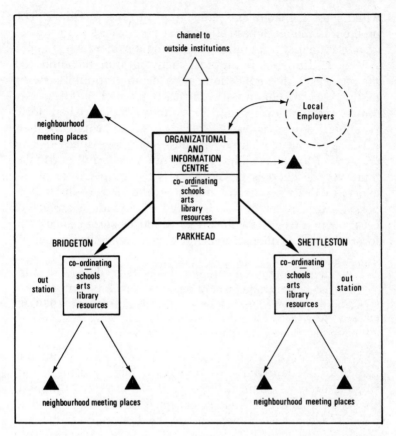

Figure 14.5 Geographic pattern of proposed local education network

expression and discovery of personal talent in art, music and drama.

(b) Kind of curriculum scope Many discussions over the last decade have circled around the question of 'relevance', raised in the Halsey Reports of 1970. Relevance to whom and for what purpose? And who is to decide? It is erroneous to seek a particular range of study topics which are deemed 'relevant' to the citizens of a deprived area. All knowledge is relevant to everybody. It is the traditional selection and even more the style of packaging and the style of measurement of success

which has alienated and failed the citizens of GEAR. The problem is therefore basically one of poor access (and thus of organisational failure) rather than of topic irrelevance as such.

If the traditional offerings lock many *out* from the enhanced life chances which education can bring, an unthinking swing to the kind of community curriculum which studies only things present locally and uses only impoverished local vocabularies can as easily lock the same people *in* their existing prison. It ill becomes those who have succeeded in the system to choose what is or is not a 'relevant' curricular topic for the citizens of GEAR. It is the proper duty of the expert to describe the full range of knowledge which it is possible to find in our society and to provide a system of access which will allow the only real judges of relevance – the local people – to choose their individual pathways through it.

> It is only the potential students themselves who can decide the most appropriate form of personal development at any particular stage of their lives . . . (Flude and Parrot, 1979, p. 106)

The difference between a deprived area and any other is just that the deprived area requires a more carefully constructed access system. If the organisational model proposed above for the GEAR area is accepted as an example of a possible access system, how should the description of its ideal curriculum run? The following list of major headings was given by Stonier (1979) and used with elaborations by Strathclyde Regional Council in its Strategy for Post Compulsory Education 1981. The present writer adds annotations.

Major Kinds of Curricula
- (i) *Education for employment* which would include:
  - basic literacy, numeracy and graphicity
  - courses for creating competences in marketable skills
  - professional
  - craft or trade
  - social and community
- (ii) *Education for life* which would include fostering ability to use 'the system':

- health education
- Organisation and managerial skills
- political education

(iii) *Education for self-development* which would include:
  - enhancement of existing work skills
  - developing new personal skills

(iv) *Education for pleasure* which would include leisure pursuits of all kinds:
  - sports
  - the arts

(v) *Education for the world* which would include:
  - locality-based environmental learning as a basis for participation in local development
  - understanding of national and international social, economic and environmental issues.

This outline packaging cuts right across traditional lines of the academic curriculum, but does not preclude major elements of that curriculum from being slotted into the framework. What is required is that this list be disaggregated further into desirable component elements and the levels of teaching ideally required. Then next, the operational sections should be defined, i.e.,

  (i) elements already provided locally in some form (most probably within the schools), requiring integration within an overall community syllabus;
 (ii) elements known to be provided elsewhere, e.g. in the institutions of further and higher education, to which access must be secured;
(iii) elements which need to be designed anew to fit local circumstances or to bring together for the first time a body of knowledge not hitherto found in a coherent form.

The Local Learning Centre will have the tasks of co-ordinating the links necessary to bring (i) and (ii) within a single access system, and of initiating the new designs of (iii).

Local environmental learning will be a particularly useful curriculum element in a deprived area. First, it is in these areas where most social, economic and physical change is taking place in our cities. It is just in such areas that most citizen participation is needed, yet where, because of the narrow educational inheritance, it is least strong. Local environmental learning would be a major investment in strengthening citizens' capability and confidence to contribute directly to the development decisions about their area.

Second, where there are numerous professionals working on the ground, there is a unique opportunity to involve a wide range of expertise in the teaching and learning about the local area – a two-way exchange of knowledge between citizens and technical workers becomes possible.

Third, the foundation of learning within familiar local contexts – whether social, economic, political or environmental – enables lines of enquiry to extend out from the locality to the national and world scales. Far from locking the student into parochial concerns, it enables him to see his local community issues within a larger whole (Forbes, 1986).

Useful experiments have already been conducted in this field in GEAR schools, linking class projects to traffic studies, playground designs and social surveys. all associated with current work by the SDA. There is a great opportunity to design such work into a future curriculum for adults.

(c) Style of operating the local education network One measure which would greatly facilitate the operation of a local system requires national policy changes which are not yet in sight. This is the extension to everyone of the right to paid educational leave. In the absence of this, the existence of a locally organised education network at least permits easy physical accessibility for part-time learning in those ranges of subjects which are provided by the local network. The guiding principle of the local system should be to deliver the learning programme as close to everyone's home as practicable (the 'meals on wheels' model of teaching and learning). This challenges remote institutions such as universities to take their knowledge to the community rather than expect citizens already alienated from big institutions, to come to them. The Local Learning Centre gives them the point of contact.

In the context of GEAR and similar areas, the curriculum should be packaged in manageable sized modules as far as possible rather than into long courses, rigidly fixed into the traditional academic year (September to June). Bryant (1982) noted the offputting effect of traditional academic packaging on unemployed people.

Modules allow wider flexibility of choice to prospective students, enabling them to tackle their learning projects in small bits and at their own pace. At the same time the OECD (1983) noted

> The modular organisation of curricula can allow
> individuals to build on their knowledge, skills and
> qualifications more quickly than through traditional long
> courses and thereby reduce the time horizon of vocational
> education. (p. 21)

Maximum use of information technology at local level will permit styles of teaching to be used which can release students from the need to travel further than the nearest terminal for parts of their learning. It can also be used to link the community information service to educational work.

In the GEAR area the technology should, however, be used strictly as the servant of an educational effort which should be founded on person to person contact. We must never lose sight of the enormous backlog of resistance to education and the deep-seated sense of personal inadequacy which affects this population. Before teaching and learning can get much further, education staff must accomplish a vast public relations task, and the continued operation of the system will require a sensitive and personal counselling service to support and guide prospective students.

Much has been made already about the need for local involvement in the design and operation of the proposed GEAR system. What has just been said may appear to make this difficult. Perhaps this will be so, at the beginning. But a local steering committee could be formed immediately by drawing in the elected regional and district and community councillors. These could be complemented by representatives of trade unions, local employers, residents' groups and the churches. Such a body would work with the technical staff of the local educational system and with others (perhaps from the universities and colleges) co-opted to advise.

The local system must be open progressively to incorporate locally derived ideas about its organisation, curriculum and style of teaching. This would be a continuous process of change, steadily refining and adapting the system to local needs, in a spirit of partnership. It will be important to set up in advance a way of monitoring what happens, so that achievements can be evaluated periodically. There are three purposes for such evaluations:

(i) to render an account to the public of successes (and failures);
(ii) to determine what aspects of the system's policy and organisation require adjustment;
(iii) to involve the steering committee and the technical officers in an exercise which is a learning experience in its own right.

7 Conclusion

The model presented here may sound elaborate and expensive. The baffled citizens of GEAR would regard it as a welcome simplification of a (to them) mysterious process. As regards expense, the models calls for one major item of capital outlay – the creation of the community learning centre – and assumes that much of the staffing of the new system would be done by relocating existing staff in new management patterns. New staff will be needed anyway in this area, regardless of the system used, if there is to be a realistic attack upon adult educational disadvantage. It is very doubtful if the modelled system would really be more expensive than a continuation of the existing fragmented and therefore wasteful one.

Those who would have to set up the new system face a difficult choice. Within a declared policy of attacking deprivation (the firm aim of Strathclyde Regional Council) one could work outwards slowly and apparently cheaply from the units one has on the ground (mostly schools) and use existing patterns of working to bring adults in. This is the 'administration-based solution'. Alternatively, one could take the opportunity offered by the special circumstances of GEAR to launch a radical experiment which departs from a failed tradition. This paper has described the possible shape of such an experiment, which is founded on the two principles of local level cross-linking and redesigning of educational offerings, and community involvement in the operation of the system. This is the 'area-based solution'.

The harsh financial circumstances in local government argue against experiment. Yet the incontrovertible facts about the state of educational need in GEAR demand something urgent and novel to provide the essential educational underpinning without which the other social and economic policies directed to this area will make little impression at all on the deprivation of its people.

15 CONCLUSIONS

David Donnison

In this final chapter we draw conclusions which may help people contending with the problems of urban renewal in other cities. This is not an evaluation of the GEAR project: we dwell on its mistakes only when there are positive lessons to be learnt from them. Nor is it a summary of our own recommendations to those responsible for the project. It is an attempt to draw on the experience of the people involved – including the people who live in the east end – and to pass on some of the lessons they have learnt from the successes and the failures of one of the biggest urban renewal schemes yet mounted in Europe.

We begin by recalling and clarifying the main problems to be tackled. They may seem obvious enough – and their symptoms certainly are – but their underlying causes are much more complex, and we cannot respond effectively to them unless those causes are properly understood. This account of the issues leads to a brief summary of the aims of an urban renewal programme. Then we turn to discuss action. This third section of the chapter may be read as a summary of the practical conclusions presented in earlier chapters, but the picture is painted with a broader brush as we focus on the larger themes which run through the whole book, and we say more than the evidence of earlier chapters would justify when it seems helpful to do so. We refer in the notes to the chapters we are drawing on to help readers who wish to turn back to them. Finally we draw some more general conclusions about urban policies and the styles of government appropriate for our times, about planning and planners, education and research.

The problems

The symptoms of urban decay are obvious enough: unemployment, squalor and disorder of various kinds, afflicting neighbourhoods where many of the people are particularly vulnerable to a harsh environment and the economic and social changes which create it – people who are unskilled;

pensioners, the sick and disabled; people caring for large families, or caring for smaller ones single-handed – many of them poor people who have nowhere else to go. Glasgow's east end is typical of the conditions to be found in many other old industrial cities of the western world.

These symptoms cluster in areas stricken by larger economic changes: the decline, reorganisation and rationalisation of obsolete forms of manufacturing, coupled with 'jobless growth' which enables more progressive enterprises to produce more with fewer workers, often switching their investment in productive machinery to more attractive smaller towns, and to places – far away, perhaps – where labour is cheaper, more docile, more easily redeployed and retrained. The cities which suffer most severely from these changes are those most firmly tied to the older industries, and those which prospered by doing things which are no longer needed – like (in Glasgow's case) provisioning, defending and trading with an empire, extracting coal and iron from deposits now exhausted, and building and maintaining a westward-voyaging merchant fleet. These problems are particularly severe in a time of depression, like the present, but they have deeper causes which will not be removed by an upswing in the national or worldwide economies.

This version of economic history is now widely understood, but the lesson took a painful long time to learn.[1] It was an important lesson because it showed that policies which assume that stricken cities and their most deprived areas can, with a little help, solve their own problems are bound to fail. That lesson may also suggest that, because a city's problems must be seen in these global terms, nothing can be done about them until the world economy takes off again or the revolution comes.

So it is important to remember that some countries not far off, with traditions not fundamentally different from our own, have managed their affairs much better. Sweden and Norway, for example, have unemployment rates running at about one-fifth of our own, and the living standards and future prospects which they offer to those who are out of work are much more generous than we offer to our unemployed. The assertion that 'there is no alternative' (whether to renascent free enterprise or to the revolution) is propaganda. However, the more successful alternatives worked out by other countries have a high political price. The Scandinavian model shows that an effective incomes policy, restraints on the export of capital, wholesale redeployments of labour, generous social security payments and effective retraining programmes – all of them measures which powerful institutions in Britain would fiercely resist – will be required. That will demand social solidarity and creative political capacities which Britain now lacks. But the development of these capacities has to begin in real places: in real communities, enterprises, trade unions and town halls. Glasgow's east end may be one of the places where these things are beginning to happen.[2]

Meanwhile citizens and civic leaders who take their responsibilities seriously cannot sit and wait for a change in the economic and political weather. Their cities may burn down around them if they do. It is in places like Clydeside, Belfast and Merseyside that the credibility of British government is being tested. Politicians, officials and other concerned citizens have to do their best to tackle the problems on their own doorstep, and in doing so they may make a larger contribution. 'Glasgow's Miles Better', the slogan of a campaign which represented a deep-rooted conviction of many people who took it up spontaneously throughout the city, could not have been so convincingly launched had the GEAR project not been at work for six years to bring some of Glasgow's revival to the east end. Newcastle is achieving a similar transformation. Britain will not be 'miles better' until many other cities are tackling similar problems effectively.

It is time to turn from these large issues to the local scale of action. The aim of urban renewal policies must be to enable people living in the most poverty-stricken neighbourhoods to achieve higher living standards, greater security and more freedom to make choices, and to do that in ways which do not merely filch these benefits from other impoverished neighbourhoods. To make progress in those directions we must first understand some of the basic mechanisms which give or withhold opportunities.

People live in households. Their capacity to 'get by' depends on the household's capacity to provide for its needs. The point is an obvious one, but it may remind us of several less obvious things. Households meet their needs by buying things in the 'formal' economy (going shopping, for example), by 'self-provisioning' (repairing their own cars, painting their own houses), and by securing things in various 'informal' economies: the 'black' market, the 'perks' and 'easements' attached to many jobs, and the economy of exchanges between relatives and neighbours (you help me fix my car and I'll help you paint your front room). The household's capacity to use all these economies depends very heavily on money, and earnings secured from work in the formal economy are far the largest source of money. (We can't exchange help in fixing cars and painting rooms unless we can afford motor spares and paint; it is difficult to keep in touch with friends and relatives if you cannot afford a telephone, a car or even bus fares; and opportunities for operating as suppliers of black markets are much greater for those who have telephones, cars, garden sheds, and the confidence and contacts which come from operating successfully in the legitimate, formal economy.) Thus, as jobs and earnings dwindle, the informal economies on which we all depend tend to dwindle too. The people who do best as customers or as suppliers of the markets in which goods and services change hands for dirty fivers out of the back pocket generally do best in the formal economy too. The same goes for whole neighbourhoods. Their residents' capacity to use all these economies depends partly on the composition of their households, and the stages of life they have reached: large households with several earners, for example, do better than small ones with none. These differences are often more important than differences between social classes. Thus a neighbourhood, like many in the east end, with a lot of pensioners living by themselves and a lot of lone parents caring for young children single-handed will be specially impoverished (Pahl, 1984).

Governments have to 'get by' too: to survive and win elections. Whatever their party, they tend in these bad times to do that by keeping the loyalty of majorities among the fully employed, the best organised, the more educated and skilled – the more demanding people. These are the people whose incomes have been rising in real terms, despite the depression of recent years; the people who have bought their own homes and put foreign holidays and the tourist trade among the most rapidly expanding industries. Meanwhile, when sacrifices have to be made, they tend to be borne by the less skilled, the marginally employed or unemployed, the unorganised.

In order to deliver social services economically, to keep potentially turbulent people under control, and to defend bureaucratic 'territories', the machinery of government tends to work through separate, specialised agencies in ways which fragment households and individuals and keep them powerless. Each service deals with a different 'need' through separate local offices whose territories form a jig-saw pattern which does not match the pattern chosen by any other service. (After six years of the GEAR project we were still unable to secure from any two public services sets of figures about their operations which dealt with the same areas.) Even within a social security office there are separate waiting rooms: one courteous, relaxed, with open counters and a plentiful supply of leaflets for the majority of workers who only come to claim insurance benefits; and the other, with chairs screwed to the floor, no readily available leaflets and massive barriers between staff and public, which deals with poorer claimants who depend on means-tested supplementary benefit. We traced a similar fragmentation, bewildering to ordinary people, in the way education is delivered to the public.[3] Low-paid temporary work is offered briefly to young workers on terms which may do more to prevent them from identifying solidly with the unemployed than to get them into lasting jobs. Public housing is usually distributed in ways which 'atomise' people, paying scant attention to family or community – despite the powerful loyalties these generate in a city like Glasgow.[4] The private sector operates in somewhat similar ways. The trade union which is prepared to defend workers' interests even to the point of bringing their industry to a halt will usually do little for them once they drop out of work – and may even ban them from union membership (McArthur, 1985).

These patterns are familiar and need not be traced at length. But the point which emerges from them is less widely understood: poverty is not distributed randomly or by accident. In the absence of any strong tradition of social solidarity, governments survive by keeping large and powerful groups happy and excluding those whose needs can be most easily disregarded. Glasgow's east end is one of the places where the trick is worked. (Middle-class people, we found, hardly ever go there, and those of them who work there do not live there.) The poor are the powerless – the people who can be most easily excluded without political turbulence from the opportunities available to the average skilled and prosperous worker. Thus policies for helping deprived people and deprived areas which do not address their powerlessness are unlikely to make a lasting impact because they are not dealing with the fundamental issue.

Aims
This brief review of the factors underlying urban deprivation should help us to formulate the aims of an effective urban renewal programme.

- It should make places nicer to live in. That will call for action inside the home, outside the home and throughout the surrounding neighbourhood to make physical improvements to buildings and the landscape, to manage polluting industry and traffic in more civilised ways, and to provide public spaces which are convenient, attractive and easy for people to supervise and control.
- More opportunities are needed for work which earns a decent wage from the formal economy, particularly for the long-term unemployed, and for people with several others depending on them. Simply to increase the numbers of jobs is not enough. Glasgow's east end, like most inner city areas, has far more work going on in it than most parts of the city. Additional jobs must be filled by those who most need them.
- In an area where most adults are not working it is equally important to increase other sources of cash income wherever possible, particularly for the unemployed, the disabled, pensioners and lone parents.
- More opportunities should be created for self-provisioning and for legitimate operations in the various informal economies – particularly for those now deprived of these opportunities. The steps which lead in that direction will vary for households in different circumstances. (For an isolated old man, opportunities of this sort may be best extended by enabling his married daughter to move closer

to him. For an active but unemployed couple, an allotment or a garden with a shed in it may be more helpful. A working couple may be looking for opportunities of buying a home of their own which they can improve or subdivide.)

– Development should be planned to create a pattern of buildings and land uses which brings within easier reach the things that people need – shops, post offices, doctors, public services, open spaces and churches. These patterns should help to define places, to identify communities and to develop humane relationships within them. (This sort of objective has sometimes been derided as naive physical determinism. But our own survey and earlier ones show that east enders are appalled by the dereliction wrought by slum clearance schemes and industrial closures and are genuinely grateful for the efforts now being made to heal these scars.)[5]

– Renewal will not succeed unless it attracts and retains a resident population which is more representative of those who live throughout the surrounding regions in terms of age, types of households and social class. This sort of objective has (with good reason) been derided when it sprang from the view that a deprived population must consist of inadequate people. That view was put to us by several of the professionals we met who work, but do not live, in the east end. It is not our view: the place is full of talented, effective people. But those in the main working age groups (between 25 and 50 years old) are thin on the ground. These are the people who bear the main responsibility for helping youngsters into jobs, for giving political leadership and establishing standards of behaviour. They number only 70 per cent of the (already rather low) proportion of the population in these age groups in the Strathclyde Region as a whole, and they have exceptionally large numbers of old people and of teenagers to care for.[6] Such demographic surpluses and shortfalls – characteristic of an area which has been losing people for a long time – lead to recurring overloads and cut-backs in schools, in the demand for housing of different types and in many other services from maternity to geriatric care.

– Decent housing of all types, sizes and tenures is therefore needed. Until recently, anyone in the east end who wanted to buy their own home was virtually compelled to move out. That deprives a community of many young families who could make an important contribution to its economy and its social life, and ensures that public and professional services – the schools, the police, health and social care – are provided and managed by people who do not live in the area. It also deprives the area of much the largest subsidy (tax relief on house-buyers' interest payments) now being put into housing – a subsidy which gives households greater freedom than tenants' subsidies do to build up and redeploy an asset in ways of their own choosing.

– Finally, an urban renewal programme should increase people's opportunities for acting collectively to meet needs which they define for themselves, to control the future development of their neighbourhoods and to deal with the public services on which they depend. That will call for initiatives from public services: initiatives which provide information in more 'user-friendly' fashion, which call upon officials to meet their customers on their own ground (not only bringing people individually to the officials' offices at the times which suit officials). These initiatives must take women seriously (for they were often the most effective representatives of their communities) and devolve power over real resources to local people wherever possible.

Even if it is successful, a demanding programme of this kind will not solve all the problems of the inner city. For that, national and global changes will be needed. Nevertheless, these aims provide a focus for the work to be done at a local scale in response to these problems. We turn next to the lessons to be learnt from the GEAR project.

Action
We traced the attempt to promote employment in the east end and in Clydebank on the other side of the city,[7] and confirmed the findings of studies made in other cities.[8] This part of the programme, carried through by the SDA, was initially the main innovation in the whole project. It succeeded in renovating derelict industrial areas which would not have been so effectively cleaned up in any other way. It does

morale good to see work going on in attractive, small workshops. And it should put the east end of Glasgow in a better position to seize new opportunities if the whole British economy revives in future. But the impact made on local rates of employment has been very small, and most of the enterprises attracted to the area would have set up somewhere on Clydeside and may therefore have been stolen from nearby areas. Those that are new are small and serve a local market, so their success may take work from other local enterprises.

Like many inner city areas, the east end already has far more jobs in relation to its population than most parts of the city, and the SDA has demonstrated that more can be brought there. The question is, who gets them? If it is the long-term unemployed who should be the centre of the target, our research suggests that less orthodox forms of not-for-profit 'community business', designed to meet the needs of the local community, do that more effectively. Some of these are now beginning in the east end. Meanwhile, if the creation of jobs is the main objective, regardless of who gets them, then public money may have been better spent on attracting private capital to build houses for sale in the neighbourhoods hitherto treated as 'no-go' areas by lenders and developers, on subsidising the improvement of private housing, and on the improvement of council housing, some of it done through the tenants' grants scheme which enabled tenants to modernise their own flats. This should not be taken as a reason for abandoning the building of small factories and workshops in inner city areas or the supporting programmes of advice and grant aid offered for new enterprises. But these policies can only be justified by arguments other than the reduction of local unemployment rates – arguments about morale, the quality of the environment and the attraction of private, wealth-creating capital to hithertho derelict industrial areas. To get people who have been out of work for a long time back into jobs other programmes will be needed: a more aggressive regional policy perhaps, direct support for local industry, and new forms of co-operative enterprise – together with larger changes operating on a national and international scale.

Meanwhile, a large proportion of east enders are pensioners, lone parents and disabled people who are not in the market for jobs. For them – as for many low paid workers entitled to housing benefit, family income supplement, free school meals and other help – their welfare rights may offer greater opportunities for increasing cash incomes. At the time of our study the Strathclyde Region's welfare rights service – the largest in the UK – estimated that one additional welfare rights worker devoting full-time to advice and advocacy would (at a cost of about £10,000 a year, together with overheads) bring an additional £150,000 a year in benefits to people living in the east end. This is money to which those people are already entitled by law. (Since then, staff of the service have improved their average 'score'. They secured a million pounds in back-pay from the social security system for homeless men living in hostels, plus a similar annual addition in benefits for them henceforth.)

Housing was the field to which the GEAR programme devoted its largest expenditures and to which we have devoted most space.[9] The scope of housing policy – often regarded as a burden imposed on the productive economy for questionable welfare purposes – has frequently been under-estimated. Glasgow, like Newcastle, Liverpool, Belfast and other cities, has shown that housing can be a leading factor in economic and social development. But, thus far, we have stumbled into this discovery, rather than making deliberate use of the regenerative powers which more carefully planned investment, co-ordinated with other services, could offer.

Private capital can be brought in to diversify tenures, modernise houses and improve the environment, even in the most unattractive areas, conferring these benefits not only upon newcomers but also upon the people already living there. But public expenditure has to lead the way, showing a solidly visible commitment to transform things, before private investment will follow. In Glasgow's east end that commitment took the form of publicly funded improvements carried out by housing associations in what had hitherto been privately owned housing, improvements made by the District Council to its own houses, and improvements made by owner-occupiers with the help of government grants, together with the environmental improvements which formed a major part of the whole GEAR project – all carried through without displacing local residents. In places where a lot of poor people live, that can only be done with the help of heavy subsidies.

The provision of cheap land by the District Council for house-builders then exerted an important influence in attracting private investment, once the other initiatives began to show what could be made of the east end.

The newcomers – first-time buyers, mostly – who bought the new houses were not, as we had feared they might be, outsiders with no commitment to the east end. They were people as strongly rooted in the area as their neighbours and probably making at least as great a contribution to its economy. The new houses are mostly quite small. The next step will be to provide larger houses which will enable these home-owners who wish to stay in the east end to do so when they have children and seek more space, a garden, and the other things a growing family needs.

Investment in housing will temporarily increase demands for construction work, and must, over the longer term, increase demands for a wide range of services which can together make a contribution to the city's economy because most of them have to be produced locally, unlike manufac-tured goods which may be made anywhere in the world. That increase may come about directly through expenditure on building, repairing and modernising houses, or indirectly by attracting to the area more home-owners who will spend money on repairing not only their houses but also their cars, washing machines, television sets and other equipment, and who seek other services nearby. A particularly vivid example of that process can be seen in the more central 'Merchant City' on the western corner of the GEAR area where the conversion of old warehouses and factories into flats has led to the development of new shops, pubs, hairdressers and other enterprises.

The development of new housing tenures may also play a part in strengthening the bonds which create a local commu-nity and give it greater control over its public services. The community-based housing associations, belonging to their own residents, which have modernised so many of Glasgow's tenements, the housing management co-operatives which took over responsibility for maintaining blocks of council housing and for allocating the houses themselves, and the homestead-ing schemes which enabled people to buy and recondition some of the least attractive council housing are now being followed by community ownership, or 'par value co-opera-tives', which will transfer blocks of council houses to their tenants (Whitefield, 1985). Together these show the influence which an innovative housing policy can exert on the community and the whole style of public administration – a point to which we return later.

The third main programme of work to which the GEAR scheme devoted resources was designed to improve the east end's physical environment.[10] Words alone can scarcely convey the scale of the devastation – the acres of rubbish and rubble, the rusting hulks of abandoned cars, the rainswept empty spaces between decaying and derelict buildings – left by completed slum clearance schemes, threatened road schemes, the abandonment of railway lines and the closure of factories. The squalor of this environment ranked high among the complaints of local people when the GEAR project was launched, but our survey and the discussions we had with groups and individuals in the east end show that the transformation wrought by the millions of pounds spent since then on landscaping, stone cleaning and the like have done a great deal to improve morale and to attract private investment.

But the cost of maintaining the landscape which has been created in the east end will be so high that much of it may eventually be allowed to run wild. We have therefore tried, by consulting local people, looking at other cities and the literature about them, and using our own imagination, to suggest other uses for this land which would meet real needs, cost less to maintain, and perhaps even raise a little revenue. More important, however, than a list of potential land uses are the principles which should guide a policy of this sort. Local people should be involved and consulted before decisions are made: local groups should, wherever possible, be given con-trol of the budget itself. Opportunities for 'self-maintenance' should be enlarged – by providing garden allotments and space for maintaining motor vehicles and learning to drive them, for example. And it must be remembered that those most crowded in their own homes and most deprived of opportunities for recreation often cannot afford to travel far; for them, attractive small open spaces widely scattered through the city will be more useful than larger attractions a long way off.

Policies for recreation pose closely related questions.[11] The dilemma central to this field is the choice to be made between high, competitive attainment and heavy usage on the one hand, and, on the other, the less glamorous provisions required to enlarge the opportunities of those now most deprived of recreation. The former priority would, in the east end, give first place to the development of the Celtic football ground – home of the first club to win the European cup for Britain – together with a major sports complex in its vicinity attracting participants and spectators from all over the Region. The latter priority would call for more generous provision for pensioners, women, the unemployed and those without cars – overlapping groups now most likely to be starved of opportunities for recreation. For them the priorities would be quite different. Pensioners need cheap and readily accessible resources: free television licences might be one of the most highly valued things they could be offered. National surveys suggest that women tend to value recreation particularly for the opportunities it affords for meeting people and getting to know them. Faced with such choices, any practical politician will want a bit of both, and rightly too. Again, a constant theme of policy should be the attempt to develop community-based projects, as has been very successfully done in Easterhouse, not far off, where the local Festival Society produced an award-winning drama, a unique mural and other remarkable projects.

Linked with all these issues are the problems of communication.[12] These have been exacerbated by the lack of any mechanism for relating decisions about different means of communication. Paving and lighting – among the first functions of local government – have been neglected, while huge sums of central government money have for years been dangled over a route for a major highway along which development has been blighted by the resulting uncertainty. But if this highway (which to us seemed to lose its justification owing to other changes which had taken place since it was first proposed) were to be abandoned, the money saved by that decision could only be used for public transport if used for capital expenditure. That would not, for example, enable the city to increase its subsidies for bus or rail services. For frail or housebound people living on their own, a free telephone might be a greater blessing than any means of transport, but public discussion of communications seldom extends to proposals of this kind which are at best regarded as a matter for the social work or social security services. This has clearly been the field of public service which has proved most difficult to incorporate effectively and humanely in the renewal of Glasgow and other cities.

Our study dealt with several other fields – notably education[13] and health care.[14] The need to rebuild communities shattered by wholesale redevelopment and to make their resources more accessible in an area which has lost two-thirds of its population within a generation – these were recurring themes. People suffer real hardships owing to our neglect of these basic concerns of good planning: the patients who will be walking or bussing further than they need have done to see a doctor in one of the awkwardly sited, new health centres; the pensioners clustered in Dalmarnock's tower blocks where there is no pharmacy within reach because a major road project has for twenty years threatened to cut through the neighbourhood and no one will build shops there; a social work area team and a major police station located on sites ill-suited for contact with the public which were chosen because the authorities happened to get their hands on land or buildings – these are some of the more striking examples.

Education presents special opportunities and problems in an area where the great majority of people left school at the earliest possible age with no qualifications, and where there are too few opportunities for them to gain second chances – no College of Further Education, for example, and no regular adult education class provided by University teachers. Various different programmes for adults are now developing, provided under different rules by teachers trained in different ways and belonging to different trade unions, and there is no single source of information about them all. There is an urgent need to get this act together. We have argued for the development of a network of learning opportunities which would operate from buildings of various kinds in each of the most accessible local centres within the east end, and a community college incorporating some of these ideas is in fact to be set up. The experience which east enders gained in school is not one which readily attracts them back into school buildings, and teachers will have to try new strategies in new settings if people are to get the second chances they need.

Some of the most productive learning we encountered took place when groups with an agenda of their own sought help with problems they defined for themselves: council tenants learning how to set up a housing management co-operative; agoraphobics meeting regularly in a 'community flat' to organise mutual support for each other; homeless men learning how to deal with hostel managers and social security officials and – when offered a flat – learning how to cook and shop for themselves; these are examples we recall. The 'teaching' was done by staff of the housing, health and social work services, and by the learners themselves. None of it was done by people officially described as 'teachers'.

Conclusion
We draw this discussion to a close by taking a brief look at some of the broader issues it touches upon. Glasgow's experience underlines the importance of sustained, consistent public leadership at national, Regional, District and more local scales. The conflicting and constantly changing policies to be seen in other cities (Parkinson, 1985; Buck et al., 1986) have been less successful. The best things happened as people in different services and different authorities looked beyond the confines of their departmental functions to grapple with broader issues on which they could collaborate. The vital contribution of the SDA was to provide some of this leadership and the resources for new initiatives on remarkably open-ended terms. For that they needed a free hand to develop a programme within broadly defined guidelines. The fact that the SDA lacked the powers of an Urban Development Corporation and therefore had to gain the support of the local authorities was probably an advantage. The fact that the area chosen for renewal was inhabited by some 40,000 fairly belligerent people who compelled the Agency to set up an office in the east end and deal frankly with them was another advantage. The London Docklands Development Corporation, which has never gained the same local credibility, and the Merseyside Development Corporation, which has carved out for itself a territory which contains no resident population at all, offer contrasting and less happy examples. In both cities

the local authorities failed to get their act together, and the central government failed to find ways of working effectively with them. The GEAR project was launched in a hurry with little experience to guide those responsible for it. Since then the SDA has perfected a much more rigorous contract for its renewal projects, specifying more limited objectives to be attained in shorter periods of time. These procedures look more businesslike and must be more attractive for officials accounting for public expenditure, but they may prove less fruitful in the long run.

Other lessons of the GEAR project have a wider relevance, not confined to urban renewal. The original intention of those responsible for it was to do better than the traditional clearance schemes which had wreaked such havoc in the past. Those clearance schemes were an example of the functional style of administration characteristic of many public bodies at that time: a centralised style, with strong links through chief officers and their committee chairmen to central departments of government responsible for the same service. That style persists today, as road planning and many branches of the health and education services show. But the GEAR project is beginning to create a system which is more issue-oriented and area-focused, and less narrowly service-oriented. (What can be done about Glasgow's east end? is the kind of question addressed by the new approach – not How many unfit houses can we replace?) The new system also pays more attention to jobs and incomes, being more economically oriented than its predecessors which assumed that the local economy would somehow look after itself, no matter how badly it was neglected, and that social benefits would reach all those who were entitled to them, without any special investment in welfare rights work.

The new system calls for closer collaboration between the public and private sectors. Our chapters on jobs and housing show that this is beginning to develop. Equally important, the system must be to a greater extent community-based. Politicians and officials are trying harder to get alongside the groups they serve, to listen to their perception of the problems, and to give them some control over the resources available for solving them. These developments are only beginning: of the services we have studied, it is the Housing Department which has probably taken them furthest in its reliance on housing associations for renewal work, and its attempts to develop housing management co-operatives and community owner- ship among its tenants. But the SDA has set an example in this respect too. 'They', we were told several times by community activists, 'are the people who will come to our meetings, and send the same person to our next meeting – in the evenings and at weekends too.' (Health service officials and highway planners were less kindly contrasted with them.)

The scope of these changes should not be exaggerated. Growing realism about the limitations of the state may encourage an ill-judged romanticism about 'privatisation' and 'community' that will lead to destructive disillusionment. The state must continue to give sustained leadership if the private sector and community-based groups are to play their parts effectively. The old, service-oriented, functional system of administration developed to cope with the tasks of the heroic age when the National Health Service was created, secondary education was reorganised, the motorways were built, and the world's largest slum clearance schemes were carried through. That system now needs to be modified, not scrapped, to cope with new tasks in a new economic environment.

Town planners have sometimes been told that renewal projects of the kind we have described, emphasising economic development and community policies, make their traditional skills obsolete. That is completely untrue. The days when the largely negative controls operated by planners could steer development into chosen places and forms have indeed gone in cities like Glasgow. If there is to be any development at all in that city's east end, public authorities have to take the lead in bringing it about and persuading the private sector to follow – and that means that agencies like the SDA, the Housing Corporation and, in local government, the housing departments play very important parts in shaping the process of urban development and renewal. But sensitivity to the physical environment and an imaginative capacity for improv- ing it, the ability to understand patterns of movement and accessibility and the ways in which communities can be strengthened or weakened by the spatial arrangement of activities on the map and the communications which link them all – all these are as important as ever. These skills need to be more closely related than hitherto with those of the people concerned with industrial and community development, housing, welfare rights, education and other services. But Glasgow's east end shows only too clearly the disasters which follow from neglect of the traditional concerns of land use planners.

These conclusions lead to a final comment on their implications for research and education in our field. Along with the old, centralised, functional style of government went an assumption that each service should be staffed by a profession armed with the authority conferred by a distinctive training approved by its own professional institute. The lawyers and doctors long ago provided the classic models and planners sought to follow them, along with the housing managers, social workers, education welfare officers and many others. The processes of urban management which we have described, and the new styles of government they are helping to call into being, do not fit this pattern at all well. The housing department of the future, if Glasgow's is any guide, will have to recruit people from the private developers' and building societies' worlds, from social work, community work, welfare rights work and other fields – people sharing a common concern for enlarging people's choices and improving housing conditions in all sectors of the market. Similar patterns are emerging in other public services.

Turning to the training of these people, it becomes clear that town planners, 'housers', industrial development officers, leisure and recreation managers and community workers have a common interest in the growth, decline and renewal of human settlements. They need a common body of knowledge based on shared research, dealing – if a label of some sort be needed – with 'urban studies'. This is a field, not a separate discipline: a field of work focused on related problems of practice and policy to which any academic discipline that seems relevant should be applied. Town planners, like 'housers' and others in this group, will need some special training of their own and perhaps an institute to speak for their profession. But their distinctive training should be regarded as a specialism built on a core of studies common to all the professions concerned with urban development, and should be pursued alongside the training of these closely related professions.

Our determination to extract useful lessons from the story we have told may encourage optimistic readers to believe that these lessons have been learnt and are now being applied in Glasgow and other cities. If so, they would be wrong. Many local services still retain a centralised, functional style of working which makes fruitful collaboration with other services very difficult and any transfer of power to the people whom they serve impossible. Central government, far from giving priority to urban renewal, has withdrawn funds on a massive scale from the support of regional policies, from local government in the old industrial cities and from the building and modernisation of housing. Housing benefits for households with low incomes are next on the list for cuts. All these expenditures play central parts in policies for urban renewal. Meanwhile, public resources have been poured into defence and into mortgage interest tax relief for house-buyers – programmes which mainly benefit the more affluent southern parts of Britain. Civic leadership, so badly needed in stricken cities, is not encouraged by a succession of unpredictable and often punitive central interventions which have destroyed in many local authorities the conviction that they have a valued contribution to make within a predictable financial environment that makes imaginative forward planning possible (Parkinson, 1985). The treatment of grants, amounting to nearly £3 million, secured by the SDA and the Strathclyde Regional Council for the GEAR project from the EEC, illustrates this pattern. They led ultimately to compensating reductions in central government funding for both bodies which meant that nearly all this money ultimately found its way into the Treasury's coffers. Only violence on the streets seems briefly to attract fresh resources for the inner cities.

But to abandon hope of progress and await instead a new government or the turbulent events which may jolt the present government into new policies would be as fatuously complacent as to assume that present policies will put things right. A new regime, more friendly towards the inner cities than its predecessors, would face the same problems and be little better equipped to deal with them unless we use the experience now being gained to formulate better ways of tackling these problems.

That is the true significance of the GEAR project. Even

when the world economy offers more opportunities for expansion and we have national, economic and social policies better equipped to seize them, a great deal of remedial action will have to be taken at the local level if the old inner city areas – or the even more impoverished peripheral housing schemes[15] – are to gain a share of these opportunities. It is to the experience of cities like Glasgow, which have done more than most to work out remedies, that people will then turn for guidelines. Some of that experience will then be seen to offer broader guidance for the general development of policy and practice throughout local government, and for research and teaching in the field of urban studies.

Notes

1   As we show in Chapters 2 and 3.

2   Some other places are mentioned in Chapter 13.

3   Chapter 14.

4   These loyalties are discussed more fully in Chapter 1.

5   Chapter 8.

6   Chapter 1.

7   Chapter 4.

8   Some of them reviewed in Chapters 2 and 13.

9   Chapters 5-7.

10 Chapter 8.

11 Chapter 10.

12 Chapter 11.

13 Chapter 14.

14 Chapter 9.

15 Chapter 9 shows that Drumchapel – not the most deprived of Glasgow's peripheral schemes – is in many ways much more impoverished than the east end.

APPENDIX

GEAR SURVEY 1982 METHODOLOGICAL REPORT
Social and Community Planning Research

1 Introduction

This report outlines the methodological details of a survey carried out by Social and Community Planning Research (SCPR) for the University of Glasgow in connection with the Glasgow Eastern Area Renewal (GEAR) Project. The project was instigated in 1976 and a previous survey of households was carried out in 1977/8. The aim of this survey was to investigate social aspects of the project by asking the residents themselves what they see as the problems of the area, and to learn about the people who live there. It was carried out by means of personal interviews conducted amongst a sample of households within the GEAR area. Although each interview was conducted with only one respondent per household (either the head of household or the housewife) information was sought on all household members. Where possible comparability was maintained with the 1977/8 Household Survey of the area.

The timetable for the survey was tight. Development work on the questionnaire started with SCPR in late December 1981, piloting in January 1982, main fieldwork from mid-February to early April, and tabulations on the data by the end of April.

2 The sample and response rate

A random sample of rateable units within the GEAR project area was selected by the University of Glasgow from the valuation roll. This source, updated in April 1981, was considered to provide the most up-to-date list of names and addresses for the area. Units were selected within the various ward boundaries and, since these do not coincide with GEAR areas, a further identity code was provided for each sampled address so that its more precise location would be identified.

Interviewers were provided with the surname of the occupier, as listed on the valuation roll, for each sampled unit. If only one household was found to live at a unit, this household was interviewed regardless of whether or not they bore the same name as the listed occupier. In cases where more than one household was found to live at a sampled unit, the listed occupier's household was interviewed, unless that household had moved, in which case the first household to be contacted by the interviewer was interviewed.

The person interviewed within each selected household was either the head of household or the housewife. At the sampling stage one-third of addresses were pre-designated as addresses at which the head of household must be interviewed. At the remainder the interviewer could interview either the head of household or the housewife, giving preference, however, to the head if both were equally available. Many of those interviewed fulfilled both the role of head and of housewife in their household (for instance, a widow or a single parent). As a result only 20 per cent of those interviewed were housewives in households in which another member was a head. Of the 80 per cent classified as household heads a large proportion were also housewives. 46 per cent of those interviewed were men and 54 per cent women.

A total of 1,300 sampled addresses were provided by the University of Glasgow at the start of the fieldwork period in the hope of achieving a final sample of some 1,000 completed interviews. A further eighty-nine addresses were added to the sample at a later date when the extent of ineligible or 'out of scope' addresses (due mainly to vacant or derelict properties) became apparent.

Of the 1,389 issued addresses, 258 (19 per cent) were found to be outside the scope of the survey (see Table A.2) thus leaving an 'in scope' sample of 1,131 addresses. The total number of analysable interviews achieved was 862. This represents a response rate of 76 per cent.

The principal reasons for non-response at 'in scope' addresses were either non-contact with potential respondents, or refusal on their part to participate. It is possible that some of those classified as non-contacts may have been vacant dwellings, and therefore technically out of scope. Detailed figures for all the non-response categories are shown in Table A.2.

Table A.1 shows the breakdown of households in the final achieved sample between the different wards.

Appendix

Table A.1: Achieved sample size by ward

	No.	%
Base: All respondents	862	100
Tollcross	268	31
Parkhead	218	25
Dalmarnock	145	17
Carntyne	80	9
Calton	75	9
Camlachie	58	7
Cambuslang East/Carmyle-Springboig	9	1
City/Townhead	9	1

3 The pilot survey

The questionnaire was tested in a pilot survey. Four interviewers, each working in a different part of the GEAR project
area between them carried out a total of twenty-three pilot
interviews. They were provided with written instructions and
briefed by telephone beforehand. No specific addresses were
issued to them; they found their own respondents within the
area that they were working, ensuring only that broad quota
requirements were fulfilled – such as an even age spread, a
good mix of men and women and of households varying in
size. Half of their interviews were carried out with people
who were heads of households and half with housewives, and
as many as possible with respondents who were in full-time
employment. These different quota criteria ensured that all
sections of the questionnaire were tested out and different
types of interviews obtained.

As in the main survey, the pilot interviews were carried out
in respondents' own homes. They involved not only question-
ing the respondent directly about himself or herself but also
obtaining certain socio-demographic details about all the other
household members, including children. Twelve out of the
twenty-three interviews were tape-recorded.

The outcome of the pilot interviews and of the survey
procedure in general was discussed at length with the
interviewers at a pilot debriefing attended by the various
University staff who were involved in the project. As a result
of this meeting and of listening to the tape-recorded interviews, the pilot questionnaire was developed into the final
version used in the main survey.

Table A.2: Statement of response

	No.	%
Addresses		
Issued	1389	
Found to be out-of-scope		
— vacant/derelict	206	
— demolished	22	
— business/industrial premises only	6	
— duplicate/interviewed on pilot	3	
— non-residential institution	1	
Assumed to be out-of-scope		
— not traced	20	
Total out-of-scope	258	
Total in-scope	1131	
Households		
Total in-scope	1131	100
Total at which analysable interview conducted	862	76
Total at which no analysable interview conducted	269	24
Reasons for non-response		
Non contact (total)	109	10
— no contact with anyone at address	90	8
— selected person away/in hospital during survey period	12	1
— selected person not contacted (e.g. never in)	7	1
Refusal (total)	107	10
— selected person personally refused	52	5
— complete refusal of information about occupants	36	3
— selected person broke appointment and could not be recontacted	13	1
— refusal, on behalf of selected person, by someone else in household	6	1
Other reasons for non-response (total)	53	5
— material lost in post	22	2
— selected person ill (at home) during survey period	13	1
— selected person senile/incapacitated	10	1
— incomplete questionnaire	8	1

There were three separate sections to the questionnaire: the main part which related directly to the respondent, an additional section which enquired about any others aged 16 years or over living in the household, and a further short section on any children aged 15 years or younger living there. The information relating to additional adults or children was either collected 'by proxy' from the respondent or, if the other household members were at home at the time of the interview, by interviewing them directly.

Broadly, the topics covered: awareness of the GEAR project, the area lived in, housing, social activities, shopping, transport, socio-demographic characteristics, activity status, employment and job details, and qualifications. Five different show cards were used in connection with the questionnaire at different points throughout the interview.

4 Data collection

The interviews lasted about 45 minutes on average. Their duration depended to a large extent on the size of the household and the amount of information to be collected.

A total of thirty-seven interviewers carried out the field-work. Each interviewer attended one of two full-day briefing conferences. Interviewing took place between 16 February and 14 April 1982.

5 Data verification and analysis

A number of quality control checks were carried out on the interviewers' work. They included personal supervision of initial interviews by an experienced supervisor, 'early work checks' where the first four or five completed questionnaires were thoroughly checked through and any errors pointed out to the interviewer concerned, and personal recalls where a supervisor went back to an address some time after the interview had been conducted to check that it had been conducted correctly.

All completed questionnaires were edited manually for any clerical errors. Where necessary, new codes were added to existing code lists. The socio-economic grouping of the respondent and of all 'additional adults' was coded, using 1971 census definitions instead of the 1981 version so that comparability could be maintained with the results of the previous GEAR survey carried out in 1977/8.

The data were then transferred to punch-cards and subject to a computer edit. Any internal inconsistencies revealed in the data by this edit were checked back to the relevant questionnaire.

A total of 259 computer tables were produced by SCPR in addition to three different hole counts of the data. The

University of Glasgow later made further analyses of the data.

All the questionnaires and show cards used in the survey were submitted with the longer version of this report sent to the University of Glasgow, but shortage of space made it impossible to reprint them here. The editors of the book will provide copies for anyone who wishes to see them.

BIBLIOGRAPHY

ABERCROMBIE, P. and MATTHEW, R. (1949), *The Clyde Valley Regional Plan 1946*, Edinburgh, HMSO.

ALDERTON, R. (1984), 'Urban development grants – lessons from America' in *The Planner*, Vol. 70, No. 12, pp. 19-21.

AMA GREEN GROUP (1985), *Green Policy*, London, Association of Metropolitan Authorities.

ANDERSON, N. (1961), *Work and Leisure*, New York, Free Press.

APPS, P. (1981), *A Theory of Inequality and Taxation*, Cambridge University Press.

BALL, MOG, TAYLOR, JOHN and BLEZARD, PAUL (1985), *First Lap: Setting up a Motor-Cycle Trail Park*, London Community Projects Foundation.

BARNETT, J. R. and NEWTON, P. (1977), 'Intra-urban disparities in the provision of primary health care: an examination of three New Zealand urban areas', *Australia and New Zealand Journal of Sociology*, Vol. 13, No. 1, pp. 60-68.

BARRETT, S. and HEALEY, P. (1985), *Land Policy: Problems and Alternatives*, Aldershot, Gower.

BASSETT, K. A. and SHORT, J. R. (1981), 'Housing policy and the inner city' in *Transactions of the Institute of British Geographics*, New Series, Vol. 6, No. 3, pp. 293-312.

BATELY, R. and EDWARDS, J. (1978), *The Politics of Positive Discrimination*, London, Tavistock.

BATTEN, ERIC (1980), 'Community education and ideology: the case for radicalism' in Colin Fletcher and Neil Thompson (eds), *Issues in Community Education*, Lewes, The Falmer Press.

BEVAN, J. (1985), 'Docklands dream is taking shape', *Sunday Telegraph*, 19 May.

BEVERIDGE, W. H. (1944), *Full Employment in a Free Society*, London, HMSO.

BILIANA, CICIN-SAM (1980), 'The costs and benefits of neighbourhood revitalisation', pp. 49-76 in D. B. Rosenthal (ed.), *Urban Revitalisation*, London, Sage Publications.

BOOTH, S. A. S., PITT, D. C. and MONEY, W. J. (1982), 'Organisational redundancy? A critical appraisal of the GEAR project', *Public Administration*, Vol. 60, No. 1.

BOWN, LALAGE (1982), 'Particpation in learning for power or powerlessness', *Journal of Community Education*, Vol. 1, No. 3.

BOYLE, R. and WANNOP, U. (1982), 'Urban initiatives and the SDA: the rise of the Area Project' in *Fraser of Allender Institute Quarterly*

Economic Commentary, Vol. 8, No. 1.

BRENNAN, T. (1957), 'Gorbals: a study in redevelopment' in *Scottish Journal of Political Economy*, Vol. 4, No. 2., p. 122.

BRENNAN, T. (1959), *Reshaping a City*, Glasgow, House of Grant.

BROADBURY, K. and DOWNS, A. (1981), *Do Housing Allowances Work?*, Washington D.C., Brookings Institute.

BROOKE, JANE (1982), 'Planning for themselves: the GEAR Schools Environmental Improvement Competition', *The Planner*, Vol. 68, No. 3.

BROOKFIELD, STEPHEN (1983), *Adult Learners, Adult Education and the Community*, Milton Keynes, Open University Press.

BRYANT, IAN (1982), 'The educational needs of the long-term unemployed', University of Glasgow, Department of Adult and Continuing Education (Mimeo).

BUCK, NICK, GORDON, IAN and YOUNG, KEN (1986), *The London Employment Problem*, Oxford University Press.

BUTT, J. (1971), 'Working class housing in Glasgow 1851-1914' in S. D. Chapman (ed.), *The History of Working Class Housing*, Newton Abbot, David and Charles.

CADMAN, D. (1982), 'Urban change, Enterprise Zones and the role of investors' in *Built Environment*, 7, 1.

CASSELL, M. (1985), 'Why new banks may appear on the Thames', *Financial Times*, 5 September.

CASTELLS, M. (1983), *The City and the Grassroots*, London, Edward Arnold.

CENTRAL ADVISORY COUNCIL FOR EDUCATION (ENGLAND) (1967), *Children and their Primary Schools*, HMSO (Plowden Report)

CHAIRMEN'S POLICY GROUP (1982), *Leisure Policy for the Future*, London, Chairmen's Policy Group.

CHECKLAND, S. G. (1981), *The Upas Tree: Glasgow 1875-1975*, University of Glasgow Press.

CHETWYND, K. (1984), 'Garden festivals: planning potential' in *The Planner*, Vol. 70, No. 7, pp. 23-5.

CHURCH OF ENGLAND (1985), *Faith in the City: A Call for Action by Church and Nation*, London, Church House Publishing.

CITY OF GLASGOW DISTRICT COUNCIL (1984a), *Annual Housing Review 1983*, Glasgow, GDC.

CITY OF GLASGOW DISTRICT COUNCIL (1984b), *Housing Plan 7*, Glasgow, GDC.

CITY OF GLASGOW DISTRICT COUNCIL (1985a), *Annual Housing Review 1984*, Glasgow, GDC.

CITY OF GLASGOW DISTRICT COUNCIL (1985b), *Community Ownership in Glasgow*, Glasgow, GDC.

CITY OF GLASGOW DISTRICT COUNCIL (1985c), *Housing Plan 8*, Glasgow, GDC.

Bibliography

CLAPHAM, D. and KINTREA, K. (1986), 'Rationing choice and constraint: The allocation of public housing in Glasgow' in *Journal of Social Policy*, 15, pp. 51-67.

COMMITTEE OF PUBLIC ACCOUNTS (1986), *The Urban Programme*, HC Paper 81, 1985-6, London, HMSO.

COMMUNITY DEVELOPMENT PROJECTS (1974) *Inter-Project Report*, CDP Information and Intelligence Unit.

CORPORATION OF THE CITY OF GLASGOW (1960), *The Survey Report of the City of Glasgow Development Plan Quinquennial Review 1960*, Glasgow.

CORPORATION OF THE CITY OF GLASGOW (1972), *Areas of Need Report*, Glasgow.

CURDS (1984), 'Functional Regions Factsheet', No. 9.

DAMER, S. (1974) 'Wine Alley: the sociology of a dreadful enclosure' in *Sociological Review*, 22, pp. 221-48.

DAMER, S. (1976), 'Property relations and class relations in Victorian Glasgow', Centre for Urban and Regional Research Discussion Paper, No. 16, University of Glasgow.

DAMER, S. (1980), 'State, class and housing: Glasgow 1885-1919' in Melling (ed.) (1980b).

DAVIES, J. G. (1972), *The Evangelistic Bureaucrat*, London, Tavistock.

DAWKINS, W. (1985), 'Labour looks to the local "resistance fighters" ', *Financial Times*, 19 August.

DAWSON, D., JONES, C., MACLENNAN, D. and WOOD, G. (1982), *The Cheaper End of the Owner-occupied Housing Market: An Analysis for the City of Glasgow 1971-1977*, Edinburgh, Scottish Economic Planning Department.

DENNIS, N. (1971), *Public Participation and Planner's Blight*, London, Faber.

DEPARTMENT OF EDUCATION AND SCIENCE (1967), *Children and their Primary Schools* (The Plowden Report), London, HMSO.

DEPARTMENT OF THE ENVIRONMENT (1973), *Making Towns Better*, London, HMSO.

DEPARTMENT OF THE ENVIRONMENT (1977a), *Policy for the Inner Cities*, Cmnd 6845, London, HMSO.

DEPARTMENT OF THE ENVIRONMENT (1977b), *Recreation and Deprivation in the Inner Urban Areas*, London, Department of the Environment.

DEPARTMENT OF THE ENVIRONMENT (1977c), *Inner Area Studies: Summaries of Consultant's Final Reports*, London, HMSO.

DEPARTMENT OF THE ENVIRONMENT (1979), *Dwelling and Housing Survey*, London, HMSO.

DEPARTMENT OF THE ENVIRONMENT (1981), *Ministerial Guidelines to Local Authorities*, July, London, DoE.

DEPARTMENT OF THE ENVIRONMENT (1982), 'Minutes of Evidence' in *The*

Problems of Management of Urban Renewal, Vol. II, Third Report from the Environment Committee, HC18II, London, HMSO.

DEPARTMENT OF THE ENVIRONMENT (1983), 'Guidance notes on the appraisal of urban programmes projects concerned with economic development'.

DEPARTMENT OF THE ENVIRONMENT (1985), *New Houses from Old*, Urban Housing Renewal Unit, London, DoE.

DOMENACH, J.-M. (1959), 'Loisir et travail' in *Esprit*, Vol. 87, No. 274, pp. 1103-10; quoted in Anderson, 1961.

DONNISON, D. V. *et al.* (1982), *GEAR Review: Social Aspects*, Department of Town and Regional Planning, University of Glasgow.

DONNISON, D. V. *et al.* (1983), *The Social Impacts of the GEAR Programme*, Reprinted by the Department of Town and Regional Planning, University of Glasgow to the Scottish Development Agency.

DUMAZEDIER, J. *et al.* (1961), 'Les loisirs dans la vie quotidienne' in *Encyclopédie Française*, T.XIV, 56.6; quoted in Anderson, 1961.

DUMAZEDIER, J. (1967), *Toward a Society of Leisure*, New York, Free Press.

ENGLEMAN, S. (1977), 'The move into council housing: The effect on quit rates' in *Urban Studies*, Vol. 14, pp. 161-8.

FIELDER, S. (1985), 'Low cost home ownership in Glasgow 1977-1983', Discussion Paper 7, Centre for Housing Research, University of Glasgow.

FLUDE, RAY and PARROT, ALLAN (1979), *Education and the Challenge of Change*, Milton Keynes, Open University Press.

FOGARTY, T. (1984), 'A study of benefits: how to evaluate financial subsidies implicit in publicly aided rehabilitation for home-owning', Pennsylvania, University of Pennsylvania (Mimeo).

FORBES, JEAN (1986), 'Continuing education and participation' in John Smyth (ed.), *Learning for Living*, Glasgow, Scottish Environmental Education Council.

FORBES, JEAN and McBAIN, I. D. (1967), *The Springburn Study*, University of Glasgow.

FORREST, R. *et al.* (1978), 'The inner city: in search of the problem', CURS WP No. 64, University of Birmingham.

FOTHERGILL, S. and GUDGIN, G. (1982), *Unequal Growth*, London, Heinemann.

FREESTONE, R. (1975), 'On urban resource allocation: the distribution of medical practitioners in Sydney', *Geographical Bulletin*, Vol. 7., pp. 14-25.

GEDDES, P. (1949), *Cities in Evolution*, London, Williams and Morgate.

GIBB, A. (1982), *Glasgow: The Making of a City*, London, Croom Helm.

GIBB, A. (1983) *Glasgow: The Making of a City*. London: Croom Helm.

Bibliography

GIBB, A. and MACLENNAN, D. (1985) (forthcoming), 'Housing in postwar Scotland' in R. Saville (ed.), *Scotland's Modern Economic History*, Edinburgh, Donald.

GIBSON, M. S. and LANGSTAFF, M. S. (1982), *An Introduction to Urban Renewal*, London, Hutchinson.

GILLETT, E. (1983), *Investment in the Environment*, Aberdeen University Press.

GOODMAN, R. (1972), *After the Planners*, Harmondsworth, Penguin.

GOW, LESLIE and MACPHERSON, ANDREW (1980), *Tell them from me*, Edinburgh, Edinburgh University Press.

GREATER LONDON COUNCIL (1983), *Small Firms and the London Industrial Strategy*, Economic Policy Group, strategy document, No. 4, London, GLC.

GREATER LONDON COUNCIL (1985a), *The London Industrial Strategy*, London, GLC.

GREATER LONDON COUNCIL (1985b), *Nature Conservation Guidelines for London*, London, GLC.

GREATER LONDON ENTERPRISE BOARD (1985), *Annual Report and Accounts to 31.3.1985*, London, GLEB.

GRIGSBY, W., MACLENNAN, D. and BARATZ, M. (1984), *Neighbourhood Conservation and Revitalisation*. Research Report Series, No. 5, Department of City and Regional Planning, University of Pennsylvania.

GROSSKURTH, A. (1983), 'Selling off the slums' in *Roof*, 8, pp. 25-8.

GULLIVER, S. (1984), 'The area projects of the Scottish Development Agency', *Town Planning Review*, Vol. 55, No. 3, pp. 322-34.

HALL, P. (1981), *The Inner City in Context*, London, Heinemann.

HALSEY, A. H. (ed.) (1970), *Educational Priority*, Vol. 1, London, HMSO.

HALSEY, A.H., HEALTH, A.F., and RIDGE, J.M. (1980), *Origins and Destinations. Family, Class and Education in Modern Britain*, Oxford, Clarendon Press.

HAMBLETON, R. (1980), 'Inner cities: engaging the private sector', School for Advanced Urban Studies Working Paper No. 10, University of Bristol.

HAMBLETON, R., STEWART, M. and UNDERWOOD, J. (1980), 'Inner cities: management and resources', School for Advanced Urban Studies Working Paper No. 13, University of Bristol.

HAMILTON, H. (1932), *The Industrial Revolution in Scotland*, Oxford, Clarendon.

HANDY, CHARLES (1984), *The Future of Work*, Oxford, Blackwell.

HANSARD (1985), *Written Answers*, 29 January, Cols 99-100.

HARRISON, P. (1983), *Inside the Inner City*, Harmondsworth, Penguin.

HART, J. T. (1971), The Inverse Care Law, *Lancet*, pp. 405-12.

HART, T. (1968), 'The comprehensive development area', Occasional Paper No. 9, University of Glasgow, Social and Economic Studies, Edinburgh and London, Oliver and Boyd.

HAWORTH, J. T. and SMITH, M. A. (1975), *Work and Leisure*, London, Lepus.

HILLMAN, M. (1973), *Personal Mobility*, London, Political and Economic Planning.

HOPKINS, E. N. *et al.* (1968), 'The relation of patient's age, sex and distance from surgery to the demand on the family doctor', *Journal of the Royal College of General Practitioners*, Vol. 16, pp. 368-78.

HOUSE OF COMMONS LIBRARY RESEARCH DIVISION (1981), 'Unemployment', Background Paper No. 92, c1534, London, House of Commons.

HOUSE OF COMMONS (1983), *Third Report from the Environment Committee Session 1982-83*, Vol. 1, London, HMSO.

HOWES, C. K. (1984), 'The ownership of vacant land by public agencies' in *Land Development Studies*, Vol. 1, pp. 23-33.

JAMES, WALTER (1982), 'Where is adult education going?', *Vocational Training Bulletin*, No. 9, September.

KEATING, M. and MIDWINTER, A. (1984), 'The Area Project approach to economic development in Scotland' in *Public Administration*, Vol. 62.

KIRBY, A. (1982), *The Politics of Location: An Introduction*, London, Methuen.

KIRWAN, R. (1981), 'The American experience' in P. Hall (ed.), *The Inner City in Context*, London, Heinemann.

KNOX, P. L. (1978), 'The intra-urban ecology of primary medical care: patterns of accessibility and their policy implications', *Environment and Planning A*, Vol. 10, pp. 415-35.

KNOX, P. L. (1979), 'Medical deprivation, area deprivation and public policy', *Social Science and Medicine*, Vol. 13D, pp. 111-21.

KNOX, P. L. and PACIONE, M. (1980), 'Locational behaviour, place preference and the inverse care law in the distribution of medical care', *Geo forum*, Vol. 11, pp. 43-55.

LAMONT, D., MACLENNAN, D. and MUNRO, M. (1983), 'New private housing in the GEAR area' in Donnison, 1983.

LANKFORD, P. (1974), 'The changing location of physicians', *Antipode*, Vol. 3, pp. 68-72.

LAWLESS, P. (1981), *Britain's Inner Cities: Problems and Policies*, London, Harper and Row.

LE BOTERF, GUY (1983), 'How should vocational training linked with regional development be planned?' in *Vocational Training Bulletin*, No. 19, December 1985, CEDEFOP, Berlin.

LECLERC, R. and DRAFFAN, D. (1984), 'The Glasgow Eastern Area

Renewal Project' in *Town Planning Review*, Vol. 55, No. 3, pp. 335-51.

LEVEN, C. L., LITTLE, J. T., NOUSE, H. O. and READ, R. B. (1976), *Neighbourhood Change: Lessons In the Dynamics of Urban Decay*, New York, Praeger.

LEVER, W. and MOORE, C. (1986), *The City in Transition*, Oxford, Clarendon Press.

LLOYD, P. and DICKEN, P. (1982), *Industrial Change: Local Manufacturing Firms in Manchester and Merseyside*, Inner Cities Research Report 6, London, DoE.

LUNDBERG, G. A. *et al.* (1943), *Leisure: A Suburban Study*, New York, Columbia University Press.

LYON, H. (1984), 'The Kingsridge/Cleddans local letting scheme', unpublished dissertation, University of Glasgow.

McARTHUR, A. A. (1985), 'Public responses to the growth of unemployment in the United Kingdom, with particular reference to action at the local scale', PhD Thesis, Department of Town and Regional Planning, University of Glasgow.

McARTHUR, A. A. (1986), 'An unconventional approach to local economic development: the role of community business' in *Town Planning Review*, Vol. 57, No. 1, pp. 87-100.

McCREADIE, D. W. A. (1974), 'Planning for primary health care in Scotland', PhD Thesis, University of Strathclyde.

McCREADIE, D. W. A. and MACGREGOR, I. M. (1979), 'Aspects of health service provision in Scotland', *Hospital and Health Services Review*, pp. 160-4.

McKEAN, R. (1975), 'The impact of comprehensive development area policies on industry in Glasgow', Urban and Regional Studies Discussion Paper No. 15, University of Glasgow.

MacKINNON, J. (1921), *The Social and Industrial History of Scotland*, London, Longman.

MACLENNAN, D. (1981), 'Tolerable survival and the central cities' in M. Gaskin (ed.), *The Political Economy of Tolerable Survival*, London, Croom Helm.

MACLENNAN, D. (1982), *Housing Economics: An Applied Approach*, London, Longman.

MACLENNAN, D., BRAILEY, M. and LAWRIE, N. (1983), *The Activities and Effectiveness of Housing Associations in Scotland*, Edinburgh, Scottish Office.

MACLENNAN, D., MUNRO, M. and WOOD, G. A. (1981), 'The structure of submarkets in two large housing systems', paper delivered at the Regional Science Association Meeting (British Section), Sheffield, September 1983.

MACLENNAN, D., ROBERTSON, D., MUNRO, M. and CARRUTHERS, D. (1984),

'The Glasgow Database Project' (Report to Glasgow District Council).

MACLENNAN, D. and BRAILEY, M. (1985), 'Housing associations and rehabilitation in Scotland', Discussion Paper 13, Centre for Urban and Regional Research, University of Glasgow.

MACLENNAN, D. and JONES, C. A. (1985), 'Credit rationing and building society lending in Glasgow' (Mimeo).

MALPASS, P. (1983), 'Residualisation and the restructuring of housing tenure' in *Housing Review*, 32, pp. 44-5.

MARWICK, W. H. (1936), *Economic Development in Victorian Scotland*, London, Allen and Unwin.

MASSEY, D. and MEEGAN, R. (1979), 'The geography of industrial reorganisation: the spatial effects of the restructuring of the electrical engineering sector under the Industrial Reorganisation Corporation' in *Progress in Planning*, 10, 3.

MEAD, M. (1957), 'The pattern of leisure in contemporary American society' in *Annals of the American Academy of Political and Social Science*, Vol. 313, pp. 1-18.

MEGEE, M. (1976), 'Restructuring the health care delivery system in the United States', in J. S. Adams (ed.), *Urban Policymaking and Metropolitan Dynamics*, Cambridge, MA, Ballinger.

MELLING, J. (1980a), 'Clydeside housing and the evolution of state rent control' in J. Melling (ed.) (1980b), *Housing, Social Policy and the State*, London, Croom Helm.

MELLING, J. (1980b), *Housing, Social Policy and the State*, London, Croom Helm.

MELLING, J. (1983), *Rent Strikes: People's Struggle for Housing in the West of Scotland*, Edinburgh, Polygon.

MILLER, D. (1986), 'Local authority economic initiatives – a booming business' in *New Socialist*, No. 36, pp. x-xi, March.

MINISTRY OF TRANSPORT (1963), *Traffic in Towns*, London, HMSO.

MORI (1986), *Public Opinion in Glasgow*, Glasgow, Glasgow District Council.

MUNRO, M. (1986), 'Testing for segmentation in the Glasgow private housing market', Discussion Paper 8, Centre for Housing Research, University of Glasgow.

MUNRO, M. and LAMONT, D. (1985), 'Neighbourhood perception, preference and household mobility in the Glasgow private housing market' in *Environment and Planning*, 17, 1331-50.

NAIRN, A. (1983), 'GEAR – comprehensive redevelopment or confidence trick?' in *Fraser of Allander Institute Quarterly Economic Commentary*, Vol. 9, No. 2.

NELSON, S. (1980), *Participating in GEAR*, Strathclyde Area Survey, University of Glasgow; University of Strathclyde.

OAKLEY, C. A. (1975), *The Second City*, Glasgow, Blackie.

Bibliography

OECD (1983), *The Future of Vocational Education and Training*, Paris, OECD.

ORTON, I. (1982), 'Whatever happened to GEAR?' *Fraser of Allander Institute Quarterly Economic Commentary*, Vol. 7, No. 3.

PAHL, R. E. (1984), *Divisions of Labour*, Oxford, Blackwell.

PARKER, S. (1971), *The Future of Work and Leisure*, London, Granada.

PARKER, S. (1976), *The Sociology of Leisure*, London, Allen and Unwin.

PARKINSON, MICHAEL (1985), *Liverpool on the Brink*, Hermitage, Policy Journals.

PARKINSON, M. H. and WILKS, S. R. M. (1983), 'Managing urban decline – the case of the inner city partnerships', *Local Government Studies*.

PAULEY, R. (1985), 'Real value of urban aid cut in 1985-86 share out', *Financial Times*, 15 January.

PHILLIPS, D. R. (1979), 'Public attitudes to general practitioner services: a reflection of an inverse care law in intra-urban primary medical care', *Environment and Planning A*, Vol. 11, pp. 815-24.

PHILLIPS, D. R. (1980), 'Spatial patterns of surgery attendance: some implications for the provision of primary health care' *Journal of the Royal College of General Practitioners*, Vol. 30, pp. 680-95.

PHILLIPS, D. R. (1981), *Contemporary Issues in the Geography of Health Care*, Norwich, Geo Books.

PLANNING (1985), 'Derelict land funds slightly up', No. 605, 15 February p. 16.

POWER, A. (1982), *Priority Estates Project 1982*, London, Department of the Environment.

RESKIN, B. and CAMPBELL, F. L. (1974), 'Physician distribution across metropolitan areas', *American Journal of Sociology*, Vol. 80, pp. 267-81.

RICHARDSON, P. (1985), 'Inner city policy in the partnerships: a case study of small industrial premises', unpublished PhD thesis, University of Reading.

ROBERTS, J. T. (1976), *General Improvement Areas*, Farnborough, Saxon House.

ROBERTS, K. (1970), *Leisure*, London, Longman.

ROBERTSON, I. M. L. (1977), *The Location of Social Facilities*, Scottish Office, Central Research Unit Papers.

ROBERTSON, I. M. L. (1984), 'Single parent lifestyle and peripheral estate residence', *Town Planning Review*, Vol. 55, pp. 197-213.

ROBINSON, R. and O'SULLIVAN, A. (1983), 'Housing tenure polarisation: some empirical evidence' in *Housing Review*, 32, pp. 116-17.

ROGER TYM AND PARTNERS (1983), *Monitoring Enterprise Zones: Year Two Report*, London, Department of the Environment.

ROGER TYM AND PARTNERS (1984), *Monitoring Enterprise Zones: Year*

Three Report, London, Department of the Environment.

SCHULLER, TOM (1979), 'The democratization of work', Schuller and Jacquetta Megarry (eds), *The World Year Education: Recurrent Education and life-long Learning*, Kogan Page.

SCOTTISH DEVELOPMENT AGENCY (no date), *GEAR: The Facts a Future*, Glasgow, Scottish Development Agency.

SCOTTISH DEVELOPMENT AGENCY (1978a), *The Future for GEAR Issues and Possible Courses for Action*, Glasgow, Scottish Development Agency.

SCOTTISH DEVELOPMENT AGENCY (1978b), *GEAR Household Su* Glasgow, Scottish Development Agency.

SCOTTISH DEVELOPMENT AGENCY (1980a), *GEAR Strategy and gramme*, Glasgow, Scottish Development Agency.

SCOTTISH DEVELOPMENT AGENCY (1980b), *Glasgow: The New East E* Glasgow, Scottish Development Agency.

SCOTTISH DEVELOPMENT AGENCY (1982), *Annual Report 1982*, Glasgo SDA.

SCOTTISH DEVELOPMENT AGENCY (1983a), 'GEAR Project Report', '8 unpublished Scottish Development Agency Report, Glasgow, SDA.

SCOTTISH DEVELOPMENT AGENCY (1983b), 'GEAR Statement of Priori ties', unpublished Scottish Development Agency Report, Glasgow, SDA.

SCOTTISH DEVELOPMENT AGENCY (1984a), *Annual Report*, Glasgow, SDA.

SCOTTISH DEVELOPMENT AGENCY (1984b), *Clydebank Task Force Position Statement*, Glasgow, SDA.

SCOTTISH DEVELOPMENT AGENCY (1985), *Annual Report*, Glasgow, SDA.

SCOTTISH EDUCATION DEPARTMENT (1975), *Adult Education and the Challenge of Change* (The Alexander Report), Edinburgh, HMSO.

SHANNON, G. W. and DEVER, G. E. (1974), *Health Care Delivery: Spatial Perspectives*, New York, McGraw Hill.

SHAW, R. (1984), 'Leisure and work' in *ESRC Newsletter*, No. 51, pp. 7-8, London. (ESRC: Economic and Social Research Council).

SILLS, A., TAYLOR, G. and GOLDING, P. (1985), 'Learning by our mistakes: experimentation and monitoring in the Inner Area Programme' in *Local Government Studies*, 11, 1.

SIMPSON, J. (1973), 'Education for leisure' in Smith et al., 1973.

SLAVEN, A. (1975), *The Development of the West of Scotland, 1750-1960*, London, Routledge & Kegan Paul.

SMITH, M. A. et al., (1973), *Leisure and Society in Britain*, London, Allen Lane.

SMITH, R. and WANNOP, U. (eds) (1985), *Strategic Planning in Action*, Aldershot, Gower.

SOULE, G. (1957), 'The economics of leisure' in Annals of the American Academy of Political and Social Science, Vol. 313.

SPARER, G. and OKEDA, L. M. (1974), 'Chronic conditions and physician use patterns in ten poverty areas', Medical Care, Vol. 12, No. 7, pp. 549-60.

STANFORTH, J. et al., (1986), The Delivery of Repair Services in Public Sector Housing in Scotland, Edinburgh, Scottish Development Department.

STEWART, M. (1983), 'The experience of inner city partnership', Memorandum to the House of Commons Environment Committee Inquiry into the Management of Urban Renewal, HC 103 vii, London, HMSO.

STONIER, TOM (1979), 'Changes in Western society: educational implications', in Tom Schuller and Jacquetta Megarry (eds), The World Yearbook of Education: Recurrent Education and Life-Long Learning, London, Kogan Page.

STOREY, D. (1982), Entrepreneurship and the New Firm, Beckenham, Croom Helm.

STRATHCLYDE REGIONAL COUNCIL (1981), 'A strategy for post-compulsory education', Report of Officer-Member Group on Further Education, Glasgow, Strathclyde Regional Council.

STRATHCLYDE REGIONAL COUNCIL (1985), 'Strathclyde Structure Plan 1981 Second Review and Alterations', Glasgow, Strathclyde Regional Council.

THOMPKINS, ERIC (1982), 'Adult education in a changing society', in Neil Costello and Michael Richardson (eds), Continuing Education for a Post-Industrial Society, Milton Keynes, Open University Press.

TOWN AND COUNTRY PLANNING (1985), 'Failing to melt the bankers' hearts', January, pp. 27-8.

TOWNSEND, P. (1974), 'Inequality and the health service', Lancet, pp. 1179-90.

TOWNSEND, P. and DAVIDSON, N. (1982) (eds), Inequalities in Health. The Black Report, London, Penguin.

VALENTE, J. and LEIGH, R. (1982), 'Local authority advanced factory units: a framework for evaluation', in Planning Outlook, Vol. 24, No. 2, pp. 67-9.

VARADY, K. (1981), 'The spillover effects from environmental factors', paper presented at a meeting of the Regional Science Association (Southern Branch), USA.

WALTERS, V. (1980), Class Inequality and Health Care, London, Croom Helm.

WANNOP, U.A. (1982), 'The future management of GEAR', Report to the Scottish Development Agency, Glasgow, University of Strathclyde.

WANNOP, U.A. (1984), 'Strategic planning and the Area development

projects of the SDA', *Regional Studies*, Vol. 18, No. 1.

WATES, NICK (1985), 'Co-op consolidation' in *The Architectural Review*, No. 1058, April, pp. 57-61.

WATTS, A. G. (1983), *Education Unemployment and the Future of Work*, Milton Keynes, Open University Press.

WEIR, DOUGLAS (1983), 'The cost of survival: choices facing post-compulsory education' in Boyd-Barrett *et al.* (eds), *Approaches to Post-School Management*, New York, Harper & Row.

WEISS, J. E. and GREENLICK, M. R. (1970), 'Determinants of medical care utilisation: the effects of social class and distance on contacts with the medical care system', *Medical Care*, Vol. 8, pp. 456-62.

WELLBORN, C. H. (1983), 'Housing and community development' pp. 151-64, in *Housing – A Reader*, Congressional Research Service, Library of Congress, Washington, US Government Printing Office.

WEST MIDLANDS ENTERPRISE BOARD (1985), *Annual Reports and Accounts*, Birmingham, WMEB.

WHITEFIELD, LESLEY (1985), 'Housing co-operatives in Glasgow: the community ownership programme', M.Phil. Thesis, University of Glasgow, Department of Town and Regional Planning.

WILLMOTT, P. and YOUNG, M. (1957), *Family and Kinship in East London*, London, Routledge & Kegan Paul.

WILLMOTT, P. and YOUNG, M. (1973), *The Symmetrical Family: A Study of Work and Leisure in the London Region*, London, Routledge & Kegan Paul.

INDEX

Index

Index